Edgar Allan Poe and His Nineteenth-Century American Counterparts

Edgar Allan Poe and His Nineteenth-Century American Counterparts

John Cullen Gruesser

BLOOMSBURY ACADEMIC
NEW YORK · LONDON · OXFORD · NEW DELHI · SYDNEY

BLOOMSBURY ACADEMIC
Bloomsbury Publishing Inc
1385 Broadway, New York, NY 10018, USA
50 Bedford Square, London, WC1B 3DP, UK

BLOOMSBURY, BLOOMSBURY ACADEMIC and the Diana logo are trademarks of
Bloomsbury Publishing Plc

First published in the United States of America 2019

Cover design by Eleanor Rose
Cover images (l-r): Engraving of the original Halls of Justice (built in 1838 in the
Egyptian Revival style), New York, Etching 1870; Engraving of the Belgian painter
Jan van Beers Borgerchout (1852-1927) © Alamy; Portrait of Edgar Allan Poe
(1809-to-1849) © Alamy; Image of Burton's Gentleman's Magazine, 1840,
courtesy of The Edgar Allan Poe Society of Baltimore

A catalog record for this book is available from the Library of Congress.

ISBN: HB: 978-1-5013-3452-8
ePDF: 978-1-5013-3453-5
eBook: 978-1-5013-3455-9

Typeset by Deanta Global Publishing Services, Chennai, India
Printed and bound in the United States of America

To find out more about our authors and books visit www.bloomsbury.com
and sign up for our newsletters.

Contents

Permissions

Acknowledgments

This book would not have been published without the generous support of many people over several years, including Beth Sweeney, Jerry Kennedy, Scott Peeples, Ben Fisher, Jeffrey Savoye, Dennis Eddings, Hanna Wallinger, Bill Engel, Philip Phillips, Paul Christian Jones, Emron Esplin, Margarida Vale de Gato, Jana Argersinger, Amy Branam Armiento, Barbara Cantalupo, Carole Shaffer-Koros, Lee Person, Alfred Bendixen, Kelly Ross, John Barton, David Schmid, Tish Crawford, Adam Bradford, Hershel Parker, Fernando González-Moreno, Margarita Rigal-Aragón, Antoine Dechêne, Michel Delville, John Jopson, Mirco Rocchi, Simonetta Berbeglia, Michela Martini, Leroy Panek, Mary Lou De Jong, Noelle Baker, Ton Fafianie, Susan Tane, Mary Balkun, Kelly Shea, John Wargacki, Rachel Warmington, JoAnn Pavletich, April Logan, Sylvia Bugbee (Special Collections, Bailey-Howe Library, University of Vermont), Patricia Zline, Albert Rolls, Lois Grubb, Haaris Naqvi, Katherine De Chant, Amy Martin, Charles Nelson, Alisha Knight, Bert Wailoo, Phil Johnson, Michael Winship, John Ernest, Elizabeth Ammons, my 2017–18 research recruit Orella Chichester, and Kean University students in my English 2220, 2403, 3221, 3223, 4415, and 4800 classes. In particular, I wish to thank Richard Kopley, Richard Katz, Joe Murphy, and especially Travis Montgomery for their careful reading of the entire manuscript and helpful suggestions for improving it.

Introduction: Dreams and Mystifications of Poe

Roughly six months before his death, Edgar Allan Poe published "A Dream within a Dream" in the March 31, 1849, issue of *The Flag of Our Union*. Although connecting the personal lives of poets with the personae they create should be done cautiously, this poem, on which Poe had worked in various forms and under different titles since the 1820s, can be read as poignant testimony to the disappointments and losses, both personal and professional, he experienced during his brief life.[1] Here is the first stanza:

> Take this kiss upon the brow!
> And in parting from you now,
> Thus much let me avow—
> You are not wrong, who deem
> That my days have been a dream;
> Yet if Hope has flown away
> In a night, or in a day,
> In a vision, or in none,
> Is it therefore the less *gone?*
> *All* that we see or seem
> Is but a dream within a dream.[2]

As Poe biographer Kenneth Silverman remarks, this intensely retrospective poem does not address "specific circumstances and persons but [Poe's] whole feeling about his life at the time."[3]

Four decades later and late in his own life, the Good Gray Poet Walt Whitman, surrounded by adoring disciples, vividly remembered meeting Poe. Most Whitman biographers believe that Poe and Whitman met only once—in the office of the *Broadway Journal* in late November or early December 1845, shortly after the latter's "Art-Singing and Heart-Singing" appeared in the magazine.[4] A Long Island native, Whitman worked as a compositor in Manhattan in 1835–36, began editing the New York *Aurora* in March 1842, and loved the fast pace of the metropolis. In *Specimen Days*, he recollects his experiences on and around its most famous thoroughfare:

> Besides Fulton ferry, off and on for years, I knew and frequented Broadway—that noted avenue of New York's crowded and mixed humanity, and of so many notables. Here I saw, during those times, Andrew Jackson, Webster, Clay, Seward, Martin Van Buren, filibuster Walker, Kossuth, Fitz Greene Halleck, Bryant, the Prince of Wales, Charles Dickens, the first Japanese ambassadors, and lots of other celebrities of the time. Always something novel or inspiriting; yet mostly to me the hurrying and vast amplitude of those never-ending human currents.[5]

It was in a building at the intersection of Broadway and Duane Street, he goes on to recall, that the meeting with Poe took place:

> I also remember seeing Edgar A. Poe, and having a short interview with him, (it must have been in 1845 or '6,) in his office, second story of a corner building. . . . He was editor and owner or part owner of "the Broadway Journal." The visit was about a piece of mine he had publish'd. Poe was very cordial, in a quiet way, appear'd well in person, dress, &c. I have a distinct and pleasing remembrance of his looks, voice, manner and matter; very kindly and human, but subdued, perhaps a little jaded.[6]

Near the end of his life, Whitman made several other observations about Poe, often contrasting his earlier views of the deceased author's writings with his current opinion of them.[7]

Thirty years after their meeting on the second floor of 304 Broadway, Whitman was the only literary figure of note to attend the ceremony in Baltimore's Westminster Burial Grounds commemorating the transfer of Poe's remains from an unmarked grave to a plot surmounted by an impressive marble monument, although the letters and poems of other authors, including Henry Wadsworth Longfellow, John Greenleaf Whittier, William Cullen Bryant, Sarah Helen Whitman, John Neal, Alfred Tennyson, and Stéphane Mallarmé, were collected in a volume memorializing the reburial the following year.[8] In a November 18, 1875, Washington *Evening Star* article about the event in Baltimore the previous day, Whitman explains that he had recently changed his mind about Poe's poetry and its significance:

> For a long while, and until lately, I had a distaste for Poe's writings. I wanted, and still want for poetry, the clear sun shining, and fresh air blowing—the strength and power of health, not of delirium, even amid the stormiest passions—with always the background of the eternal moralities. Non-complying with these

requirements, Poe's genius has yet conquer'd a special recognition for itself, and I too have come to fully admit it, and appreciate it and him. Even my own objections draw me to him at last; and those very points, with his sad fate, will make him dearer to young and fervid minds.[9]

Known for poems that powerfully celebrate the vastness and diversity of the United States, especially the epic-like *Song of Myself*, Whitman acknowledges here that he has come to see that the nation and its literature can encompass both his own upbeat, expansive, and concrete vision and Poe's often gloomy, claustrophobic, and dreamlike worldview. Reiterating the point while writing about Poe in 1886, he declares, "The Poetic area is very spacious—has so many mansions!"[10]

In the *Evening Star* item, Whitman recounts a vivid dream he had that he associated with Poe:

> I saw a vessel on the sea, at mid-night, in a storm. It was no great full-rigg'd ship, nor majestic steamer, steering firmly through the gale, but seem'd one of those superb little schooner yachts I had often seen lying anchor'd, rocking so jauntily, in the waters around New York, or up Long Island sound—now flying uncontroll'd with torn sails and broken spars through the wild sleet and winds and waves of the night. On the deck was a slender, slight, beautiful figure, a dim man, apparently enjoying all the terror, the murk, and the dislocation of which he was the centre and the victim. That figure of my lurid dream might stand for Edgar Poe, his spirit, his fortunes, and his poems—themselves all lurid dreams.[11]

Each of the things we associate with Whitman and his writings has a dark counterpart in his dream of Poe: daytime versus midnight, consciousness versus dream state, security versus chaos, heroism versus victimization, harmony versus discord, celebration versus foreboding, optimism versus pessimism, potentiality versus devastation, connection versus alienation, direction versus aimlessness, fixity versus dislocation, and realism versus fantasy. Yet this is Whitman's "lurid dream," not Poe's. The figure, who "might stand" for Poe, in fact, represents the Poeish side not only of Whitman himself but the United States and American literature with which Whitman, in his later years, and the nation in the final decades of the nineteenth century, were gradually but inevitably becoming reconciled.

A generation earlier, however, it would hardly be surprising if Poe, in the last year of his life, had come to regard as little more than fading dreams the most prominent of his long-held aspirations, namely national and international recognition for his contributions to literature; ownership and complete editorial control of a remunerative, influential, interregional literary magazine; and the establishment of what he termed "a republic of letters," a genuine literary culture in the United States. "A Dream within a Dream" concludes as follows:

> I stand amid the roar
> Of a surf-tormented shore,
> And I hold within my hand
> Grains of the golden sand—
> How few! yet how they creep
> Through my fingers to the deep,
> While I weep—while I weep!
> O God! can I not grasp
> Them with a tighter clasp?
> O God! can I not save
> *One* from the pitiless wave?
> Is *all* that we see or seem
> But a dream within a dream? (*CW*, I 452)

Because so many of Poe's poems have deliberately indistinct, oneiric settings, this one, by addressing the very subject of dreams, occupies a significant place within his oeuvre.

* * *

Beyond but also on account of the connections between Poe's writings and dreams, his life and art have generated many myths, the consequences of a process of mystification he himself initiated and early editors, biographers, and translators significantly expanded. Soon after his demise, Poe became the victim of a smear campaign by his literary executor, Rufus Griswold, which falsely portrayed him as vindictive, friendless, and mentally unbalanced. Yet first abroad and later in this country, thanks largely to the efforts of the Frenchmen Émile Daurand Forgues, who wrote an early article about him, and especially Charles Baudelaire, who translated and championed Poe's writings, his stature grew steadily—and exponentially.[12] Beginning in the second half of the twentieth century and continuing to this day, filmmakers, television writers, composers, rock musicians, comic book artists, and even an NFL team, not to mention legions of authors around the globe, have paid him homage, and today his contributions to poetry, literary criticism, science fiction, horror literature, and detective and mystery writing are indisputable.

In part because of his popularity and ubiquity, people today think they know all about Poe. Out and out falsehoods—for example, that he traveled as a young man to Greece and St. Petersburg (a quasi-Byronic adventure of Poe's own concoction) and that he habitually used drugs—have been thoroughly disproven, yet erroneous suppositions about him and his writings persist.[13] *Edgar Allan Poe and His Nineteenth-Century American Counterparts* addresses four widely held misconceptions. First, by devoting attention to the writer's nonfiction and to his detection respectively, Parts 1 and 2 endeavor to counter the mistaken belief in Poe's one-dimensionality, summed up in the following lament by art historian Fernando González-Moreno and literary scholar Margarita Rigal-Aragón: "We, as modern readers, are used to the crude images created by contemporary artists who have focused on the most macabre and morbid aspects of the tales, offering a reductionist image of the author. Poe has been transformed almost exclusively, and unfortunately, into the master of horror."[14] Second, most people do not know that Poe—as I discuss in Chapters 1, 2, and 3—attempted to support his young wife Virginia (who was also his cousin), his mother-in-law Maria Clemm (who was also his aunt), and himself primarily by working as a magazinist, and that, consequently, he likely wrote more criticism, in the form of reviews and essays (both signed and unsigned), than he did creative works during his lifetime. Third, many readers fail to attribute the striking effects Poe achieves in his writings to deliberate design and meticulous craftsmanship—something I address in my discussion of his ratiocinative tales and their impact in Chapters 4, 5, and 6. Finally, during the last few decades, diligent scholars have largely but—as I argue in the Coda—by no means fully succeeded in discrediting a fourth myth: the assumption that Poe's characters, several of whom commit murder, otherwise engage in aberrant behavior, and have lost their sanity, are reflections of the writer himself.[15]

Beginning this process of demystification, the three chapters that make up Part 1, "The Quixotic Quest for Literary Fame, Financial Stability, and a Republic of Letters in Antebellum America," devote attention to Poe's unrealized ambitions as a literary artist in the 1830s and 1840s. The first contrasts the trajectory of his life with that of the quintessential American success story as outlined by Benjamin Franklin in his *Autobiography*. The second discusses Poe as both an insider and outsider in connection with the nation's literary hub, Lower Manhattan, as evidenced by his nonfiction series *Doings in Gotham* and *The Literati of New York City*, as well as his short story "The Cask of Amontillado." The third contends that there was likely a biographical as well as an autobiographical dimension to Herman Melville's "Bartleby, the Scrivener: A Story of Wall-Street," with Poe serving as a model for the forlorn, enigmatic copyist. The three chapters that compose Part 2, "The Competition in Cunning: Ramifications of and Responses to Poe's Ratiocinative Tales," concentrate on his technique in his detective stories and the ways in which white and black writers in the second half of the nineteenth century respond to them. Chapter 4 elaborates the three levels of competition that Poe incorporates into his stories featuring C. Auguste Dupin, as well as their implications for the detective genre. Chapter 5 examines texts by canonical white males that respond directly or indirectly to Poe by utilizing elements of detection. Opening with a discussion of "The Gold-Bug," in which Poe explicitly introduces the subject of race into modern detection, Chapter 6 looks at the intertextual relationships among a trio of woman-authored narratives that, like Poe's story, concern cunning, madness, and the racist ideology that enables both slavery and Jim Crow. Interrogating (mis)readings of Poe's reviews of Nathaniel Hawthorne generally and his statements about that writer's story "The Minister's Black Veil" in particular, the Coda of this book demonstrates that certain myths about Poe continue to flourish.

Part One

The Quixotic Quest for Literary Fame, Financial Stability, and a Republic of Letters in Antebellum America

I'll tell you a plan for gaining wealth,
Better than banking, trade or leases—
Take a bank note and fold it up,
And then you will find your money in creases!
This wonderful plan, without danger or loss,
Keeps your cash in your hands, where nothing can trouble it;
And every time that you fold it across,
'Tis as plain as the light of the day that you double it!

Edgar Allan Poe, "Epigram for Wall Street,"
Evening Mirror, January 23, 1845

Poor Edgar's Almanac: E. A. Poe's Money Woes

In respect to the other features of the Penn Magazine, a few words here will suffice. It will endeavour to support the general interests of the republic of letters, without reference to particular regions; regarding the world at large as the true audience of the author. Beyond the precincts of literature, properly so called, it will leave in better hands the task of instruction upon all matters of *very* grave moment. Its aim chiefly shall be *to please*; and this through means of versatility, originality, and pungency.

Edgar Allan Poe, Prospectus of the Penn Magazine, August 1840

Depend upon it, after all, Thomas, Literature is the most noble of professions. In fact, it is about the only one fit for a man. For my own part, there is no seducing me from the path. I shall be a *littérateur*, at least, all my life; nor would I abandon the hopes which still lead me on for all the gold in California. Talking of gold, and of the temptations at present held out to "poor devil authors," did it ever strike you that all which is really valuable to a man of letters—to a poet in especial—is absolutely unpurchaseable? Love, fame, the dominion of intellect, the consciousness of power, the thrilling sense of beauty, the free air of Heaven, exercise of body & mind, with the physical and moral health which result—these and such as these are really all that a poet cares for:—then answer me this—*why* should he go to California?

Edgar Allan Poe to Frederick W. Thomas, February 14, 1849

In April 1849, Edgar Allan Poe published "Eldorado," a poem about a long, unfulfilled quest that critics have read in connection with get-rich-quick schemes, particularly the California Gold Rush.[1] It begins as follows:

Gaily bedight,
A gallant knight,
In sunshine and in shadow,
Had journeyed long,
Singing a song,

In search of Eldorado.
But he grew old—
This knight so bold—
And o'er his heart a shadow
Fell, as he found
No spot of ground
That looked like Eldorado. (*CW*, I 463)

Appearing a half year before his death, these stanzas depicting a searcher "Singing a song" might also be read in relation to Poe's own long-held, unrealized dreams of wealth, fame, and a republic of letters.

Poe's ambitions, attitudes, and experiences in connection with money and art come into clearer focus when contrasted with those of the man who epitomized the American success story. Widely recognized as American geniuses, Benjamin Franklin and Edgar Poe were born in Boston and spent key periods of their lives in Philadelphia. However, their theories about art, their attitudes toward money and the means of acquiring it, and the paths of their lives differ markedly. The prototypical self-made man, Franklin was born in 1706 and became a key figure in the Enlightenment, insisting that people could use reason to improve themselves and their society. Through the very profitable guise of Poor Richard Saunders, he offered practical advice on the Way to Wealth, and in his old age had the leisure to tell his own story, consciously crafting the first part of his memoirs into a rags-to-riches tale for his posterity to emulate. Such prosperity, however, would elude Poe. Born a century after Franklin, he led a peripatetic life during which he faced, as he himself put it in an October 28, 1844, letter to James Russell Lowell, "a host of troubles growing from the *one* trouble of poverty,"[2] and he passed away at forty under mysterious circumstances, never having achieved financial self-sufficiency.[3] Three economies—literary, national, and personal—worked against Poe. As he was acutely aware, and as scholars have often noted, supporting oneself through writing alone was all but impossible in antebellum America. Moreover, soon after he left the South to pursue a literary career in the nation's largest city, the country was gripped by the Panic of 1837, the effects of which would linger well into the 1840s. Additionally, Poe's circumstances and tendencies greatly complicated matters for him: he had the education and the tastes but not the independent means of an aristocrat; he frequently attacked people in print, often to his own detriment; he had a problem with alcohol that tended to erupt at just the wrong time; and he was admirably committed to his art but suffered financially because of this.

As he was starting out in earnest to be a writer in the early 1830s, Poe rejected Franklin's ideas, incorporating a nonpragmatic artistic philosophy into the Prologue to the *Tales of the Folio Club* and parodying *The Autobiography of Benjamin Franklin* in the process.[4] Although Poe wrote the Prologue with his tongue firmly in his cheek, it nevertheless anticipates the ideas he would elaborate at various times, including his August 1840 *Prospectus for the Penn Magazine*, an excerpt from which serves as the first epigraph to this chapter. Whereas the practical, didactic Franklin believed that writing should instruct readers on how to better themselves and inspire them to do good things, the artist and aesthete Poe held that literature's sole purpose was to delight. This can be seen in the striking differences between the Junto and the Folio Club.

The Autobiography recounts that while Franklin was as a fledgling printer in Philadelphia he "form'd most of [his] ingenious acquaintance into a club, for mutual improvement, which we called the Junto"[5] and explains at some length how the group, which met weekly, initially in an "alehouse," operated:

> The rules I drew up, required that every member in his turn should produce one or more queries on any point of Morals, Politics, or Natural Philosophy, to be discuss'd by the company, and once in three months produce and read an essay of his own writing on any subject he pleased. Our debates were to be under the direction of a president, and to be conducted in the sincere spirit of enquiry after truth, without fondness of dispute, or desire of victory. (168–69)

Franklin proceeds to identify and briefly describe the ten other original members of the Junto, which endured for almost forty years and was, as he puts it, "the best school of philosophy, morals and politics that then existed in the province" (170) of Pennsylvania. Poe's narrator likewise describes his own club as a "Junto," albeit a "Junto of *Dunderheadism*" (*CW*, II 203),[6] and, like Franklin, he devotes considerable attention to the way it operates:

> A clause in the Constitution then adopted forbade the members to be other wise than erudite and witty: and the avowed objects of the Confederation were "the instruction of society and the amusement of themselves." For the latter purpose a meeting is held monthly at the house of some one of the associational when each individual is expected to come prepared with a "Short Prose Tale" of his own composition. Each article thus produced is read by its author to the company assembled over a glass of wine at dinner. Much rivalry will of course ensue— more particularly as the writer of the "Best Thing" is appointed President of the Club *pro tem*, an office endowed with many dignities and little experience,

and which endures until its occupant is dispossessed by a superior *morceau*. The father of the Tale held, on the contrary, to be the least meritorious, is bound to furnish the dinner and wine at the next similar meeting of the Society. (*CW*, II 204)

Similar to the Junto, the "number of the [Folio] Club is limited to eleven" (*CW*, II 204), and Poe's narrator, echoing Franklin, names and tersely characterizes each of the other ten members.

Despite their common features, there can be no mistaking the differences between the two organizations. The egalitarian Junto serves as a kind of "school" for a group of tradesmen, who, lacking formal education, join together for "mutual Improvement," take "truth" as their goal, and present queries and essays on morals, politics, and science. Meanwhile, the "erudite" members of elitist Folio Club seek "solely," as the current president tells Poe's narrator, to "amuse" themselves through the reading of original works of fiction. Moreover, whereas Franklin's group strictly forbids "dispute" and "desire of victory" at its meetings, monetarily penalizing those who engage in "warmth, all expressions of positiveness in opinion, or of direct contradiction" (169), the one described by Poe's narrator encourages considerable "rivalry," rewards the "Best" story, and mandates that the author of the worst tale host the next gathering.

With one key exception, Franklin does not indicate the specific subject of any of the Junto's debates. Rather, he emphasizes the practical benefits that membership in the club had for his printing shop—the other members of the Junto, as he explains, "exerting themselves in recommending business to us" (173). The one topic of discussion that Franklin does divulge is the question of whether more paper money should be introduced into the provincial economy. "Our [Junto] debates possess'd me so fully of the subject," he recollects, "that I wrote and printed an anonymous pamphlet on it" (186), the effect of which was to convince a majority in the legislature to vote for more paper currency. Once again the result was personal gain for Franklin because the members of the House supporting the measure, "who conceiv'd I had been of some service, thought fit to reward me, by employing me in printing the money, a very profitable Job, and a great help to me" (186). Such writing holds few charms for the brash young *littérateur* Poe. Just as the Folio Club, in contrast to the Junto, devotes its meetings strictly to entertainment as opposed to professional advancement, so, too, Poe, in his projected collection of stories, sought, unlike Franklin, merely to delight rather than morally uplift or enrich his readers. Thus, in the *Folio Club* Prologue, a piece written at the onset of his professional literary career, Poe in effect declares his independence from didactic, profit-driven writing epitomized by *The Autobiography*.[7] Such a commitment to an art that pleases rather than instructs, clearly reflected in the Poe's 1840 *Prospectus*, would have significant consequences for his life and career.

* * *

How did people acquire wealth and secure economic well-being in the United States in the 1830s and 1840s, an era that Heinz Tschachler has characterized as "a world of banking collapse, financial panics and bankruptcies, and grinding depression"?[8] Some inherited money or property, others had the talent or good fortune to secure gainful employment in the private sector, a few individuals had the connections to obtain a government job, a handful invested in risky enterprises that beat the odds and proved successful, and a small number entered into marriages with persons of means. At various times, Poe pinned his hopes on each of these options. None of them, however, would change his fortunes.

Orphaned as a toddler, Poe was raised by a prosperous Richmond couple, a family situation that seemed to bode well for his future. However, he often traded harsh words with John Allan, who never legally adopted him. After amassing huge gambling debts at and consequently dropping out of the University of Virginia, Poe had a highly successful two-year stint as a soldier, but, with no means of advancement as an enlisted man, he decided to become a cadet at West Point. However, when Allan started a new family following the death of his first wife, Poe, apparently realizing that he would never be his foster father's heir, got himself court-martialed. Shortly thereafter, he embarked on a career in letters at a time when American publishers could reprint the works of established foreign authors without paying royalties, the United States lacked an established and knowledgeable audience for books and literary journals, critics at home and abroad evinced considerable prejudice against native writers, and the nation's population was widely spread out, making the distribution of printed materials difficult. Thus, Poe could hardly have picked a less-promising means of earning a living.

Poe's life of privation began in earnest in early 1830s Baltimore, where he lived with his poor Poe relatives. During this period, he sought full-time employment as a newspaperman and a teacher, but, without well-connected family members and friends to recommend him, he failed to secure a position. Applying himself to his newly chosen career, Poe sent five tales to the *Saturday Courier* of Philadelphia, all of which would appear in the paper during 1832 without revealing the identity of the author and, very likely, without putting any money in his pocket. These stories were part of a projected volume, which he alternately titled *Eleven Tales of the Arabesque* and *Tales of the Folio Club*. Over the next four years, Poe attempted to get his book published, but it suffered the same fate as Nathaniel Hawthorne's proposed short story collections *Tales of My Native Land* and *Provincial Tales* a few years earlier and never saw print. Poe did, however, place some of this fiction, along with poems, critical essays, and occasional pieces, in the Baltimore *Saturday Visiter* in 1833. In October of that year, his "MS. Found in a Bottle" won the $50 first prize in the fiction portion of a contest held by the *Visiter*. Through this competition, he gained a much-needed friend and patron in John Pendleton Kennedy, the author of *Swallow Barn; Or, A Sojourn in the Old Dominion* (1832), who, when Poe declined a dinner invitation because he had nothing appropriate to wear in early 1835, provided the struggling author with funds for clothes, meals, and even a horse to ride. It was at Kennedy's urging that Poe began to submit fiction, poetry, and criticism to the *Southern Literary Messenger*, which had been founded the previous year in Richmond. This eventually led to Poe being hired in August 1835 as an assistant editor at the *Messenger* with a salary of $520 a year, his first steady employment since his days as an army enlisted man six years previously. Two months later, Poe brought his young cousin Virginia Clemm, whom he would marry in May 1836, and her mother, Maria Clemm, to live with him in Richmond, where over a period of a year and a half he gained notoriety as a slashing book reviewer for, a frequent contributor to, and the de facto editor of the *Messenger*. In a rare upbeat letter dated January 22, 1836, Poe told Kennedy, "My health is better than for years past, my mind is fully occupied, my pecuniary difficulties have vanished, I have a fair prospect of future success—in a word all is right" (*CL*, I 81).

Such euphoria did not last; by January of the following year, Poe had either quit or, more likely, been fired from the *Messenger*, and, accompanied by his fourteen-year-old wife and Mrs. Clemm, he moved to New York City the next month to pursue a writing career. However, a major economic downturn made literature, as Arthur Hobson Quinn puts it, as "unsalable . . . as any other form of luxury,"[9] frustrating Poe's search for employment and publishing opportunities. It is known that his aunt took in boarders to make ends meet, but what Poe did to support the family during their fifteen-month stay in Gotham remains a mystery, as only a small handful of writings by him from this period have survived. In 1838, he moved to Philadelphia, where he would scrape by financially for six years, despite becoming widely known as an editor and critic, penning many of his most famous tales, and delivering well-received literary lectures. Having been unable to find a firm willing to bring out *Tales of the Folio Club* in the early and mid-1830s, Poe continued to hope that publishing books would advance his career and improve his finances, yet neither the novel *The Narrative of Arthur Gordon Pym*, which he completed in 1837 and eventually appeared in New York in 1838, nor *Tales of the Grotesque and Arabesque*, published in Philadelphia in late 1839, sold well. In fact, the only book of Poe's to go into a second edition during his lifetime was decidedly nonliterary, *The Conchologist's First Book*, a treatise on seashells to which he lent his name. After two and a half years without full-time employment, Poe became an editor of *Burton's Gentleman's Magazine* in Philadelphia in June 1839, the front page of which featured a drawing of Benjamin Franklin. Following William Burton's sale of the journal to George Graham in 1840, Poe became an editor of the newly formed *Graham's Magazine*. Resigning from his $58-a-month position there in the spring of 1842, he found himself once more in desperate straits, telling James Herron, "The renewed and hopeless illness of my wife, ill health on my own part, and pecuniary embarrassments, have really driven me to distraction. My only hope of relief is the 'Bankrupt Act,' of which I shall avail myself as soon as possible" (*CL*, I 198–99).

Without inherited wealth and only barely able to survive as a magazinist, Poe pursued other ways of changing his fortunes. Shortly after relocating to Philadelphia, he sought employment from James Kirke Paulding, an established author and friend of Washington Irving, who had recently been named secretary of the navy. Two years earlier, Paulding had tried to place Poe's *Tales of Folio Club* with New York publishers, and, when this came to naught, he counseled Poe to shift from short fiction to book-length narratives. In his desperate letter to Paulding, Poe asks for "the most unimportant Clerkship . . . *any thing, by sea or land*—to relieve me from the miserable life of literary drudgery to which I now, with a breaking heart, submit, and for which neither my temper nor my abilities have fitted me." He goes on to assert that living by his pen alone has prevented him from prospering, stating that were he to secure such a position he "could then, (having something beyond mere literature as a profession) quickly elevate myself to the station in society which is my due" (*CL*, I 175). Failing to obtain a post in the War Department from Paulding, Poe tried to land a job in the Philadelphia Customs House, convinced that the light duties and regular income of such a situation would make it possible for him to devote himself properly to a literary career and manage a cutting-edge literary journal. For months he believed a position was forthcoming from the Tyler administration, and he even made a self-sabotaging trip to the nation's capital in connection with it. However, unlike his literary counterparts Paulding, Kennedy, Hawthorne, Irving, Whitman, James Fenimore Cooper, and Herman Melville, all of whom were able to obtain governmental appointments, he never got the job. Bruce I. Weiner aptly observes of Poe, "No other writer in America yearned more for the ideal poetic life and no other writer was more involved in the literary marketplace"; as a result, he became, in Tschachler's words, "a strange synthesis of art and commerce, a public intellectual transformed into a commercial writer."[10]

For several years, Poe sought financial backers and subscribers for a magazine of his own, convinced that taking the gamble on becoming a publisher would change his economic status. After trying and failing to launch the *Penn* (later renamed the *Stylus*) magazine in Philadelphia between 1840 and 1844, he did, briefly, realize one of his long-held aspirations, that of editing and owning a journal. In early 1845, roughly a year after moving back to New York and in the wake of the sensation created by "The Raven," Poe became coeditor of and acquired a one-third interest in the *Broadway Journal*. In time he became the sole editor and, after borrowing heavily, the sole owner of the magazine. Despite assuming the role of proprietor, as opposed to a mere employee, his finances remained as precarious as ever because he received no pay for all the work he did for the *Journal*, which ran into money problems and folded at the end of 1845. He never completely abandoned his dream of launching his own magazine, however, soliciting funds and striving to secure patrons for such a project during the final years of his life.

Poe would make one more attempt to achieve financial stability. Following the death of his wife in 1847, he courted a series of women, including the poet Sarah Helen Whitman, who agreed to marry him in 1848, as did his first sweetheart Sarah Elmira Shelton, by then a wealthy widow, the following year. However, rumors about Poe caused Whitman to break off the engagement, and his untimely death in Baltimore, while he was on his way to New York for the purpose of relocating Maria Clemm in Richmond, prevented the marriage to Shelton. As this overview suggests, Poe's choice of profession and unfavorable circumstances conspired to keep him down.[11]

As I move from the literary and the national to Poe's personal economy, let me return to the contrast with Franklin, who, especially in Parts 1 and 2 of the *Autobiography*, highlights habits and practices that increase an individual's chances for success. These include the virtues of diligence, thriftiness, and temperance as well as pragmatic strategies that continue to be valuable in the business world today, namely networking, image manipulation, and, for want of a better term, schmoozing.[12] Given how much high-quality and carefully crafted writing Poe produced, there can be no denying his industriousness; moreover, biographical accounts and his correspondence attest to the trying circumstances that made frugality a necessity for him. However, these sources also document his sporadic bouts of intemperance—alcohol-fueled sprees resulting in erratic behavior, physical illness, and extreme regret and embarrassment—that often occurred at the most inopportune moments, such as when he was looking for employment or trying to make arrangements with a potential publisher or patron. The biographer Jeffrey Meyers identifies what he sees as "a recurrent pattern" in the writer's life: "He would strive intensely for a desperately desired goal and, when it was in reach, destroy his own chance of achieving it."[13] Poe was able to cultivate personal and literary friendships, especially during his Baltimore and Philadelphia years, yet he often picked fights with powerful people. As early as 1833, Poe demonstrated his willingness to stand up for what he believed in no matter what it cost him financially and professionally. He confronted John Hill Hewitt over the results of the poetry portion of the Baltimore *Saturday Visiter* literary contest, accusing him of unethical behavior. A poem that Hewitt, who edited the *Visiter*, submitted under a pseudonym was chosen as the $25 prize winner over Poe's "The Coliseum" even though the judges subsequently admitted that they preferred the latter. This encounter, which reportedly led to physical violence, apparently caused the *Visiter* to renege on its plans to print *Tales of the Folio Club* on a subscription basis, as had been announced in the paper before Hewitt and Poe quarreled,[14] and episodes similar to this one would occur in the years to follow. Over a decade later, in a letter to Lowell, Poe alludes to his self-damaging propensity, which he elsewhere refers to as "the imp of the perverse": "I am *not* ambitious— unless negatively. I now and then feel stirred up to excel a fool, merely because I hate to let a fool imagine that he may excel me" (*CL*, I 255). As a result of this tendency, he gained many enemies throughout his life who were only too happy to see him struggle and fail.

There was one more means of becoming financially secure in United States prior to the Civil War that highlights the contrast between Franklin and Poe: working at a trade. The former complained about his apprenticeship, which required him to work without wages and made him subject to beatings, yet being bound to his brother taught him nearly all there was to know about printing. As a result, Franklin acquired valuable skills that enabled him to support himself when he fled Boston for Philadelphia at seventeen and eventually made it possible for him to retire at forty-two and devote himself to philanthropic projects, scientific research, and colonial and international politics. As a newspaperman and magazinist, Poe followed developments in printing and illustration technology,[15] and, according to Lambert Wilmer, who knew him in Baltimore, attempted to learn lithography, much to the detriment of his health.[16] Moreover, in an ironic link to Franklin (who famously wheeled the paper he purchased through the streets of Philadelphia to showcase his diligence), Robert T. P. Allen, a West Point classmate, claimed in a 1875 letter to *Scribner's Monthly* to have been told in 1834 that *"Poe was then working in a brick-yard in Baltimore, being engaged in wheeling clay in a wheel-barrow."*[17] Bred to be a Southern gentleman, however, Poe never worked at a trade for any significant period of time—unlike Whitman and Mark Twain, both of whom, like Franklin, worked in the printing business. Rather, he made his avocation—literature—his career.

The *Autobiography* makes plain that another personal trait contributed greatly to Franklin's success—what his admirer and one-time secretary Benjamin Vaughn aptly termed his "disinterestedness."[18] Whatever endeavor Franklin tried his hand at, he studied carefully, learning its rules and devising a means by which to be successful at it. Anticipating his later scientific work, he experimented with different methods, pursuing those that proved effective and abandoning those that did not. Printing appealed to Franklin because of his love for reading and books, but it is clear that he would have done well in any trade or métier he devoted himself to, as his many useful inventions, groundbreaking investigations into electricity, and celebrated civic, political, and diplomatic initiatives attest. Poe, like Franklin, had a healthy sense of humor and was often quite calculating in his efforts to draw attention to himself. However, he cared too deeply about his art to be detached about it. In a November 30, 1845, appeal for money, he told George Poe, Jr., "I have perseveringly struggled, against a thousand difficulties, and have succeeded, although not in making money, still in attaining a position in the world of Letters, of which, under the circumstances, I have no reason to be ashamed" (*CL*, I 303). This statement reveals Poe's belief in the impossibility of both earning a literary reputation through talent alone and prospering. In connection with his writing, had Poe been more like his character C. Auguste Dupin, whose detachment resembles Franklin's, he very likely would have supported himself more successfully and achieved financial stability, but his art presumably would have suffered as a consequence. Poe seems to have recognized this, connecting the inspiration of the Muses with indigence by observing, "Never sing the Nine so well as when penniless,"[19] in a scathing attack on a tin-eared affluent poet in 1843. His Philadelphia employer George Graham was thus, at best, half right in claiming that Poe "cared little for money and knew less of its value" (*PL* 381). Throughout his life, Poe frequently made choices based on principle or personal animus that cost him financially; however, because of the deprivation resulting from such choices and the other factors making a literary career in the 1830s and 1840s all but untenable for someone without means or powerful connections, Poe knew only too well the value of the money he did not have.

Poe's dire circumstances during his second extended stint in New York compelled him to publish the travelogue-like *Doings in Gotham* series in 1844 and the gossipy installments of *The Literati of New York City* in 1846; however, he continued to write imaginative literature until the end of his life, producing some of his finest poems and tales in his later years. Had he cared less about and been more practical in connection with his art, he might have fully embraced fact-based writing, which proved to be an avenue to wealth and fame for a few of his contemporaries. One of these was Nathaniel Parker Willis, Poe's employer at the New York *Evening Mirror* in late 1844 and early 1845, who carved out a lucrative career for himself through accounts of exotic places and reports on high society. Another was Joel Tyler Headley, who achieved unprecedented success for an American author by means of travel writing and popular history. Today these more practical and, consequently, more celebrated and richly rewarded contemporaries of Poe have been all but forgotten. People recall Willis mainly because he was the original publisher of "The Raven," the object of a dismissive allusion in Emerson's "The American Scholar," and the man who employed Harriet Jacobs as a nanny for many years. As for Headley, if he is remembered at all, it is because one of his sketches about Italy partly inspired Poe's "The Cask of Amontillado."

I opened this chapter by quoting the first half of Poe's poem in which a "gallant knight" begins to lose heart as he continues his quixotic pursuit of Eldorado. Allow me to quote the rest of it:

> And, as his strength
> Failed him at length
> He met a pilgrim shadow—
> "Shadow," said he,
> "Where can it be—
> This land of Eldorado?"

"Over the Mountains
Of the Moon,
Down the Valley of the Shadow,
Ride, boldly ride,"
The shade replied—
"If you seek for Eldorado!" (*CW*, I 463)

Unfavorable literary, national, and personal economies doomed Poe—in so many ways the anti-Franklin—to a short life of grinding poverty, financial insolvency, and unrealized aspirations. However, precisely because of his commitment to an art that delights rather than instructs or blatantly self-promotes, ever since his passing, and with increasing frequency and intensity, Poe has become a figure on whom readers, writers, visual artists, and composers, as well as filmmakers and animators, have projected their own dreams—and nightmares.

Outside Looking In: Poe and New York City

Born in Boston but raised in Virginia, Poe lived in New York City for two extended periods, from early 1837 to early 1838 and from April 1844 until his death in October 1849. After establishing himself as an editor, critic, and literary artist at (and being forced out of) the *Southern Literary Messenger* in Richmond, he came as an outsider to the nation's most important publishing hub because it appeared to offer him opportunities to advance his literary career. His toast at the March 30, 1837, Booksellers Banquet—"The Monthlies of Gotham— Their distinguished Editors, and their vigorous Collaborateurs"[1]—indicated his desire to play a role as an insider in the city's publishing industry, but the severe economic depression that began shortly thereafter frustrated his ambitions, and by the following spring he had moved to Philadelphia.[2] During the first sixteen months that followed his return to New York, he experienced high points, such as the sensations created by the "The Balloon Hoax" (which ran in the *New York Sun* on April 13, 1844) and "The Raven" (published in the *American Review's* February 1845 issue as well as the *New York Evening Mirror's* January 29, 1845, issue), invitations to literary soirées, and sole editorial control (and shortly thereafter outright ownership) of a magazine in the latter half of that year. These successes have led J. Gerald Kennedy to refer to 1844 as Poe's "annus mirabilis."[3] However, late the following year and early the next, his fortunes began to plummet. A disastrous reading at the Boston Lyceum in October 1845 was followed by the demise of the *Broadway Journal*, which ceased publication with the January 3, 1846, issue, and, soon afterward, a scandal involving the poets Frances Osgood and Elizabeth Ellet led to fallacious reports that Poe had been institutionalized for mental illness. This combination of misfortunes resulted in his being effectively exiled from the New York publishing world. That spring both he and his wife were ill, making it difficult for Poe to work, and he produced far fewer texts, especially fictional ones, in 1846 than he had during the previous two years. The nadir came in December 1846 when there were appeals for donations to support Poe, his dying wife, and his mother-in-law, who were described as living in extreme poverty in the Bronx (*PL*, 577–85, 614–15, 622–24, 672–78).

During his second extended New York period, Poe published two nonfiction series about the city loosely structured around an opposition between inside and outside, as well as a short story concerning a rivalry between an insider and an outsider that turns deadly. *Doings in Gotham* (seven installments, May 18 to July 6, 1844, in the *Columbia* [Pennsylvania] *Spy* newspaper) is a kind of travel journal by a nonnative who shares what he has learned about the city with provincial readers, and *The Literati of New York City* (six installments, May through October 1846, in the Philadelphia-based *Godey's Lady's Book*), provides a mix of gossipy portraits and glib assessments of New York writers from the perspective of a purported insider.[4] One of Poe's best-known stories, "The Cask of Amontillado" (*Godey's* November 1846), tells the tale of an out-of-favor nobleman who walls up his popular foe in a crypt.[5]

Poe relies on several oppositions in *Doings* and the *Literati*, notably quacks versus geniuses, public/printed opinion versus private/spoken opinion, fancy versus imagination, nonsense versus sense, and the provinces versus New York City. Similarly, "Cask" pits the well-liked, happy-go-lucky Fortunato, who is a Mason, against the disliked and disgruntled Montresor, who does not belong to the secret society. All of these dichotomies might be subsumed under the in-out opposition. In *Doings*, Poe presents himself as an outsider looking in on New York, identifying himself as someone familiar with Philadelphia and its environs, which he often uses as points of comparison while describing the larger metropolis. Located in New York and providing inside information about it to an audience of outsiders, he nevertheless writes as an outsider in *Doings*. In the *Literati*, he again writes about New York City for an outside, provincial audience—although the highly successful *Godey's* was distributed nationally. This time, however, he does so as a self-proclaimed insider, an author based in New York, someone privy to inside opinion and thereby uniquely qualified to share gossip with his audience of outsiders. Although Poe was still living in Manhattan when the *Literati* began to appear, he had by that time, as noted earlier, once again become an outsider vis-à-vis the New York literary scene, a status that was reinforced when he and his family moved thirteen miles outside of the city to a cottage in Fordham in May 1846, in part because of his consumptive wife's precarious health (*PL*, 638–39).

Poe decries the cruel dynamics of the antebellum literary scene in his letters and several works published before the *Literati*, most notably "Some Secrets of the

Magazine Prison-House," which appeared in the *Broadway Journal* in February 1845. The lack of an international copyright law makes the publication of books by American writers rare because publishers can print volumes by established foreign authors without having to pay royalties. As a result, magazines have become the only practical means of finding an audience; however, the "poor devil authors" receive little or nothing for periodical publication.[6] He explains the harmful effects this situation has had on "our national literature" in a September 1845 *Marginalia* entry. It keeps out of print "the efforts of our men of genius, for genius, as a general rule, is poor in worldly goods and cannot write for nothing." Meanwhile, "editors and proprietors" put into their magazines, typically without compensation, the writings of "gentlemen of elegant leisure," who "have been noted, time out of mind, for the insipidity of their productions," their "obstinately conservative" nature, and their "imitation of foreign, more especially of British models."[7] Because the wages (and, as the cliché goes, the stakes) were so low, the antebellum publishing world not only bred enmity between writers of "genius" and "quacks" but also spawned bitter personal animosities. After two years in the crucible of the New York literary scene, having seen his fortunes rise and precipitously fall and having written extensively about the factors responsible for the mediocre quality of American letters, Poe wrote a story devoted to the rivalry between an insider and an outsider, "The Cask of Amontillado," his only new work of fiction to be written and published in 1846. In the light of Poe's experiences in New York in 1844, 1845, and 1846, we can fruitfully see him and, I contend, he must to a certain extent have seen himself as both the outsider Montresor and insider Fortunato.

Looking in on Gotham

As Scott Peeples has discussed, the writing of a series of letters from and about New York had become a popular practice by the early 1840s, one in which Nathaniel Parker Willis, Lydia Maria Child, and George G. Foster participated. Whereas Child and Foster wrote for specific outside audiences—Bostonians, abolitionists, Fourierists—Willis, portraying himself as the consummate insider, wrote for people residing inside the city *and* for those outside of it. As Peeples notes, Poe clearly had Willis in mind while penning *Doings*, mentioning him several times, quoting his poems in full, and even, at least initially, affecting the style of the man who would employ him at the *New York Mirror* from the fall of 1844 until the spring of the 1845, publish "The Raven" in late January 1845, and staunchly defend him against his many detractors after his death in 1849. According to Peeples, "reading 'Doings in Gotham' against other New York Letters series deepens our appreciation for how enmeshed Poe was in the network of New York journalism."[8] Yet despite its links to other such New York series and the writings of Willis in particular, Poe unmistakably left his own fingerprints all over *Doings*.[9]

The first paragraph of the initial installment alerts readers that Poe's approach to his task will be random because, as he explains, "I must deal chiefly in *gossip*," an "unlimited" subject "engrossing at least seven-eighths of the whole waking existence of Mankind" that has "neither beginning, middle, nor end" and recognizes no "law."[10] Therefore, he reserves the right to swerve from his "avowed purpose" of depicting New York, indulging in "a frequent hop-skip-and-jump, over the hedges, into the tempting pastures of digression" and "touching . . . upon everything and something besides."[11] Although I agree with Peeples's observation that Poe abandons a Willisesque style after the opening paragraph, I must take exception to his contention that "throughout most of 'Doings in Gotham,' Poe presents himself not as the new arrival that he was but as a curmudgeonly Knickerbocker."[12] Poe decidedly does not adopt the pose of a New York insider in the series. Described by the *Spy* as a correspondent "from the City of New-York, where he has taken up residence for the present" (rather than a native New Yorker or a permanent transplant),[13] Poe frequently aligns himself with his provincial readers, evoking the gingerbread "in some of the Dutch boroughs of Pennsylvania," referring to an article in "a Philadelphian paper," and contrasting New York's most famous thoroughfare with those in the "city of Brotherly Love": "Foreigners are apt to speak of the great *length* of Broadway. It is no doubt a long street; but we have many much longer in Philadelphia."[14] Through his use of the first-person plural, he clearly dissociates his readers and himself from New Yorkers (whom he refers to as "the"—rather than "we"—"Gothamites" throughout the series).

At times, Poe assumes the role of the literary traveler. He walks the streets, paddles about in boats, describes merchants' wares, remarks landmarks, deplores city noise and street filth, and critiques architecture and urban planning. Two instances, in particular, stand out. He memorably offers the following advice to his readers, should they ever journey to the city:

> When you visit Gotham, you should ride out the Fifth Avenue, as far as the distributing reservoir, near forty-third street, I believe. The prospect from

the walk around the reservoir, is particularly beautiful. You can see, from this elevation, the north reservoir at Yorkville; the whole city to the battery; with a large portion of the harbor, and long reaches of the Hudson and East rivers.[15]

Poe's peregrinations about New York do not occur solely on foot, as he also observes the city from the East River, telling readers in the third installment:

A day or two since I procured a light skiff, and with the aid of a pair of *sculls*, (as they here term short oars, or paddles) made my way around Blackwell's [now Roosevelt] Island, on a voyage of discovery and exploration. The chief interest of the adventure lay in the scenery of the Manhattan shore, which is here particularly picturesque. The houses are without exception, *frame*, and antique. Nothing very modern has been attempted—a necessary result of the subdivision of the whole island into streets and town-lots. I could not look on the magnificent cliffs, and stately trees, which at every moment met my view, without a sigh for their inevitable doom—inevitable and swift. In twenty years, or thirty at farthest, we shall see here nothing more romantic than shipping, warehouses, and wharves.[16]

Poe accurately predicts that the pace of change in the metropolis, so noticeable to him after an absence of a half a dozen years, will not only continue but accelerate, and, along with it, the loss of natural beauty.

At other times, Poe delivers inside opinions on the visual arts, local and national politics, corruption, "mob-disorder," celebrated trials, and, of course, writers and the publishing world. Rufus Griswold, in particular, suffers at the hands of Poe the critic, who as early as the mid-1830s was given the nickname the "tomahawk man" for the scathing reviews he published in the *Southern Literary Messenger*. In the sixth installment of *Doings in Gotham*, after mentioning that Griswold served for a time as the editor of *The Opal*, a holiday annual, Poe states:

By the way, if you have *not* seen Mr. Griswold's "American Series of the Curiosities of Literature," then look at it, for God's sake—or for mine. I wish you to say, upon your word of honor, whether it is, or is not, *per se*, the greatest of *all* the Curiosities of Literature, or whether it is as great a curiosity as the compiler himself.[17]

Poe does not specify exactly what makes Griswold's contribution to Isaac Disraeli's *Curiosities of Literature* so odd. On the one hand, some of its contents make fascinating reading even today, including "Bold Hawthorne," a ballad about the commander of the *Fair American*, written by the ship's surgeon, which Griswold recovered and first reprinted in 1842. The "noble captain," as Griswold explains, "wounded in the head by a musket ball" while battling the British during the Revolutionary War, was "an ancestor of the inimitable author, Nathaniel Hawthorne, of Salem."[18] On the other hand, "The Curiosities of American Literature" contains notable errors, such as the assertion that Anne Bradstreet's verse was first printed "at Cambridge in 1640."[19] What may in particular have irked Poe was Griswold's decision "to exclude everything relating to contemporaries" from the "Curiosities,"[20] meaning, of course, that there would be no mention of Poe. As for Griswold's own eccentricities, Poe may have already divined these from his personal dealings with the man, whom he first met in 1841, and the accounts of others.[21] In the seventh and final letter of *Doings*, Poe returns to the subject, dispelling any possible ambiguity his previous comments may have generated: "It is preposterous, also, to hear anything like commendation of that last and greatest of all absurdities, Griswold's Appendix to D'Israeli's 'Curiosities of Literature.'"[22]

Miscellaneous items in *Doings* often let readers in on subjects that relate in fascinating ways to Poe's own life and writings. In the first installment, he talks about the ongoing "bustle of the first of May," the date on which so many New Yorkers, particularly boarders like Poe and his family, move out of one place of residence and into another.[23] The third letter contrasts Edward Bulwer-Lytton's visit to the United States with that of Charles Dickens, whom Poe met in Philadelphia in 1842. In the fourth installment, he describes the sensation created by a "foot-race" watched by 11,000 people, yet he is not impressed by the winner's time—"Touching the actual feat in question—ten miles within the hour—I have not only accomplished it myself, but firmly believe that there are at least one thousand men, in our western districts, who could perform, with proper training, *twelve*, with all ease," adding that, because gentlemen do not "contend, in public," such contests only involve athletes who come from "'the lower classes' of society" and do not feature "the most active men—those in the highest physical condition."[24] Poe also alludes to his own publications. The use of the esoteric word *porphyrogenitus*, which he translates as "born in the purple,"[25] in the opening paragraph of the series recalls his 1839 poem "The Haunted Palace," later incorporated into "The Fall of the House of Usher." References to detection, stereotomy (a type of pavement), Mary Rogers, and "gift-books" evoke the Dupin trilogy—"The Murders in the Rue Morgue," "The Mystery of Marie Rogêt" and "The Purloined Letter." The latter story appeared in the *The Gift* for 1845 (meaning that it was available in the second half of 1844), a volume that Poe predicts "will bear away the palm" among the Christmas annuals for that year.[26]

A long paragraph in the fourth installment about Antarctic exploration, which includes two mentions of "Reynolds," relates to his 1838 novel *The Narrative of Arthur Gordon Pym* (as well as to accounts of the supposed ravings of a delirious Poe while on his deathbed).[27] Moreover, he makes explicit reference to his own "Balloon Hoax," recently perpetrated in New York, which he compares and contrasts to Richard Adams Locke's earlier "Moon-Story," thereby anticipating his long discussion of Locke's hoax two years later in the final installment of the *Literati*.[28]

Letting Some Secrets of the New York Literati Out

Portraying himself as an insider lifting the veil to reveal what is really true about the New York literary scene by sharing what writers and editors actually say about their peers behind closed doors, Poe makes the outside-inside opposition that is implicit in *Doings* overt in the *Literati*. He asserts, "With one or two exceptions I am well acquainted with every author to be introduced, and shall avail myself of the acquaintance to convey, generally, some idea of the personal appearance of all who, in this regard, would be likely to interest the readers of the magazine."[29] In doing so, he further emphasizes the opposition, often criticizing the inaccuracy of official (public, outside) portraits, which he remedies by offering his own (private, inside) descriptions of people's physical characteristics. He explains that he limits himself to "New York literature" not because it is unique but rather because it "may be taken as a fair representation of that of the country at large. The city itself is the focus of American letters. Its authors include, perhaps, one-fourth of all in America," and their influence is "extensive and decisive."[30] Over a year previous to this, an anonymous New York *Evening Mirror* item entitled "Why Have the New Yorkers No Review" that biographers have attributed to Poe, asserted, "We are the chief city in the Union in all respects, and in no respect more especially than in the number and eminence of our literary men—in the number and merit of the books they write."[31]

Poe's ambition to reshape American letters has been the subject of recent criticism. The 2012 essay collection *Poe and the Mapping of Antebellum Print Culture* focuses on Poe "not because of any assumed preeminence among contemporary literati," as J. Gerald Kennedy, one of the coeditors, explains, but rather "because he was among the first to regard the republic of letters then emerging in the United States as a community imaginable across boundaries of region, party, and clique, and beyond differences of gender. His involvement in the magazine world and print culture . . . make him singularly representative of the practical realities of antebellum literary production."[32] In particular, as Kennedy goes on to state, "his various efforts to construct an idea of the literary nation and to install himself as critical kingpin, comprise an illuminating yet largely unappreciated dimension of Poe's achievement."[33] Kennedy convincingly argues that just as Poe intended to incorporate the *Literati* into his subsequent unrealized projects, *The Living Writers of America* and *Literary America*, the origins of the 1846 *Godey's* series can be traced back to his series on "Autography" in the *Southern Literary Messenger* in 1836. This was a project he would resurrect and significantly expand in *Graham's Magazine* in 1841 and which, along with the *Literati* and other similar projects, complemented his long-term effort to found his own journal devoted to the productions of prominent writers from all regions of the United States.

Given the exhaustive nature of Kennedy's project to enumerate Poe's multiple endeavors to map American literature and publishing in the antebellum United States, it is somewhat surprising that he makes no mention of Poe's extensive review of *The Complete Poetical Works of William Cullen Bryant*, published in *Godey's* the month before the start of the *Literati*. Poe refers to this critique in the opening sentence of the series: "In a criticism on Bryant published in the last number of this magazine, I was at some pains in pointing out the distinction between popular 'opinion' of the merits of cotemporary authors and that held and expressed of them in private literary society."[34] Even though it was not officially part of the series that began in *Godey's* in May, Poe saw his April review as a key precursor to the *Literati* and an integral part of his larger project to chart the republic of letters because of Bryant's well-established position in the New York publishing scene as both one of the nation's most lauded poets and the editor of the *New York Evening Post*.

In the Bryant review, Poe adopts the pose of a literary (and New York) insider. Referring to members of "private literary circles," he states:

> The fact is, that when brought face to face with each other we are constrained to a certain amount of honesty by the sheer trouble it causes us to mould the countenance to a lie. We put on paper with a grave air what we could not for our lives assert personally to a friend without either blushing or laughing outright. That the opinion of the press is not an honest opinion, that necessarily it is impossible that it should be an honest opinion, is never denied by the members of the press themselves.[35]

The next month in the initial installment of the *Literati*, he returns to this subject:

> But the very editors who hesitate at saying in print an ill word of an author
> personally known, are usually the most frank in speaking about him privately.
> In literary society, they seem bent upon avenging the wrongs self-inflicted upon
> their own consciences. Here, accordingly, the quack is treated as he deserves—
> even a little more harshly than he deserves—by way of striking a balance. True
> merit, on the same principle, is apt to be slightly overrated; but, upon the whole,
> there is a close approximation to absolute honesty of opinion.

As a result of this private veracity and public dishonesty, "the most 'popular,' the
most 'successful' writers among us, (for a brief period, at least,) are, ninety-nine
times out of a hundred, persons of mere address, perseverance, effrontery—in a
word, busy-bodies, toadies, quacks"; meanwhile, "men of genius," who refuse to
"resort to these manœuvres," struggle "because genius involves in its very essence
a scorn of chicanery."[36] After repeating almost verbatim what he said about lying,
blushing, and laughing outright in the Bryant review, he proceeds in the initial
installment of the *Literati* to contrast the reputations of Nathaniel Hawthorne
and Henry Wadsworth Longfellow in order to illustrate the "very remarkable
discrepancy between the apparent public opinion of any given author's merits
and the opinion which is expressed of him orally by those who are best qualified
to judge." The former, a "poor man" who is not a "ubiquitous quack," "is scarcely
recognized by the press or by the public, and when noticed at all, is noticed
merely to be damned by faint praise" even though his "extraordinary genius"
has "no rival either in America or elsewhere."[37] In contrast, popular opinion
regards Longfellow, "a man of property and a professor at Harvard" as "a poetical
phenomenon, as entirely without fault as is the luxurious paper upon which his
poems" are printed, yet in "private society he is regarded . . . as a determined
imitator and dexterous adapter of the ideas of other people."[38] Poe implicitly
associates himself with Hawthorne, a "poor devil author" at the mercy of the
"fat," "pursy 'editor[s]'" and "bottle-nosed 'proprietor[s]'" he describes in "Some
Secrets of the Magazine Prison-House."[39]

In the *Godey's* series, Poe delivers on his promise to provide two types of
often-conflicting inside information—his "own unbiased opinion of the
literati (male and female) of New York" and that of "conversational society in
literary circles."[40] In the six installments, he profiles thirty-seven authors and
editors, including Willis, Evert Duyckinck, Margaret Fuller, Lydia Maria Child,
and Catherine Sedgwick. Some of these figures he flatters, some he ridicules,

and others he analyzes extensively and meticulously. Along the way, he often lashes out at Bostonians, particularly the Transcendentalists, and, once again, raises concerns about the editorial choices and critical assessments of Rufus Griswold, who would exact a notorious and nearly century-long revenge on Poe for this and other actual and perceived slights. Poe refers to Griswold by name seven times in the *Literati*, sometimes noting his errors, sometimes indirectly criticizing him, and sometimes openly questioning his judgment. In the section on James Aldrich in the third installment, after mentioning that "three (or four)" of Aldrich's poems appeared in Griswold's *The Poets and Poetry of America*, Poe accuses Aldrich of plagiarizing Thomas Hood, implicitly chiding Griswold for including the poems in his collection.[41] In the Henry Cary section in the same installment, Poe skewers Griswold, Charles F. Briggs (his one-time coeditor and coproprietor at the *Broadway Journal*), and Cary himself. The article begins by noting Griswold's inaccuracies: "Doctor Griswold introduces *Mr. Cary* to the appendix of 'The Poet[s] and Poetry,' as Mr. Henry Carey, and gives him credit for an Anacreontic song of much merit entitled, or commencing, 'Old Wine to Drink.' This was *not* written by Mr. C. He has composed little verse, if any, but, under the *nom de plume* of 'John Waters,' has acquired some note by a series of essays in 'The New York American' and 'The Knickerbocker.'"[42] Poe upbraids Briggs at considerable length for overpraising Cary, whom Poe judges to be a "fifth or sixth rate" essayist. Echoing his September 1845 *Marginalia* item, Poe faults Briggs and Griswold for promoting businessmen who dabble in literature: "Mr. Cary is what Doctor Griswold calls a 'gentleman of elegant leisure.' He is wealthy and much addicted to letters and *virtû*. For a long time he was President of the Phœnix Bank of New York, and the principal part of his life has been devoted to business."[43] For Poe, the frequency with which men of affluence and status such as Cary appear in periodicals contributes to the inferior quality of American writing.

He also decries a related problem: the tendency of critics to overpraise authors. In the initial section of Part 5 of the *Literati* devoted to Charles Fenno Hoffman, Poe accuses Griswold of indulging in crude favoritism:

> Whatever may be the merits of Mr. Hoffman as a poet, it may be easily seen that these merits have been put in the worst possible light by the indiscriminate and lavish approbation bestowed on them by Doctor Griswold in his "Poets and Poetry of America." The compiler can find *no* blemish in Mr. H., agrees with everything and copies everything said in his praise—worse than all, gives him more space in the book than any two, or perhaps three, of our poets combined.

All this is as much an insult to Mr. Hoffman as to the public, and has done the former irreparable injury—how or why, it is of course unnecessary to say.[44]

In the opening section of the fourth installment, on Sarah Margaret Fuller, Poe evokes Griswold's "Curiosities," as he did in *Doings*: "'Woman in the Nineteenth Century' is a book which few women in the country could have written, and no woman in the country would have published, with the exception of Miss Fuller. In the way of independence, or unmitigated radicalism, it is one of the 'Curiosities of American Literature,' and Doctor Griswold should include it in his book." Poe acclaims Fuller, whom he regards as the antithesis of dilettantes such as Cary, because of her "genius (for high genius she unquestionably possesses)."[45] He implies that just as Griswold has missed Aldrich's plagiarisms, puffs amateurs like Cary, and allows bias to dictate his editorial decisions, he lacks the ability to recognize true genius such as Fuller's.[46]

Similar to *Doings*, Poe does not hesitate to make several explicit and covert references to himself in the *Literati*, ranging from the increase in circulation he effected at the *Southern Literary Messenger* to items he published in the *Broadway Journal* and *Godey's* to a facetious offer to forgive to Lewis Gaylord Clark for reviewing *The Raven and Other Poems*. Although the controversial nature of the *Literati* made it quite popular, the series did nothing to change Poe's marginal position in the New York publishing world; rather, it led to counterattacks and even a protracted libel suit Poe brought against the New York *Evening Mirror* in 1846.

Inside and Out: Revenge in "The Cask of Amontillado"

Just as the Bryant review, published in the April 1846 issue of *Godey's*, serves as a kind of preface to the six installments of the *Literati*, "The Cask of Amontillado," which appeared in the November issue of the magazine, might be regarded as a fictional culmination to the series. In the tale, a man of French descent living in Italy recounts how fifty years earlier he exacted revenge on Fortunato, an Italian. A "quack" in his knowledge of "painting and gemmary," Fortunato, like Montresor himself, takes pride in "his connoisseurship in wine" (*CW*, III 1257). As he lures his foe to the fatal crypt, their conversation indicates Montresor's outsider status. Referring to the possible ill effects of the damp, nitre-encrusted catacombs on their health, he contrasts himself with the popular, contented Fortunato: "You are rich, respected, admired, beloved; you are happy, as once I was. You are a man to be missed. For me it is no matter" (*CW*, III 1259). Moreover, when Fortunato makes a gesture that Montresor does not comprehend, the former declares, "Then you are not of the brotherood," referring to the Masons, a fraternal order to which he does and Montresor does not belong. Choosing carnival season so that both he and Fortunato are in costume and ensuring that his servants have left the house, Montresor uses a pipe of Amontillado as the MacGuffin to lead his enemy first into his family's catacombs, then inside "a deep crypt" in which there is an "interior crypt," which itself has "a still interior crypt or recess" that "seemed to have been constructed for no especial use within itself." When his victim enters this innermost crypt following his declaration "herein is the Amontillado," Montresor chains Fortunato to the back of this "niche" and walls up the "figure within" (*CW*, III 1260, 1261, 1262). Thus, in achieving his vengeance, Montresor transforms his enemy from a figurative, that is, social, insider into a literal one.

In writing the story, Poe drew inspiration from an account of a literal insider— actually a mummy—in a church wall. Since 1934 when *American Literature* published Joseph Schick's article on the subject, scholars have acknowledged the striking similarities between "Cask" and "A Man Built in a Wall," an account of an upright skeleton J. T. Headley claimed to have seen in a church south of Florence in 1843.[47] Prompted by the claim of a physician accompanying him that the cause of death was suffocation, Headley tells a tale of vengeance in which the man was sealed alive behind the wall as his bitter enemy looked on. Although other sources have been proposed as the inspiration for Poe's story, none resembles it as closely as "A Man Built in a Wall." Like Poe, Headley asserts that the victim and the man responsible for his live burial were "men of rank," claims that the latter "stood leaning on his sword—a smile of scorn and revenge on his features—and watched the face of the man he hated," details the walling up of the immobilized victim tier by tier by a mason using a trowel, emphasizes the placing of the final stone to complete the entombment, and alludes to the death of the killer many years after he committed the murder.[48] Additionally, to underscore the excruciating nature of the means by which the man died, Headley twice uses the phrase "At length," the same words Poe italicizes at the start of the third sentence of his story when Montresor states, "*At length*, I would be avenged" (*CW*, III 1256).

Surprisingly, no Poe scholar has ever, apparently, attempted to establish the veracity of Headley's story. Had such a person done so, he or she would have discovered not the "skeleton" Headley writes about but a mummy known locally as *l'uomo murato* (the walled man). Wally, as I will refer to him, was found when some repairs were undertaken in the Church of San Lorenzo in San Giovanni Valdarno in 1780 and was put on semipublic display there in 1820. He has been the subject of articles in history books, scholarly journals, and local magazines; is mentioned on several travel websites; and can even be seen in a three-minute YouTube video.[49] (See the image of *l'uomo murato* on the back cover of this book.) Although nothing definitive is known about Wally's identity, people over the years have speculated that he might have been someone famous, including San Giovanni Valdarno's favorite son, the artist known as Masaccio, a friend of Donatello and an innovator who had a profound influence on Michelangelo. Others, however, assert that it is much more likely that Wally was a criminal originally buried in unconsecrated ground whose family had enough influence to arrange to have the body secretly buried in the church. Headley himself contributed to the interest in Wally among foreign tourists. The 1843 edition of the *Handbook for Travellers in Central Italy*, which Headley almost certainly read, contains a brief description of Wally. Likely because of the stature Headley had achieved as a writer in the interim, the 1850 edition of the same guidebook quotes "A Man Built in a Wall" extensively, presenting it as if it were historical fact.[50]

A travel and nature writer, popular historian, and politician, Joel Tyler Headley was born in Delaware County, New York, in 1813. He earned a divinity degree and briefly served as a minister in Stockbridge, Massachusetts, before suffering a breakdown in 1842, which led to his embarking on a long European tour. Between January 1843 and February 1844, the *New York Tribune* published twenty-seven of his "Letters from Italy." In March of 1844, twenty-two of Headley's letters, nearly all of which had appeared in the *Tribune*, were published in *Italy and the Italians*.[51] Neither the *Tribune* series nor *Italy and the Italians* included "A Man Built in a Wall," which first appeared in the August 1844 issue of the *Columbian Magazine*, the same issue in which Poe's "Mesmeric Revelations" was published. From that point on, Headley became increasingly visible in the New York publishing world. Between November 1844 and July 1845, he published at least fifteen "Alpine Sketches" in the *New York Observer*, a virulently anti-Catholic religious weekly. In spring 1845, articles by Headley appeared in *Graham's Magazine*, the *Democratic Review*, the *American Review*, and the *Christian Parlor*, a New York monthly magazine for which Headley would become the editor in 1847. Late June 1845 saw the appearance of Headley's *Letters from Italy*, containing forty-nine letters, the thirty-ninth of which was

"A Man Built in a Wall." The book sold well and garnered considerable and mainly favorable critical attention, with some of the reviewers commenting specifically on or quoting from "A Man Built in a Wall." In connection with the publication of *Letters from Italy*, the weekly *New York Mirror* printed "A Man in Built in a Wall" in its July 12, 1845, issue.[52] From September 1845 through August 1846, the *Christian Parlor* printed ten installments of Headley's "Rambles about Paris and London" series, late in 1845 Headley's *The Alps and the Rhine* appeared, and between February and June 1846 the *Observer* published seven installments of Headley's new series, the "Sacred Mountains."

In spring 1846, Baker and Scribner published Headley's initial foray into popular history, *Napoleon and His Marshalls*, Scribner's first bestseller, which was so successful that by 1861 it was in its fiftieth printing. The book received long, mostly positive, reviews in the leading newspapers and journals of the day, and, because it was published in two volumes, there were often multiple reviews in the same periodical, frequently accompanied by extended excerpts. In September 1846, Baker and Scribner published notices in the *Tribune* stating that Headley's *The Sacred Mountains* would be published in early October as an elaborately engraved gift book. Despite being available for sale in early fall 1846, this volume bore the date 1847 because of a printer's error, which led to a federal court case involving copyright infringement. For several months during 1847, Headley engaged in a public battle with Rufus Griswold arising from competing books about George Washington and his generals prepared by the two men, a feud Headley effectively won when the *New York Daily Tribune* printed a letter in which he declared,

> I should not have taken the trouble to contradict the ridiculous accusations he made, if your paper had been confined to the city where he is understood. A man to whom even his friends have been accustomed to say, "is that a Griswold or a fact," I can well let pass where he is known, but in other parts of the country where *The Tribune* circulates, people are not well acquainted with matters.[53]

Having continued to publish works of history and travel, as well as a volume on the Adirondack Mountains, Headley sold an astounding number of books— over 200,000 copies—by 1853.[54] The next year, as a member of the nativist, anti-Catholic Know Nothing Party, Headley was elected to the New York state assembly; from 1855 to 1858 he served as secretary of state for New York; and, when he died in 1897, he had published a total of thirty books. However, it was the period from mid-1844, when "A Man Built in a Wall" was first published, through fall 1846, when *The Sacred Mountains* appeared that transformed Headley from a fledgling writer into a literary star. As noted earlier, these two and a half years would be pivotal and remarkably productive for Poe as well, although 1846, Headley's banner year, was Poe's *annus horribilis*.

There were numerous connections between Poe and Headley in 1844, 1845, and 1846. Duyckinck, who corresponded with both men, edited and actively promoted two books by each writer in 1845, Poe's *Tales* and *The Raven and Other Poems* and Headley's *Letters from Italy* and *The Alps and the Rhine* in Wiley and Putnam's American Library series. Moreover, Poe reviewed Headley's books positively in the *Broadway Journal*.[55] His assessment of *Letters from Italy*, in fact, explicitly mentions the "Man in the Wall" but does not comment further on it.[56] Anne C. Lynch attested that Poe and Headley attended a party she hosted on January 10, 1846, and it seems likely that the men interacted socially on other occasions during 1845 and early 1846 when Poe was a frequent guest at New York literary gatherings (*PL*, 619–20). Although some scholars have argued for an earlier composition date, Poe told Philip Pendleton Cooke in an April 16, 1846, letter, "I am now writing for Godey a series of articles called 'The N. Y. City Literati'" (*CL*, I 564). Two weeks later, he asked Duyckinck to supply him with the autographs of several authors, including Headley, indicating the intention to write something about him (*CL*, I 570). Another key link between the men, hitherto unnoticed by scholars, concerns the commencement exercises held at the University of Vermont in August 1846. In April, Poe was invited by members of the school's literary societies to serve as commencement poet, an offer he declined, citing "a multiplicity of engagements" and what he termed "serious and, I fear, permanent ill health." When Duyckinck loyally complied with Poe's request that he publicize this honor, getting a brief notice about the university's invitation printed on the second page of the May 1 issue of the *Tribune*, it was overshadowed by Margaret Fuller's lengthy page one review of the initial volume of *Napoleon and His Marshalls*.[57] Three months later, on August 8, the front page of the *Tribune* featured a glowing account of the address Headley had delivered at the University of Vermont four days earlier.[58] Perhaps not coincidentally, in a letter to Cooke written the very next day, Poe discusses his renewed plans for establishing the *Stylus*, a magazine which would pit "men of genius" such as himself against "those dunces the men of talent" (*CL*, I 597), a group that included successful writers such as Headley.

The clearest link between Poe and Headley has always been the former's savagely funny, posthumously published review of *The Sacred Mountains*, which appeared under the title "Joel T. Headley" at roughly the same time in the *Southern Literary Messenger* and the third volume of *The Works of the Late Edgar Allan Poe*, edited by Griswold. It describes Headley as the "Autocrat of all the Quacks" and asserts that "the thing he 'does' especially well is the public."[59] The review begins, "The *Reverend* Mr. Headley—(why *will* he not put his full title in his title pages)," a reference to the fact that the author's name appears on the title page of this and other books simply as "J. T. Headley," which is also the way it is printed at the start of "A Man Built in a Wall" in *Columbian Magazine*.[60] The word "Reverend," which Poe italicizes, likely alludes as well to Headley's practice of using the byline "Rev. [or The Rev.] J. T. Headley" when he published articles in the *Observer* and the *Christian Parlor*. This was also the way he was sometimes referred to in the *Tribune*, including the article about his Vermont commencement address. Many scholars have accepted Rufus Griswold's contention that "Joel T. Headley" was directly connected with the larger Literati project on which Poe was at work during his final years, even though the piece in question is clearly a review as opposed to a wide-ranging evaluation of a writer's life and career, which is the way Poe conceived of the installments of the Literati series. Because much of *The Sacred Mountains* was published in the *New York Observer* by "Rev. J. T. Headley" in the spring of 1846 while Poe was at work on the New York Literati series and the book itself appeared in print in early October of that year, I suspect that Poe wrote the review of Headley's book sometime in the fall of 1846, perhaps trying and failing to place it in a periodical or deciding for some reason not to publish it.

If my theory is correct, then it is possible that Poe wrote *The Sacred Mountains* review within a few weeks of completing "The Cask of Amontillado," which was available to the public when the November issue of *Godey's* went on sale on October 20. Poe's statements about *The Living Writers of America*, one of the names for the larger Literati project, bolster this argument. In his December 16, 1846, letter to George Eveleth, Poe says that in the *Living Writers* he will address "Historical Writing," very likely a reference to Headley (*CL*, I 602). Moreover, in his manuscript for the *Living Writers*, which contains nothing to indicate that it was written after 1846, Poe devotes a paragraph to Headley, signaling his plan to include an article about him in the series. In it Poe refers to four articles and book reviews Headley published between 1844 and 1846 and characterizes him as "nervous," unimaginative, and easily "impressed," as well as a writer with an "Irish headstrong style" and a dearth of "powers of reason." The paragraph begins with the note, "See scrap in bundle," no doubt a reference to his previous reviews of Headley's books in the *Broadway Journal* (one of which refers to Headley's "Irish *abandon*") but very likely to *The Sacred Mountains* review as well.[61]

In asserting that "The Cask of Amontillado" was to some extent a response not simply to "A Man Built in a Wall" but also to the meteoric trajectory of Headley's career, I do not mean to suggest that he regarded this prolific author as an enemy who had done him an evil turn in the way that critics such as Francis Dedmond see Poe using "Cask" to settle scores with the writer Thomas Dunn English and the editor Hiram Fuller, key figures in the aforementioned libel suit.[62] Rather, because wherever he looked in 1846 Headley was in (and Poe was out)—in New York dailies, in the pages of leading journals, and even in the ceremonies at the University of Vermont—he may have regarded Headley as epitomizing "the duncees the men of talent" (i.e., the "quacks"), who, in stark contrast to Poe, a writer "of genius," undeservedly enjoyed financial success and public acclaim. Thus, Headley, for Poe, may have represented fortune's favorite— that is, Fortunato—someone "respected, admired, beloved, . . . happy . . . a man to be missed," as Poe once was. What better way to get vengeance not on Headley per se but instead on fate itself than to use the semi-fictional sketch about Italy, "A Man Built in a Wall," by this exceedingly verbose writer (whom undiscriminating critics and the fickle public had anointed that year's literary celebrity) as the basis for a true work of art, a remarkably concise tale of incredible power with an Italian setting?

"The Cask of Amontillado" reflects Poe's experiences in New York in a variety of ways. On one level, he likely identified with the outsider Montresor's desire to obtain revenge on one of the "quacks" and "duncees the men of talent" who thrived in the antebellum publishing world.[63] A key critical question about "Cask" concerns who gets the last laugh—Montresor or Fortunato. Poe may have enjoyed the first chuckle in writing the story—and in penning his hilarious assessment of *The Sacred Mountains* shortly thereafter. However, by the time the review appeared in print in 1850, the popular, successful, respected insider Headley, who would hike in the Berkshires with Hawthorne and Herman Melville in August of that year, could easily laugh off this attack from an outsider who had self-destructed so infamously and was the ongoing subject of one of the most vicious character assassinations in literary history, perpetrated by Rufus Griswold. Yet, 170 years later it is Poe—or, if not Poe, then his audience— who has come out on top. As noted in the Chapter 1, the only reason anyone remembers Headley at all today is that his "A Man Built in a Wall" served as a key source for one of the most memorable and most carefully constructed tales by an undisputed master of the short story form. On a different level, as someone thoroughly familiar with the cutthroat world of literary publishing, possessing a love for a good joke, and willing to share the inside dope no matter what the cost to himself, Poe quite plausibly identified with the insensitive, carefree (and inebriated) insider Fortunato in opposition to humorless, deceitful, distrusted, and vindictive Montresor-like men such as Griswold. However, on yet another level, Poe had to know that he himself, an insider and an outsider—and not English, Fuller, Griswold, Headley, or anyone else—was often his own worst enemy. Throughout his career, but especially in 1845 and 1846, Poe's tendency to attack people kept hurrying him to his destruction. And how can we imagine that the author of "The Imp of the Perverse," published in the summer of 1845 and addressing this very subject, was not acutely aware of this?

Only an insider and an outsider could have produced both *Doings in Gotham* and *The Literati of New York City*. In the former, having recently returned to the city after a six-year absence, Poe the nonnative notes how drastically things have changed in New York and accurately predicts how rapidly they will continue to do so. Meanwhile, with considerable experience as not only an editor for several magazines (and even, briefly, the proprietor of a doomed one) but also a "poor devil" author, Poe uniquely had the inside knowledge—as well as the temerity—to publish the "honest opinions" of the latter series. Similarly, what makes several of Poe's stories, foremost among them "The Cask of Amontillado," which followed immediately on the *Literati*'s heels, so fascinating is that they can be convincingly interpreted in at least two (often diametrically opposed) ways. One group of critics has read this tale as a story about a man who plans and successfully executes the perfect act of revenge, and thus they regard Montresor as a reliable narrator. Meanwhile, an opposing critical camp deems Montresor, like other narrators in the writer's most famous tales, to be unreliable and unsuccessful in punishing his foe "with impunity."[64] Relating "The Cask of Amontillado" to Poe's experiences as a New York outsider and insider who strove but failed to realize his literary dreams, we can profitably read the story in a third way, one in which we see him as Montresor, as Fortunato, and as both Montresor *and* Fortunato.

Eddy P., the Scrivener: Biography and Autobiography in Herman Melville's "Story of Wall-Street"[1]

This country & nearly all its affairs are governed by sturdy backwoodsmen—noble fellows enough, but not at all literary, & who care not a fig for any authors except those who write those most saleable of all books nowadays—ie—the newspapers, & magazines. And tho' the number of cultivated, catholic men, who may be supposed to feel an interest in a national literature, is large & every day growing larger; yet they are nothing in comparison with the overwhelming majority who care nothing about it. This country is at present engaged in furnishing material for future authors, not encouraging its living ones.

Herman Melville to Richard Bentley, July 20, 1851

It was rather a step downward, after being the chief editor of several monthlies, as Poe had been, to come into the office of a daily journal as a mechanical paragraphist. It was his business to sit at a desk, in a corner of the editorial room, ready to be called upon for any of the miscellaneous work of the day.

Nathaniel Parker Willis to George Pope Morris, 1859

Following the tepid reception of *Moby-Dick* (1851) and the panning of *Pierre* (1852), which resulted in Herman Melville no longer being able to find a publisher for his books, "Bartleby, the Scrivener: A Story of Wall-Street" appeared in the November and December 1853 issues of *Putnam's Magazine*. Critics have variously read this story about the death of a legal copyist and putative Dead Letter Office worker as Melville's statement about failed attempts at communication, the lack of an audience for the American literary artist, and his own increasingly futile search for readers. As he penned "Bartleby," Melville may have had in mind another author of serious and significant literature compelled to eke out a living by writing for magazines. That author was Edgar Allan Poe, who, having been unable to launch a national journal of his own in Philadelphia, labored at hack work a mere seven blocks away from Wall Street from late 1844 to early 1845 to support himself and his family. Likely drawing on the recollections of friends, acquaintances, and business associates who knew the ill-fated writer, Melville describes his scrivener in terms that recall contemporary accounts of Poe during his New York years, and his story alludes to "Some Secrets of the Magazine Prison-House" (1845) and "The Cask of Amontillado" (1846). Although critical essays and scholarly books have noted references to Poe in several of Melville's writings, including "Bartleby," none has argued, as does this chapter, that descriptions of Poe's appearance, accounts of his work habits, and the perils of his situation as a magazinist with ambitious literary aspirations influenced Melville's narrative, enhancing its emotional power.

After returning from his maritime travels in October 1844, Melville divided his time between New York City, his birthplace, and upstate Lansingburgh, and three months later he was living in Lower Manhattan when "The Raven" caused a sensation. His first two books, *Typee* (1846) and *Omoo* (1847), both set in the South Seas, met with commercial (and critical) success, making it possible for Melville, his new wife, and several other family members to move to 103 Fourth Avenue in the East Village, close to the recently constructed Grace Episcopal Church, which stands there to this day. In 1850, by which time he had published five books and was well established as a writer in New York, Melville began work on what would become *Moby-Dick*, but he made drastic changes to the manuscript after he and his family moved to Pittsfield, Massachusetts, in the Berkshires, where he met Nathaniel Hawthorne. Well before the book appeared in print, Melville confided to Hawthorne in an early May 1851 letter that he felt economically harassed, intellectually exhausted, and artistically compromised:

> The calm, the coolness, the silent grass-growing mood in which man *ought* always to compose—that, I fear, can seldom be mine. Dollars damn me; and the malicious Devil is forever grinning in upon me, holding the door ajar. My dear Sir, a presentiment is on me—I shall at last be worn out and perish, like an old nutmeg-grater, grated to pieces by the constant attrition of the wood, that is, the nutmeg. What I feel most moved to write, that is banned—it will not pay. Yet, altogether, write the *other* way I cannot. So the product is a final hash, and all my books are botches.[2]

Though considered today to be among the greatest novels ever written, *Moby-Dick* received mixed reviews and failed to sell out its 1851 first edition of 3000 copies. If *Moby-Dick* was a severe disappointment for Melville, his next book was a disaster, prompting critics "to question [his] very sanity," and eight months after the 1852 publication of *Pierre*, over 2000 copies of the initial print run had not been purchased; these books, along with the unsold copies of *Moby-Dick*, went up in smoke in a December 1853 warehouse fire.[3] Dan McCall says of this low point in Melville's career and its effects upon him:

> We should remind ourselves that when he wrote his first short story, he had undergone the crushing experience of writing *Moby-Dick* only to see its commercial defeat; he had suffered through *Pierre* and the unanimous critical disapproval of it. He was exhausted, hurt beyond bearing, by all the heroic work he had done and by the world's rejection of it.

Nevertheless, "his furious habit of composition continued,"[4] and Melville turned to periodicals as the only available outlet for publication.

This creative crisis informs much of the scholarly commentary on "Bartleby." As James C. Wilson states in a 1981 essay, "Since Melville's literary resurrection in the 1920s, many critics have read [this story] as an allegory of Melville's own plight as an artist in nineteenth-century America."[5] Building on biographical readings by Richard Chase (1949) and Newton Arvin (1950), Leo Marx in a 1953 study describes the tale as a response to "Melville's own fate as a writer," in which the walls represent those forces that "hem in the meditative artist and for that matter every reflective man." Asserting that "Bartleby" "was written in a time of deep hopelessness" and that "it reflects Melville's doubts about the value of his recent work," Marx notes that "the story *is* about a kind of writer, a 'copyist' ... who obstinately refuses to go on doing the sort of writing demanded of him." He contends, moreover, that "'Bartleby' is not only about a writer who refuses to conform to the demands of society, but it is, more relevantly, about a writer who forsakes conventional modes because of an irresistible preoccupation with the most baffling philosophical questions." In sum, "Bartleby, the Scrivener" stands, in Marx's view, as "the most explicit and mercilessly self-critical statement of his own dilemma that Melville has left us."[6] Subsequent critics have echoed Marx. According to Laurie Robertson-Lorant's 1998 biography, "On one level, Bartleby may represent the writer who is forced to produce books easily classified and marketed by publishers, as well as the writer whose family is trying to force him to give up writing for a secure government job," as Melville's was attempting to do. Likewise, Andrew Delbanco's 2006 observation that "Bartleby" may be "a story about Melville's own fall into obscurity" indicates that biographical readings of the tale have not waned since the 1950s.[7]

Yet beyond the autobiographical dimension of the story, there are compelling links to Poe. As soon as "Bartleby" was published, readers connected its style and mood with the deceased writer's texts, and, ever since, as McCall remarks, "Like a jack-in-the-box, the figure of Poe pops up repeatedly in the critical commentary."[8] In December 1853, the *Literary World*, edited by Evert Duyckinck, referred to it as "a Poeish tale," and, three years later, writing about *The Piazza Tales* (in which "Bartleby" was republished with minor changes), a reviewer in the *Democratic Review* raised the possibility that this "wild, weird tale" might be "an imitation" of Poe because of its "concentrated gloom."[9] What these reviewers suggested critics would later confirm. Although he never specifically comments on the ways in which "Bartleby" invokes the spirit of Poe, Perry Miller nevertheless designates Poe and Melville as two key figures in *The Raven and the Whale*, a pioneering 1956 study of antebellum literary culture.[10] Like Miller, Harry Levin in 1958 places Poe and Melville within the same creative orbit; moreover, comparing Melville's copyist, a man "croaking a negative answer to all requests and queries," to the Raven, Levin regards such correspondences as evidence for a deep imaginative kinship between Melville and Poe, writers whose work exhibits "the power of blackness" and conveys a worldview at odds with the idealism of other American authors.[11]

Such responses have led later scholars to investigate ways in which the writings and example of Poe shaped "Bartleby." Listing "similarities of mood, method, structure and literary devices" in "Bartleby" and "The Raven," details that had not escaped previous critical notice, James L. Colwell and Gary Spitzer consider the two works psychological studies in which the "narrators find their lives forever changed by experiencing forms of the irrational which serve somehow to develop their involvement in humanity."[12] Detecting other evidence of Poe's influence, R. Bruce Bickley, Jr., who takes a critical cue from John Seelye, links Melville's story "to the popular tradition of the 'mysterious stranger'" seen in texts by American authors, including Poe's "The Man of the Crowd" (1840). Arguing that "Bartleby" lampoons Duyckinck as the lawyer, Cornelius Mathews as Turkey, and Poe as Nippers, Daniel A. Wells reads it as an attack on the nationalistic Young America literary movement that Poe supported—with his nose held—during his tenure as contributor, editor, and eventually owner of the *Broadway Journal* in 1845.[13] In addition, Melville biographer Hershel Parker connects the story to Poe's "The Business Man," which appeared "in the *Broadway Journal* of August 2, 1845."[14]

Bolstering the claims of critics who hear echoes of Poe in "Bartleby" are Melville's allusions to the writer or his works in other texts. According to Mildred Travis, Melville evokes Poe repeatedly in *Pierre*, and Harrison Hayford insists that the tract-selling beggar of *The Confidence Man* (1857) is a parody of Poe.[15] Furthermore, there can be no doubt that Melville has Poe in mind when he famously asserts in "Hawthorne and His Mosses" (1850), "for spite of all the Indian-summer sunlight on the hither side of Hawthorne's soul, the other side—like the dark half of the physical sphere—is shrouded in a blackness, ten times black." Melville not only draws the phrase "Indian-summer sunlight" from, but is also responding to, the final paragraph of Poe's 1847 *Godey's Lady's Book* review of Hawthorne's *Twice-Told Tales* and *Mosses from an Old Manse*, in which Poe states, "for allegory is at war with the whole tone of his [Hawthorne's] nature, which disports itself never so well as when escaping from the mysticism of his Goodman Browns and White Old Maids into the hearty, genial, but still Indian-summer sunshine of his Wakefields and Little Annie's Rambles."[16] Clearly, Melville knew Poe's writings and at times engaged with them directly.

Even if no planned or accidental meeting brought Poe and Melville together in the small world of antebellum literary New York, the latter, well-versed in the former's fiction, criticism, and poetry, very likely heard about Poe from several people, most notably the bookseller William Gowans, the editors Duyckinck and Charles Frederick Briggs, and the artist Felix Darley. Gowans had boarded with Poe, his wife, and Mrs. Clemm in New York in 1837, and both Poe and Melville "were patrons of the antiquarian's 97 Nassau Street establishment."[17] Thus, the very real possibility exists that Gowans and Melville talked about Poe. In 1845, Poe met Duyckinck, who was instrumental in getting both *Tales* and *The Raven and Other Poems* published that year in the American Library series, which he edited. Thanks to the efforts of Melville's brother Gansevoort, who received a diplomatic posting to London in the summer of 1845, the first edition of *Typee* appeared in London in February 1846, and the same version was published by Wiley and Putnam in the United States a month later. In the summer of 1846, Melville became acquainted with Duyckinck, who oversaw the publication of the expurgated second edition of *Typee*. Parker suggests that Melville may have first gleaned specific information about Duyckinck, prior to meeting him, via Poe's profile of the editor in his New York Literati series published in "the July 1846 issue of *Godey's Magazine and Lady's Book*."[18] Duyckinck later became a good friend to Melville, championing his writing and enlightening him about the inner workings of the New York literary world.

Briggs, who had extensive business dealings with Melville, penned accounts of Poe that resemble the tale's description of the troubled scrivener. Shortly after writing to James Russell Lowell in early 1845 that New Yorkers were "raven mad" about Poe's latest poem, Briggs briefly coedited and co-owned the *Broadway Journal* with Poe, an experience that left him embittered.[19] Although the exact nature of his relationship with Melville remains unknown, Briggs worked at *Putnam's* from 1852 until his dismissal late in 1854, handling not only "Bartleby," about which he expressed great enthusiasm, but also other pieces Melville submitted to the magazine.[20] Looking back on his experiences with Poe, Briggs recalled the "sad and tearful look" of Poe's "large grey eyes," described his clothing as "always scrupulously neat" and his behavior as "perfectly respectable and deferential," and asserted, "He never laughed and rarely smiled; but when he did smile there was always a partially-suppressed expression of sadness."[21] These statements closely tally with the narrator's descriptions of the gray-eyed Bartleby as "pallidly neat, pitiably respectable, incurably forlorn," and characterized by a "wonderful mildness"—as someone whose "poverty is great" and whose "solitude" is "horrible," a man "absolutely alone in the universe." "A bit of wreck," the narrator observes with apparent compassion, "in the mid Atlantic."[22]

Darley may also have provided Melville with information about Poe. In 1843, Poe had contracted with Darley to supply illustrations for the never-realized journal the *Stylus*, and the artist executed the artwork for "The Gold-Bug" later that year.[23] By early August 1853, Darley had become a good enough friend of Melville to visit his Massachusetts home, Arrowhead. Parker speculates that "Darley must have talked to Melville about his friend Poe" at that time—a likely supposition, which, coupled with the fact that the composition of "Bartleby, the Scrivener" occurred "between mid-August and . . . mid-September" 1853, bolsters the likelihood that Melville wrote the story with Poe in mind.[24]

Driven to writing for magazines to find an audience and earn a living, Melville would naturally think about the author of "The Raven." At the time of Poe's death in October 1849, Melville was living in New York, embarking shortly thereafter on a trip to England and the Continent. He no doubt read or heard about the infamous "Ludwig" obituary, in which Rufus Griswold erroneously claimed that Poe "had few or no friends," an assertion that Melville's story appears to echo in the lawyer's reference to his employee's "miserable friendlessness and loneliness" ("Bartleby," 27).[25] The accounts of Poe's means of earning a living in New York, his clothing, the color of his eyes, his looks, and his personal life that appeared in the press after his death, combined with the recollections of Melville's intimate associates Duyckinck and Darley (and, quite possibly, those of Gowans and Briggs) may have inspired the depiction of Bartleby.

Melville's copyist bears particularly striking similarities to Nathaniel Parker Willis's account of Poe, which served as an obituary notice in the *Home Journal* and was reprinted in Griswold's 1850 edition of Poe's works. Melville could easily have encountered either of these texts, in addition to Griswold's obituary, before penning "Bartleby." In his tribute, Willis relates some memories of Poe, who worked under him for a few months at the *Evening Mirror*. Especially interesting is the passage in which Willis describes Poe the magazinist:

> He was invariably punctual and industrious. With his pale, beautiful and intellectual face, as a reminder of what genius was in him, it was impossible, of course, not to treat him always with deferential courtesy. . . . With a prospect of taking the lead in another periodical, he, at last, voluntarily gave up his employment with us, and, through all this considerable period, we had seen but one presentment of the man—a quiet, patient, industrious, and most gentlemanly person, commanding the utmost respect and good feeling by his unvarying deportment and ability.[26]

Willis indicates, however, that this portrayal lacks completeness. Noting the testimony of others who saw Poe inebriated, he concludes that "two antagonistic spirits" warred within the author's soul.[27] Like Willis, Melville's lawyer admires his talented employee's professional skills but struggles to understand the man's profound unhappiness. The narrator recalls, "At first Bartleby did an extraordinary quantity of writing. As if long famishing for something to copy, he seemed to gorge himself on my documents. There was no pause for digestion. He ran a day and night line, copying by sun-light and by candle-light. I should have been quite delighted with his application, had he been cheerfully industrious. But he wrote on silently, palely, mechanically" (19–20).

Willis's portrait of Poe and the narrator's description of Bartleby have notable similarities. Remarkable for their pallor and noiseless diligence, Poe, as Willis depicts him, and Bartleby are surprisingly productive, yet they ultimately find their work, with its drudgery, unsatisfying.[28] Paralleling Poe, who quit the *Evening Mirror* to become an editor of the *Broadway Journal*, Bartleby withdraws from copying, declaring that he prefers not to do it anymore.[29] On one occasion, the troubled scrivener utters his memorable phrase ("I would prefer not to") with "his glance fixed upon [the narrator's] bust of Cicero"—the representation of a man who, in his opposition to Caesarian tyranny, embodied the republican values that many of Melville's readers associated with American institutions (30). Expressing personal preference while looking at a symbol of liberty, Bartleby voices a longing for freedom analogous to the literary aspirations of Poe, who hoped that taking over the *Broadway Journal* would free him to publish and promote writing of lasting value. Melville, undoubtedly aware that Poe's dreams for sustained editorial and artistic independence failed to materialize, created a narrative about a man whose skills cannot secure for him the life he desires—a story about a thwarted writer, a figure whom Melville, in all probability, feared he had become in 1853.

Other details in Melville's tale suggest the influence of Willis's remarks about Poe, including the setting of the story. Much of "Bartleby" takes place in a law office on Wall Street, but, as Wells observes, this place, where quill pens scratch incessantly across sheets of paper, resembles an "editorial office."[30] Willis recollects that at the New York *Evening Mirror*, a hive of activity in which Poe's professional assiduity earned the respect of his employer, Poe "was at his desk . . . from nine in the morning till the evening paper went to press"[31]—an image that prefigures Bartleby, the indefatigable scrivener who "ran a day and night line, copying by sun-light and by candle-light" (19). Of similar interest is the language that Willis uses in an 1859 letter (see the second epigraph to this chapter) to his quondam business associate, George Pope Morris, describing Poe's duties at the *Mirror* as those of a "mechanical paragraphist" required to "sit at a desk, in a corner of the editorial room, ready to be called upon for any of the miscellaneous work of the day." Willis also notes that Poe "was a man who never smiled, and never said a propitiatory or a deprecating word."[32] Melville could not have seen the letter to Morris before "Bartleby" appeared in print, but Willis's epistolary account of Poe's toil closely resembles Melville's description of the "very dull, wearisome, and lethargic" work required of Bartleby. Such drudgery, the narrator remarks, is decidedly unsuitable for "sanguine temperaments"—such as that of the "poet Byron" (20) with whom Poe sometimes identified himself.[33]

The copying that takes place in the lawyer's office might also have symbolic significance, especially for the literary artist. According to Robert Weisbuch, such "drudge-work . . . gestures toward the chief anxiety of influence—that there is nothing but copying left for the self to write, nothing left for the self to be a self about."[34] Thus, the scriveners of Melville's tale resemble American writers pressured to imitate literary celebrities, furnishing text for a publishing world in which the profitable trumps the original. As noted in Chapter 2, Poe made his disgust for this state of affairs well known, and his frustration surfaces in an 1848 letter that Willis includes in "Death of Edgar A. Poe." In this missive, Poe presents a plan for achieving artistic autonomy: "My general aim is to start a Magazine, to be called 'The Stylus;' but it would be useless to me, even when established, if not entirely out of the control of a publisher. I mean, therefore, to get up a Journal which shall be *my own*, at all points."[35] As Poe knew, the literary wage-laborer experiences little artistic liberty, and true independence requires ownership of the means of production. Without such control, writers face, as Melville's tale suggests, a dismal life of copying.

If the office in "Bartleby" represents an editorial establishment, then Willis himself might have been the model for Melville's lawyer. The latter, "a conveyancer and title hunter," manages "rich men's bonds and mortgages and title-deeds" while supervising copyists, who supply the labor essential to his legal enterprise (19, 14). Their drudgery makes possible the lawyer's pursuit of "the easiest way of life" (14). Related to the conveyancer was the entrepreneurial literary editor of nineteenth-century America, and Willis, a star among antebellum editors, benefited from the sensational success of "The Raven," which appeared in the January 29, 1845, issue of the *Evening Mirror*.[36] Monetary rewards did not, however, trickle down to Poe, and although Willis employed Poe and respected him, the professional bond between them had an exploitative dimension.[37] As Scott Peeples observes, the two men maintained a "complicated relationship," to which Poe responded creatively in his fictional and critical writings, in part because "Willis enjoyed the level of success and control over the publication and distribution of his writing that Poe experienced only on rare occasions."[38] If he read Willis's account of Poe, Melville may have noticed such unpleasant truths, which Willis, however well intentioned, may not have fully realized. At any rate, in "Bartleby," Melville laments the plight of writers like Poe, who must struggle for artistic independence in a world of professional thralldom.

Creative crises of that order were consequences of what Charles Sellers has termed the "Market Revolution," the flood of commercial energy that carried America into modernity. Although many profited from industrialization and its effects, others struggled to find their places in a shifting world, and some unfortunates, including large numbers of workers and artisans, were crushed under the wheels of change.[39] The emergence of authorship as a profession occurred during this time, so Melville's thoughts about the life of writing reflected larger social concerns. Casting a cold eye on the Macaulayite fervor that characterized many of his fellow citizens, Melville lingered over the ruins of the Market Revolution, gazing, like "the angel of history" that Walter Benjamin envisions, at the waste in the wake of the "storm . . . we call progress."[40] The memory of Poe, a writer of genius who perished in this tempest, must have unsettled Melville as he struggled to fashion a new authorial identity for himself after his reputation as a novelist steeply declined. This struggle animates "Bartleby," augmenting its impact.

The tale ends with Bartleby's death in the New York City prison known as The Tombs, and this harrowing conclusion is, perhaps, one more nod to Poe, whose 1845 article titled "Some Secrets of the Magazine Prison-House" exposes the evils common to periodical publishing. Appearing in the *Broadway Journal* around the time Poe left the *Evening Mirror*, this essay indicts

> Magazine publishers (who sometimes take upon themselves the duplicate title of "editor *and* proprietor,")—publishers, we say, who, under certain conditions of good conduct, occasional puffs, and decent subserviency at all times, make it a point of conscience to encourage the poor devil author with a dollar or two, more or less as he behaves himself properly and abstains from the indecent habit of turning up his nose. (*CW*, III 1207)

Underpaid—if paid at all—and underfed, the periodical writer "dies, and by the good luck of his decease (which came by starvation) the fat 'editor and proprietor' is fatter henceforward and for ever to the amount of five and twenty dollars, very cleverly saved, to be spent generously in canvas-backs and champagne" (*CW*, III 1208–09). The famished writer is a prisoner trapped in a system that is rigged against him, a condition that Poe knew all too well, having suffered hunger on many occasions while editors and publishers ate their fill. Like Poe and the other poor devils, Bartleby, a man who makes his living by writing, eats little and refuses food while in prison, noting grimly that he is "unused to dinners" (44). Describing Bartleby's demise, Melville, who had joined the rank of struggling scriveners, quite possibly thought of Poe, a writer walled in by circumstances, many of which were beyond his control—for "Bartleby" commemorates authors at the mercy of publishers, those wardens of the magazine prison house.

Significantly, Melville's "Story of Wall-Street" contains a reference to Poe's equally famous story about walls, "The Cask of Amontillado," published in 1846.[41] Wishing to "rid" himself of the scrivener but unable to bring himself to "thrust . . . the poor, pale, passive mortal" and "helpless creature out of [his] door," the lawyer states, "Rather would I let him live and die here, and then mason up his remains in the wall" (38). In Poe's story, Montresor, a vindictive and deceitful man unlike Melville's indulgent and at times compassionate narrator, lures Fortunato to his family's catacombs, chains him to the wall in a small niche, and seals him up behind a wall of mortar stone he erects with the aid of a trowel. The lawyer's thought of walling up Bartleby comes shortly after his extended reference to a grisly 1841 incident that occurred a mere five blocks from Wall Street. In an office building at midday, John C. Colt used a hatchet to kill Samuel Adams, crated up the body, and tried to send it by ship to New Orleans. In the long paragraph in Melville's story that discusses the case, the lawyer emphasizes the fact that Adams and Colt, like Bartleby and himself in his own second-floor place of business, "were alone": "It was the circumstance of being alone in a solitary office, up stairs, of a building entirely unhallowed by humanizing domestic associations—an uncarpeted office, doubtless, of a dusty, haggard sort of appearance;—this it must have been, which greatly helped to enhance the irritable desperation of the hapless Colt" (36). McCall has shown that, in order to stress the "solitary" situation in which the narrator finds himself with the scrivener, Melville altered the facts of the murder case:

> The Judge in the Colt-Adams trial called the scene of the crime "the most frequented house in the most populous city in the union: the time midday, and separated only by a folding door was a schoolroom filled with scholars." That is curious, for Melville uses the phrase "solitary office"; he even repeats it, and elaborates it at some length.[42]

In "The Cask of Amontillado," Montresor prides himself on cleverly ensuring that there are no servants at home so that he and Fortunato are entirely alone on the night that he kills him. The lawyer's use of the words "mason up his remains in the wall," his comparison of his own situation with the scrivener to that of Colt and Adams shortly before this, and his stress on isolation in connection with both the famous murder case and his dilemma over Bartleby all serve to connect Melville's story about walls to Poe's.

These textual reverberations reinforce the link between Poe and "Bartleby," a tale of creative crisis. Thwarted expression is, of course, an important theme in the epilogue of Melville's story. Here, the lawyer repeats a "vague report," which has "a certain strange suggestive interest to" him, "that Bartleby had been a subordinate clerk in the Dead Letter Office at Washington, from which he had been suddenly removed by a change in the administration" (45). By focusing attention on dead letters, which, by definition, are ones that have not found their addressees, the final section of Melville's story highlights failed attempts at communication.[43] The lawyer declares:

> Dead letters! Does it not sound like dead men? Conceive a man by nature and misfortune prone to a pallid hopelessness, can any business seem more fitted to

heighten it than that of continually handling these dead letters, and assorting them for the flames? For by the cart-load they are annually burned. Sometimes from out the folded paper the pale clerk takes a ring:—the finger it was meant for, perhaps, moulders in the grave; a bank-note sent in swiftest charity:—he whom it would relieve, nor eats nor hungers any more; pardon for those who died despairing; hope for those who died unhoping; good tidings for those who died stifled by unrelieved calamities. On errands of life, these letters speed to death. (45)

Accustomed to being well paid for anything that he (or any of his subordinates) writes, the lawyer strays widely from the "eminently *safe*" path he has pursued throughout his life by putting pen to paper and telling the tale of the scrivener (14). Clearly this "rather elderly man" without family and friends has, like many of Poe's narrators vis-à-vis other characters, been deeply affected by Bartleby, whose profound loneliness to a large extent resembles his own (13). If, in considering the narrative autobiographically (in relation to Melville) and biographically (in relation to Poe) we agree with Jonathan Elmer that on some level the story "is in a basic way about an attempt at literature," then the issue of its success or failure—that is, whether it does or does not find an audience— deserves our attention. Obviously we do not know definitively whether the narrator ever attempts to publish his account of the singular law-copyist. Yet, whether he chooses not to share what he has written about the scrivener with others, tries but is unable to get it printed, or succeeds in publishing his narrative but fails to find sympathetic readers, his consciously crafted recollection— "interpretation," as Elmer puts it—of Bartleby itself amounts to a dead letter.[44] A similar failure is most likely what Melville in 1853, with the example of Poe in mind, feared would be the result of his own attempts to reach an audience.

Part Two

The Competition in Cunning: Ramifications of and Responses to Poe's Ratiocinative Tales

What a curious thing a "detective" story is. And was there ever one the author needn't be ashamed of, except "Murders in the Rue Morgue"?

Mark Twain's Notebook (1896)

Character Rivalry, Authorial Sleight of Hand, and Generic Fluidity in the Dupin Trilogy

> It is just possible that you may have seen a tale of mine entitled "The Murders in the Rue Morgue".... The *theme* was the exercise of ingenuity in the detection of a murderer. I have just completed a similar article, which I shall entitle "The Mystery of Marie Rogêt—a Sequel to the Murders in the Rue Morgue." The story is based upon the assassination of Mary Cecilia Rogers, which created so vast an excitement, some months ago, in New York. I have, however, handled my design in a manner altogether *novel* in literature. I have imagined a series of nearly exact *coincidences* occurring in Paris.... My main object,... as you will readily understand, is an analysis of the true principles which should direct inquiry in similar cases.
>
> Edgar Allan Poe, Letter to George Roberts, June 6, 1842

The era in which Poe founded modern detective fiction was an era known for its hoaxes. In *Humbug: The Art of P. T. Barnum*, Neil Harris attributes the legendary showman's success in attracting people in the early 1840s to spectacles such as the "Fejee Mermaid" (a monkey's head and hands sewn to a fish's body) and the "Great Buffalo Hunt" (the pursuit of a pitiful collection of undersized and frightened bison into a New Jersey swamp) to a "national tolerance for clever imposture."[1] This was an era that saw the *New York Sun* publish a report of the telescopic sighting of people with wings on the moon and a second highly technical but totally false account of a three-day Atlantic crossing in a balloon. Harris explains that Barnum and others used a scientific methodology and technical jargon to hoodwink an American public captivated by marvelous new innovations such as the steamboat and the railroad. These frauds appealed to the public because they were essentially competitive games that allowed people to match their wits with the bamboozler's. Such entertainments provided diversions from the often hard business of earning a living and the challenges of adapting to a rapidly changing society. Even though these amusements were rigged in the house's favor, the stakes were low enough that losing had no lasting consequences. Provided the counterfeit was ingenious and well executed, people did not mind being swindled, especially if the con artist elucidated the method for perpetrating it.

Harris links the aforementioned "Balloon Hoax," written by Poe, to Barnum's early humbugs and credits them both, along with Richard Adams Locke (the man responsible for the Moon Hoax), with a keen grasp of "an aesthetic of the operational, a delight in observing process and examining for literal truth" (79). "Experiencing a complicated hoax was pleasurable," explains Harris,

> because of the competition between victim and hoaxer, each seeking to outmaneuver the other, to catch him off-balance and detect the critical weakness. Barnum, Poe, and Locke didn't fear public suspicion; they invited it. They understood . . . that the opportunity to debate the *issue* of falsity, to discover how deception had been practiced, was even more exciting than the discovery of fraud itself. (77)[2]

During this same period in American history, Poe invented—and then reinvented—what we now know as detective fiction. Despite the manipulation, readers eagerly read Poe's tales to their conclusions to find out where they have fallen short in their supposed competition with the detective. In this sense, the author's "ratiocinative tales," as he referred to them, resemble Barnum's frauds and hoaxes, about which a ticket seller is reported to have said, "First he humbugs them, and then they pay to hear him tell how he did it."[3] As created by Poe in three stories featuring C. Auguste Dupin, the genre entails the clever humbugging of readers; however, the battle between author and reader is but one type of rivalry Poe incorporates into the form. Competition on three distinct levels constitutes Poe's most important contribution to detection.

First, and on the most basic level, Poe stages a series of contests between characters: Dupin versus the narrator and Dupin versus the police prefect G----- in "The Murders in the Rue Morgue," Dupin versus various newspapermen in "The Mystery of Marie Rogêt," and Dupin versus the master criminal D----- in "The Purloined Letter." To underscore the competitive nature of detection and explain the analytical ability that enables the protagonist to come out on top, Poe makes reference to games of skill and games of chance, and, in the final story, depicts Dupin's recourse to the stratagems of disguise and masquerade to ensure victory. As Leroy L. Panek remarks, "Clearly one way in which the analyst's abilities are conceptualized is through the metaphor of the game player."[4]

Second, Poe, as author, conceives of detection as competition between himself and his readers. Supposedly providing all the information necessary to decipher the puzzle, he challenges those who read the tales to arrive at a solution before the denouement begins, deflecting agency by using a first-person narrator who is not the detective to heighten the illusion of a fair contest. What Poe said of his protagonist C. Auguste Dupin in an August 9, 1846, letter to Philip Pendleton Cooke holds true for other literary detectives:

> You are right about the hair-splitting of my French friend:—that is all done for effect. These tales of ratiocination owe most of their popularity to being something in a new key. I do not mean to say that they are not ingenious—but people think them more ingenious than they are on account of their method and *air* of method. In the "Murders in the Rue Morgue," for instance, where is the ingenuity of unravelling a web which you yourself (the author) have woven for the express purpose of unravelling? The reader is made to confound the ingenuity of the supposititious Dupin with that of the writer of the story. (*CL*, I 595)

In other words, detective fiction fools readers into believing that they are in competition with the detective rather than recognizing that this central figure is simply one among many means of getting the better of them.

Third, by weaving authorial competition into the fabric of detective fiction (i.e., by striving to rework and outdo what he has already done), Poe not only anticipates texts that manipulate the conventions of detection for comic ends (a parodic reworking of the genre that he himself pioneers in the 1844 story "Thou Art the Man") but also makes it possible for a diverse range of authors to use the form openly or obliquely to address issues of morality, class, gender, sexuality, nation, and race. Thus, in his detective stories following "Murders," Poe essentially competes with himself. In founding detection in this manner, he has inspired subsequent writers to compete with him and each other to bring innovations to the form; moreover, in doing so, Poe initiated a malleable genre, one that has enabled authors of all different stripes to find new ways to outwit, enlighten, educate, and politicize readers and one that has reflected and responded to the evolution of modern society.

In developing the first two parts of this argument, I build on the approaches of critics who emphasize Dupin's deceptions and dubious motives and those who concentrate on Poe's manipulations of the reader. Members of both camps have commented on the appropriateness of the detective's surname. Peter Thoms asserts that it "reflects his acts of duping"; similarly, Burton R. Pollin observes, "whatever the origins of Dupin's name, Poe the humorist may have silently been adding to it the letter g."[5] The depth and breadth of the protagonist's wiles are indeed considerable, and he certainly is, as Daniel Hoffman asserts, "one of Poe's finest creations, his most believable portrait of the Man of Thought."[6] However, because Dupin serves as only one means by which Poe successfully manipulates readers, the ultimate focus of our attention must be the author himself—and not merely his competition with readers but also his competition with himself and, by extension, later writers of detective fiction.

The Murders in the Rue Morgue

In the originary tale, Dupin projects an air of objectivity, abstraction, and aloofness, yet he actually takes the case for personal reasons. An avid and expert game player, Dupin demonstrates his superior analytical skills, formulating and adhering to a methodology combining ratiocination, observation, and imagination that enables him to defeat his opponents with ease. The story opens with an explanation of the methodology employed by the analytical genius,[7] who, Dupin's companion the narrator explains, enjoys all forms of problem solving:

> As the strong man exults in his physical ability, delighting in such exercises as call his muscles into action, so glories the analyst in that moral activity which *disentangles*. He derives pleasure from even the most trivial occupations bringing his talent into play. He is fond of enigmas, of conundrums, of hieroglyphics; exhibiting in his solutions of each a degree of *acumen* which appears to ordinary apprehension preternatural. His results, brought about by the very soul and essence of method, have, in truth, the whole air of intuition. (*CW*, II 528)

Unlike mere calculation or simple ingenuity, analysis requires discipline and creative thinking, and thus, although less complex than chess, draughts and whist better showcase the capacity of someone like Dupin to throw "himself into the spirit of his opponent" (*CW*, II 529) and trick that person into committing a mistake. An individual with this extraordinary mental power has the capacity to look beyond the rules of the game, to see more than simply the pieces on the board or the cards on the table. He questions the premises that limit other people's reasoning, demonstrating the ability to think outside the enclosed spaces (or, in this first case, the supposedly locked room) that so obsess the police. Like the protagonist vis-à-vis other characters, in "Murders" Poe succeeds in winning the contest with his readers, accomplishing this through multiple deceptions.

The narrator relates how he serendipitously met and came to lead a secluded, homosocial life with Dupin, a "young gentleman . . . of an excellent—indeed of an illustrious family" living in greatly reduced circumstances, who takes pleasure in his "peculiar analytic activity" (*CW*, II 531, 533). To illustrate the remarkable talent that enables Dupin to defeat his opponents, the narrator describes an incident in which Dupin deduces his companion's thoughts even though no words have passed between them for fifteen minutes. This episode, the initial instance of analysis and competition in the Dupin tales, serves as a microcosm for the series. In it, the hero challenges his companion to figure out how he was able to accomplish such a feat. Totally unequal to the task, the narrator beseeches Dupin to reveal his method. In a passage that dominates the entire scene, Dupin explains that he approached the problem as he does any other, devising a logical method for arriving at a correct solution. Because he is intimately acquainted with his friend's mind, knowing what the narrator knows, Dupin reasons that he can use his highly developed imagination to foresee the mental associations his companion is likely to make, as well as rely on his keen powers of observation to confirm his knowledge-based predictions. He anticipates the course of the narrator's thoughts and then uses such details as his friend's facial expressions and posture to verify the imaginative leaps he has made. The ability that Dupin demonstrates here at the start of "Murders" to formulate a well-reasoned plan to solve a puzzle, to imagine the mental steps another person has made or will make, and to note everyone and everything carefully foreshadows the methodology he will employ to solve mysteries and outwit not only the narrator and G----- later in this story but also his rivals in its two sequels.

Immediately following this illustration and explication of Dupin's powers of analysis, the narrator presents information relating to the grisly deaths of two women, a mother and daughter, thereby introducing the theme of female victimization into detection. Maurice S. Lee notes, "Particularly in nineteenth-century America, where domestic ideology made a kind of religion out of the sanctity of the home and the sexual purity of women, 'The Murders in the Rue Morgue' is especially horrifying as a kind of home invasion."[8] The case provides the occasion for a second private competition between Dupin and his companion as well as a public contest between Dupin and G-----, the Prefect of police. From a Parisian newspaper, the narrator quotes twenty-two paragraphs about the killings, beginning with the headline "EXTRAORDINARY MURDERS" and concluding with a condemnation of the police for failing to get to the bottom of this bizarre crime (*CW*, II 537, 544). Just as Dupin knows the narrator and his limitations well, he is thoroughly acquainted with G-----, who tends to look at things too closely or to seek too deeply for the truth. Dupin proposes to the narrator that they launch an investigation of their own, indicating a pair of personal motives for doing so. First, echoing the story's initial comparison between the analyst and the strong man who "exults in his physical ability" (*CW*, II 528), Dupin asserts, "An inquiry will afford us amusement," signaling that he welcomes the chance to compete once again with his companion (*CW*, II 546). The inappropriateness, if not the callousness, of this statement made in connection with the gruesome deaths of two women causes the narrator, who otherwise exhibits nothing but admiration for and awe toward the detective, to comment on its oddity. Second, Dupin proceeds to explain that he owes a favor to the man whom the police are holding for the crime, which also suggests that he looks forward to the opportunity to defeat the Prefect. To solve the crime and triumph over the narrator and G-----, Dupin relies on the same methodology he used to read his companion's mind. Dupin knows that, in order to be victorious, he must make a superior play, not only proving the fallacious nature of the hypotheses advanced by his adversaries but establishing the truth of his own to their satisfaction.

In this sense, his friendly competition with the narrator serves as a trial run for the more serious one with the Prefect. In the former, Dupin creates and strives to maintain the illusion of a fair contest between himself and his companion. Each has read and considered the facts of the case, each examines the crime scene, and each proposes a solution to the mystery. As for G-----, he has already played his hand, arresting a bank clerk for the killings because he was the last person known to have seen the victims alive and was aware of the bags of money in the apartment. Unlike the Prefect and his men, who allow the strangeness of the killings to baffle them and appear willing to turn to the supernatural to explain the crime, Dupin regards the "*outré*" character of the mystery as a help rather than a hindrance and rejects any solution that relies on the occult: "Madame and Mademoiselle L'Espanaye were not destroyed by spirits. The doers of the deed were material, and escaped materially" (*CW*, II 547, 551). Thus, he goes to the crime scene seeking the answers to two major questions: How did the perpetrator or perpetrators get into and out of the building—described by John T. Irwin as "the tale's initial mystery"—and what is the identity of the killer or killers—described by Irwin as "the tale's principal mystery"?[9] After using his ratiocinative and observational skills to best both G----- and his companion in answering the former, Dupin relies on his imagination to figure out the latter.

In contrast to the police, who erroneously conclude from their imperfect observations that the room was sealed at the time the crime was committed, Dupin reasons that despite appearances there had to have been a way into and out of the room. Demonstrating the difference between his methods and those of both G----- and the narrator, Dupin begins by carefully looking outside the building rather than examining the room where the killings occurred: "Before going in we walked up the street, turned down an alley, and then, again turning, passed in the rear of the building—Dupin, meanwhile, examining the whole neighborhood, as well as the house, with a minuteness of attention for which I could see no possible object" (*CW*, II 546). As Ronald Thomas states, "Dupin's framework for solving the case is distinguished from the overly empirical approach of the police by virtue of its *tour de force* of imaginative construction, which looks for the truth outside as well as inside the locked room."[10] Once he enters the apartment, Dupin takes a series of rational steps to determine how the killer or killers entered and departed. Ruling out the doors and the chimney as the means of access, he concludes that one of the two apparently locked windows must have been used. Knowing that the assailants or assailant could not have fastened them after leaving the building, he surmises that the windows must have a means of fastening themselves. Finding the spring lock to the unobstructed window and satisfying himself that the perpetrator or perpetrators could not have used this casement because it was indeed firmly nailed shut, Dupin concludes that the means of entrance and escape must have been the other window. His explanation of his procedure at this point in his investigation underscores his competitive nature:

> You will say that I was puzzled; but, if you think so, you must have misunderstood the nature of the inductions. To use a sporting phrase, I had not been once "at fault." The scent had never for an instant been lost. There was no flaw in any link of the chain. I had traced the secret to its ultimate result,—and that result was *the nail.* (*CW*, II 553)

As Irwin notes, through the use of the terms "sporting phrase" and "scent," Dupin "hints at the solution to the larger mystery of the killer's identity, in that it calls to mind the sport of hunting and suggests that the object of Dupin's pursuit is in fact an animal."[11] Locating the spring for the second window, Dupin confirms his supposition that the nail, which appears to keep it permanently shut, is broken, allowing it to be opened and closed. Having determined which window was used, Dupin draws on the observations he made before entering the building to conclude that a single perpetrator climbed the lightning rod to reach the fourth floor, used one of the shutters to swing from the rod into the room through the window, killed the women, and then exited the room through the window, which sprang shut upon this departure.

After using his ratiocinative and observational skills to best both G----- and his companion in solving the riddle of how the killer went into and out of the room, Dupin turns to the question of the identity of the perpetrator. Unlike the police and the narrator, who are confounded by the conflicting testimonies of the people who heard voices in the room where the killings took place, Dupin seizes on "the peculiarity of the evidence," namely the unanimity among the witnesses that "no sounds resembling words" were discernible in the utterances of one of the voices (*CW*, II 549, 550). In order to prolong the competition—or rather the illusion of it—between them, Dupin shares what he observed at the crime scene and its significance with the narrator. Instead of revealing his entire hand all at once, Dupin lays his cards on the table one by one, offering a series of hints to his friend about the identity of the killer:

> My ultimate object is only the truth. My immediate purpose is to lead you to place in juxta-position, that *very unusual* activity of which I have just spoken [ascending the rod and swinging into the room via the window], with the *very peculiar* shrill (or harsh) and *unequal* voice, about whose nationality no two persons could be found to agree, and in whose utterance no syllabification could be detected. (*CW*, II 555)

As Irwin observes, "Dupin conceives of this method of revelation as a game played with his friend the narrator," a contest that "is at once a part and a figure of the game the author plays with the reader."[12] Sensing his companion's continued bemusement, the detective attempts to prod his friend by stressing the "*excessively outré*" (*CW*, II 557) aspects of the crime: in contrast to the Prefect's theory, it lacks a human motive because nothing was stolen; moreover, its violence not only represents "something altogether irreconcilable with our common notions of human actions" (*CW*, II 557) but also required more than human strength. Having related the fruits of his ratiocination and observations to his companion, Dupin gives the narrator one last chance to arrive at a solution to the mystery. Like that of the Prefect earlier, the narrator's hypothesis—that an escaped lunatic killed the women—falls far short of the mark because he lacks Dupin's superlative imagination. Just as Dupin quickly dispensed with G-----'s theory about the guilt of the bank clerk by pointing out that no money was taken from the apartment, Dupin refutes the narrator's supposition by pointing out that even the most deranged people speak in syllables.

Rather than announcing his solution to the narrator, however, Dupin offers proof of its accuracy in the form of a tuft of coarse and tawny hair he extracted from Madame L'Espanaye's body,[13] a facsimile of the impression made by the immense hand that throttled Mademoiselle L'Espanaye, and a description of the attributes of an orangutan supposedly written by the zoologist Georges Cuvier that tallies point for point with the actions performed by the perpetrator of the killings as he has reconstructed them. As Thomas puts it, "Dupin imagines the culprit to be a beast he has never seen by 'constructing' its existence out of scant physical evidence that corresponds to a passage he has read from Cuvier's text on animal physiology."[14] The narrator concedes that the killer must have been an ape, yet he remains confused by certain aspects of the mystery, especially the fact that the deponents claimed to have heard two voices in the apartment, one of them belonging to a Frenchman. It is at this point that Dupin discloses the existence of a witness who will shortly arrive to confirm his "full solution to the riddle" (*CW*, II 560) to the satisfaction of not only the narrator but also the Prefect, and thereby ensure his victory in both his private and public competitions. The discovery of a sailor's hair ribbon at the base of the lightning rod enabled Dupin to imagine the scenario by which the orangutan made its way to Paris, and immediately after leaving the crime scene the detective placed a newspaper advertisement designed to bring the owner of the ape to his place of residence.

Though a mere pawn in Dupin's contests with his companion and the Prefect, the sailor, too, finds himself unwittingly embroiled in a competition with the aristocratic sleuth. Despite being a powerful man wielding a large oaken cudgel, the sailor quickly sees that he is outclassed by Dupin, whose advertisement has lured him into a trap, whose pistols force him to curb his violence, and whose knowledge of his role in the killings and appeal to "honor" compel him to tell all he knows in order to secure the release of an innocent man. The sailor recounts the ape's initial capture in an East Asian colonial outpost, its transportation to Paris, its escape into the night armed with a razor, its entrance into the apartment in the Rue Morgue, and its frenzied killing of the two women.[15] The sailor definitively establishes the validity of Dupin's solution to the satisfaction of the narrator and forces the Prefect not only to acknowledge the falsity of his own hypothesis by letting the bank clerk go but also to accept, albeit with some grumbling, the truth of Dupin's own: "This functionary . . . could not altogether conceal his chagrin at the turn which affairs had taken, and was fain to indulge in a sarcasm or two, about the propriety of every person minding his own business" (*CW*, II 568). Dupin makes no reply to his vanquished opponent; however, he later contentedly remarks, "Let him talk. . . . I am satisfied with having defeated him in his own castle" (*CW*, II 568), using language, specifically the image of the castle, that Stephen Knight describes as "fascinatingly aggressive" and "competitive."[16] Thus, in this first tale detailing his exploits, the detective delights in matching wits with the narrator, the Prefect, and, briefly, the sailor, emerging victorious in each of these contests.

Poe likewise emerges triumphant, using not only Dupin's deceptiveness but also an apparently trustworthy narrator, the structure of the story, the withholding of key information, and a shift from one mystery to another to humbug his readers. Choosing to focus on the main character rather than his creator, Thoms asserts that Dupin successfully manipulates other characters as well as those who read the tale. Certainly, detection causes readers to become detectives and detectives to become readers—Dupin having to peruse newspaper accounts of the killings, the traces the killer leaves behind, and Cuvier's description of orangutans accurately to solve the crime. Thoms goes a step further, however, asserting that the protagonist becomes a writer as well, authoring "the hidden story of the crime,"[17] so that he can divert attention from his own dubious motives and actions. Dupin does indeed deceive readers, as Thoms contends, but the detective's slipperiness is but one aspect of Poe's larger pattern of manipulation. Just as Dupin strives to create and maintain the illusion of a fair contest between himself and his companion as each attempts to solve the case, Poe uses the device of a seemingly reliable first-person narrator, a close friend and companion of the detective, to create the illusion of fair play. As Hoffman states, "To create Dupin, . . . Poe had to invent his bland and dim narrator."[18] Designed through his naiveté to serve as a model or stand-in for the reader, the narrator, as Warren Hill Kelly notes, never realizes the extent to which Dupin withholds information from him, nor does he ever question the detective's ratiocination; rather, like Dr. Watson in the Sherlock Holmes stories, as Robert Daniel observes, he treats Dupin as a miracle worker who should be regarded with nothing short of reverence.[19] Summing up the contrast between them, Jeffrey Meyers remarks, "Though Dupin's mind is a mystery to the narrator, his thoughts are transparent to Dupin."[20] Perhaps the final word on the subject should rest with Pollin, who points out, in a statement regarding the mind-reading episode that holds true for the relationship between the detective and his companion generally, "The 'stooge' of Dupin must be able to forget almost everything, and Dupin nothing."[21] Thus, the narrator provides no indication of the cunning manner in which Poe deceives readers, even though he himself functions as the mouthpiece for the author's manipulations.

Careful examination of the construction of the mind-reading episode offers clues to Poe's ingenious method of structuring the story as a whole, a method he explains in the 1846 letter to Cooke quoted earlier. The first part of Dupin's explication of how he came to know the narrator's thoughts (which bears no small resemblance to Poe's explanation in "The Philosophy of Composition" of how he wrote "The Raven") enumerates—in reverse order—the mental sequence that led the narrator to muse about the insufficient height of the shoemaker-turned-actor Chantilly: "'I will explain,' he said, 'and that you may comprehend all clearly, we will retrace the course of your meditations, from the moment in which I spoke to you until that of the *rencontre* with the fruiterer in question. The larger links of the chain run thus—Chantilly, Orion, Dr. Nichol, Epicurus, Stereotomy, the street stones, the fruiterer'" (*CW*, II 535). The word "retrace" indicates a movement forward in time; meanwhile, the phrase "from the moment in which I spoke to you until that of the *rencontre* with the fruiterer" suggests a movement in the opposite direction. The slippage between chronology and causation here and in other passages hints at Poe's method of writing the tales (i.e., backward), which he elaborated to Cooke.

Even more deviously, in this first tale of detection, Poe persuades readers that they are playing one game when they are actually playing another, thereby anticipating hard-boiled novels which concern themselves not with who did what but rather, in Raymond Chandler's words, "what the hell went on."[22] The newspapers and the police mistakenly believe the killings to be murders, when, in reality, and despite the story's misleading title, no murder has taken place because the perpetrator is not human. Consequently, Poe deceives readers into erroneously regarding "The Murders in the Rue Morgue" as a whodunit, the tale's title reflecting, as Thoms notes, "the incorrect assumptions of journalists and the police."[23] Dupin actually solves a wholly different type of mystery, one in which he detects a missing beast solely from the marks that have been left behind. In doing so, the protagonist allies himself with a long line of literary characters who figure out the properties of an absent animal (or person). In one of the oldest recorded versions of the story, the three princes of Serendip (a bygone name for Sri Lanka) detect a lame, half-blind camel with a missing tooth they have not seen (and also deduce that it carried sugar and butter and was ridden by a pregnant woman). Horace Walpole coined the word "serendipity" in a 1754 letter to Horace Mann, deriving it from "a silly fairy tale called *the three Princes of Serendip*." The story originally came from late thirteenth- and early fourteenth-century Persia, according to Joseph Schick, although it was not translated into English until 1722. Schick also traced the origin of stories about the detection of unseen animals to India, where the beast in question was a pachyderm (six hundred years before Mark Twain's "The Stolen White Elephant").[24] Other detective figures who solve missing animal mysteries include Voltaire's Zadig, who minutely describes a dog and a horse he has not caught sight of, and, more recently, Brother William of Baskerville, who, at the start of Umberto Eco's *The Name of the Rose*, enumerates the physical characteristics of the abbot's missing prized steed.[25] In "Murders," Poe slyly hints at his own bait-and-switch in his presentation of the facts of the case when he has the narrator quote a newspaper article about the killings that raises the question of what kind of a crime has been committed: "A murder so mysterious, and so perplexing in all its particulars, was never before committed in Paris—*if indeed a murder has been committed at all*" (my emphasis, *CW*, II 544).

An ardent and consistently victorious competitor and a clever manipulator with questionable motives, Dupin is only one means by which Poe deceives his audience. As a result, readers never have a legitimate chance to solve the mystery in "Murders" before the detective announces his solution. Nevertheless, because of the sheer ingeniousness of the author's multifaceted deceptions, people continue to read, reread, and marvel at this story and have made the genre it originates enormously popular. Although the results are far from satisfactory, by deciding to bring Dupin and his companion back for a second outing in "The Mystery of Marie Rogêt," the author introduces a third level of competition into detective fiction that has had far-reaching consequences.

The Mystery of Marie Rogêt

Revisiting but also reconceiving the form he created in "Murders," Poe chooses to impose limitations on his detective and himself in "Mystery," which recounts Dupin's "armchair" detection in a case based on an actual unsolved death in which a woman, once again, is the victim. As Daniel Stashower remarks, "In the saga of Mary Rogers, Poe appeared to have found a young woman culled from one of his own works. The victim was not only young and beautiful, but an aura of melancholy and injustice hung over the crime."[26] Anonymous writers of newspaper articles advancing theories about the case, as critics have noted, replace the narrator and the Prefect as Dupin's opponents. Like the conflicting eyewitness accounts in "Murders," the newspaper articles in "Mystery" function as both sources of information to be evaluated and straw men for the detective to rebut. A considerable portion of the tale, by far the longest of the trilogy, involves the detective's point-by-point refutation of the hypotheses of these journalists. Rather than matching wits, Dupin and his companion now work as a team, the former doing the analysis and the latter the legwork. Likewise, the Prefect no longer serves as the protagonist's primary adversary. Instead, acknowledging his own deficiencies as an analyst, G----- hires Dupin to determine what happened to Marie Rogêt for a "liberal" fee, "the precise nature of which" the narrator refuses to divulge (*CW*, III 728). Although the detective is credited with solving the mystery and, as a result, collects the reward, the second story lacks a moment of complete triumph for Dupin attesting to his peerless reasoning prowess. Poe himself fares even worse than his main character, failing to effect a clever humbug and falling short of equaling, much less surpassing, what he accomplished in his previous effort. Nevertheless, by making Dupin the protagonist of a second story and having the narrator quite explicitly refer to both the detective's previous case and his own chronicling of it (*CW*, III 724), the author incorporates repeatability, self-referentiality, and authorial competition, as well as subversion, variation, and parody, into detection.

Because "Mystery," unlike the tales that precede and succeed it, provides no opportunity for Dupin to exercise his observational skills, he must rely on ratiocination and imagination alone to best his rival crime solvers. In "Murders," Dupin and his companion read about the events in the Rue Morgue shortly after they occur and examine the crime scene and the bodies of the victims. In contrast, it is more than three weeks after the discovery of Marie Rogêt's corpse that they hear about the case from a desperate G-----. Having dozed behind green eyeglasses in an armchair while the Prefect long-windedly offered opinions about the mystery, Dupin sends his companion out the following day to secure a full report of the evidence from the police and to obtain a copy of every newspaper containing any information relating to the case. From these, the narrator collates what he deems to be the relevant facts as well as the most prominent conjectures advanced by the press about what happened to the attractive salesgirl. Asserting that submerged bodies rarely surface in less than a week, *L'Etoile* speculates that the corpse said to be Marie's may not be hers because it was found floating in the Seine less than seventy-two hours after her disappearance. *Le Commerciel* reasons that because no one remembers seeing the widely known Marie walk to either the area close to where the body was found or her aunt's residence, it is likely that she was abducted shortly after leaving her home by a gang who gagged her with the piece of her petticoat found wrapped around her neck. Responding to more recent discoveries, *Le Soleil* argues that Marie's grass-and-mildew-covered outer garments, found along with other evidence in a wooded area many days after her death, prove she was killed at that location.

Commencing his entirely textual investigation, Dupin notes that it differs markedly from his previous case. People mistakenly assumed that the strangeness of the occurrence in the Rue Morgue made it difficult to solve. The death of the *grisette*, in contrast, he remarks to his companion, "is an *ordinary*, although an atrocious instance of crime. There is nothing peculiarly *outré* about it. You will observe that, for this reason, the mystery has been considered easy, when, for this reason, it should have been considered difficult, of solution" (*CW*, III 736). The killings of Madame and Mademoiselle Espanaye stumped G----- and his men because only a highly imaginative person could have arrived at a solution that would explain all the facts. However, it is precisely because the police have been able to fancy "many modes" and "many motives" to account for this second mystery that they have been unable to determine the correct sequence of events (*CW*, III 736). Before attempting to arrive at his own solution, Dupin uses his ratiocination to ascertain whether the body recovered is in fact Marie's, thereby ensuring that he will be able to collect the reward. This leads him to disprove *L'Etoile*'s contention that, because "all experience has shown that drowned bodies, or bodies thrown into the water immediately after death by violence, require from six to ten days for sufficient decomposition to take place to bring them to the top of the water" (*CW*, III 743), the corpse found cannot be Marie's. Summing up his refutation, Dupin states, "Both science and experience show that the period of [drowned bodies'] rising is, and necessarily must be indeterminate"; more to the point, bodies deposited in the water right after violent death do not fill with water and sink the way those of drowning victims do, and thus Marie "might have been found floating at any period [after death] whatever" (*CW*, III 744). These facts, combined with the corpse's positive identification and the presence of Marie's clothes on it, remove all doubt as to whether the body is hers and she may still be alive.

If ignorance disqualifies *L'Etoile*'s theory, faulty premises doom *Le Commerciel*'s suggestion that a gang bears responsibility for the girl's demise. The claim that

Marie must have been seized soon after leaving her home because someone as well known as she could not have taken a stroll without being recognized would only be valid if she were known to follow a specific route on a regular basis; however, as "the walks of Marie may, in general, be supposed discursive," it is likely "that Marie might have proceeded, at any given period, by any one of the many routes between her own residence and that of her aunt, without meeting a single individual whom she knew, or by whom she was known" (*CW*, III 749). Likewise, the assertion that the streets would have been filled with people when she departed at nine in the morning lacks validity because the day in question was a Sunday and at that hour most people are "*preparing for church*" (*CW*, III 750). Dupin disposes of the paper's additional claim that the piece of petticoat around Marie's throat indicates that "fellows who had no pocket-handkerchief" perpetrated the crime by observing that gang members are "people who will always be found to have handkerchiefs even when destitute of shirts" (*CW*, III 750). As for *Le Soleil*, Dupin ridicules its lack of originality, not even bothering to dispute its conjectures at this point in the story.

Having disproved the theories of two of his opponents and expressed his utter contempt for the third, Dupin starts to formulate his own. He begins by broadening the scope of the investigation so as to "divert inquiry, in the present case, from the trodden and hitherto unfruitful ground of the event itself, to the cotemporary circumstances which surround it" (*CW*, III 752). Just as the narrator could not fathom why Dupin commenced his inquiry in "Murders" outside the apartment where the killings occurred, he cannot understand why the detective scrutinizes newspaper accounts about Marie's first disappearance three and a half years earlier as well as others concerning events transpiring after the discovery of her body, namely the press's reception of letters attempting to assign blame in the case and reports of the theft of a boat that had been found floating empty on the Seine the day after Marie went missing. The former suggests to Dupin a pattern in Marie's life while the latter provides insight into the mind of the person responsible for her death. Returning home a week after her first disappearance, which attracted much notoriety, Marie claimed she was simply visiting her aunt; however, it was subsequently revealed that she had eloped with "a young naval officer" (*CW*, III 753) with whom she later quarreled. Dupin asserts that it is reasonable to assume that the second disappearance relates to the first, an elopement with the same man, whose profession entails long absences, being a likely possibility. He detects a pattern, that is, efforts by the culprit to divert attention from himself, in the fact that someone has been contacting the press in an attempt to cast suspicion on both a person whom the police have already exonerated and *Le Commerciel's* improbable gang. Because the unlikely discovery of Marie's garments three weeks after her death fits into this pattern, he chooses at this point to refute the statements made by *Le Soleil* in some detail. In contrast to what the paper claims, no evidence exists to suggest "that the articles discovered had been there more than a very few days in the thicket" (*CW*, III 758), grass being capable of growing several inches a day and mildew developing in as little as twenty-four hours. Meanwhile, three considerations undermine the journal's contention that Marie's death occurred at the location where her possessions were found: it is highly unlikely that the articles would have escaped notice for over three weeks in a well-populated area, the items were arranged in a totally unnatural way, and thorns alone could not have torn out entire strips of Marie's frock.

After examining all the evidence, Dupin uses his imagination to envision the aftermath of Marie's demise, concludes that a lone perpetrator must be responsible for her death, proceeds to theorize about this person's identity, and logically outlines the steps to be taken to bring about this individual's apprehension. The traces of some kind of struggle in the thicket further discount *Le Commerciel's* theory, for "what *struggle* could have taken place . . . between a weak and defenceless girl and the *gang* of ruffians imagined?" (*CW*, III 763). Bolstering the case for a single assassin, Dupin attempts to conjure up the thoughts of the perpetrator immediately following the shop girl's death:

> Let us see. An individual has committed the murder. He is alone with the ghost of the departed. He is appalled by what lies motionless before him. . . . His is none of the confidence which the presence of numbers inevitably inspires. He is *alone* with the dead. He trembles and is bewildered. Yet there is the necessity of disposing of the corpse. He bears it to the river, but leaves behind him other evidences of guilt; for it is difficult if not impossible to carry all the burthen at once. (*CW*, III 764)

The sole assailant theory explains certain particulars of the mystery, such as why some of Marie's clothes were left behind, why it was necessary to rig some means of dragging or carrying the victim to the water, and why the body was not weighted down so that it would sink. Again Dupin enters the mind of the guilty party the day after he disposed of the body: "let us pursue our fancies.—In the morning, the wretch is stricken with the unutterable horror at finding the boat [from which the corpse was dumped into the Seine] has been picked up at a locality which he is in the daily habit of frequenting—a locality, perhaps, which his duty compels him to frequent. The next night, . . . he removes it" (*CW*, III 771). Who might this man be? Reasoning that only someone connected with the navy would have been able to steal the boat from the barge office and that a man at a higher rank than a common sailor would be better able to write letters to the press deflecting suspicion from himself, and keeping in mind that "a young naval officer" had eloped with Marie previously, Dupin sketches a plan for tracking down this person. The first step is to find the missing boat, for "with the first glimpse we obtain of it, the dawn of our success shall begin. This boat shall guide us, with a rapidity which will surprise even ourselves, to him who employed it in the midnight of the fatal Sabbath. Corroboration will rise upon corroboration, and the murderer will be traced" (*CW*, III 771).

In stark contrast with the first Dupin story, however, the second offers no independent confirmation of the protagonist's solution. Moreover, because "Mystery" stops short of the "dawn" referred to in the previously quoted passage, only "tracing to its *dénouement* the mystery," as the narrator puts it (*CW*, III 772), the detective does not savor a moment of total victory the way he does in the initial tale. Even though the editors of "the Magazine in which the article was originally published" supposedly insist that "the result desired was brought to pass; and that the Prefect fulfilled punctually, although with reluctance, the terms of his compact with the Chevalier [i.e., Dupin]" (*CW*, III 772), the sequel features neither an eyewitness account of the crime, similar to the sailor's in "Murders," proving the protagonist's theory, nor a scene in which Dupin's opponents are forced to acknowledge the validity of his solution. As Daniel Stashower states:

> Poe's cunningly deceptive editorial note gave the impression that Dupin had emerged triumphant, but it scrupulously avoided giving any detail. The passage revealed only that "the result desired was brought to pass," but gave no information as to the identity of the villain or the exact nature of what transpired. In effect, Poe claimed to hold a winning hand without actually showing his cards.[27]

Or, as Meyers somewhat more concisely puts it, although Dupin "suggests how the crime *could* be solved, he never actually names the murderer."[28] Thus, in this second outing, Dupin experiences at best a hollow triumph.

Heightening the contrast with the previous tale, Poe does not succeed in manipulating readers successfully in "Mystery"; furthermore, he fails to produce a story superior to "Murders." As Meyers puts it, "Poe seemed more concerned with suggesting a solution to the crime than with writing a good story."[29] Ironically, the author had the tables turned on him as he was publishing the sequel, the facts of which he patterned on the sensational case of the Mary Rogers. As a result of a confession from one of the parties involved, what Poe believed to be a murder proved, like the first Dupin tale, to be something else, namely death resulting from a botched abortion.[30] Similar to the humbugged reader of "Murders," Poe mistakenly believed the game he was playing was a whodunit. To his chagrin, he found himself at the last minute groping to figure out "what the hell went on." Although he made revisions in the light of this information when the story was later reprinted, "Mystery" would remain "the ugly stepsister of the trio," as Patricia Merivale has wryly termed it.[31]

In conceiving the Dupin tales as a series, however, Poe bequeaths repeatability and self-referentiality to the form. As problematic as "Mystery" may be, detective fiction could not begin to become a literary genre until the second story in a sequence had been written. By composing more than one Dupin story, Poe, as Terence Whalen remarks, made detection into something capable of being reproduced:

> Despite numerous efforts to project the entire history of the detective novel back onto "The Murders in the Rue Morgue," the tale of ratiocination only became a form when it was repeated enough times to establish its generic elements. In the case of the detective story, of course, Poe himself wrote two more Dupin tales, thereby transforming his own creation into the origin of a series, if not of a full-fledged genre.[32]

By having the narrator refer to "Murders" in "Mystery," Poe initiates the convention of paying some type of homage to earlier detective texts, a practice subsequent writers have continued, either implicitly, as in Wilkie Collins's "Who Is the Thief?" (1858), or explicitly, as in Arthur Conan Doyle's *A Study in Scarlet* (1887).[33] Referring to the problems connected with Poe's tale based on the life and death of Mary Rogers, Hoffman observes, "Dupin is essentially a creature of dreams, not of facts; the crimes he solves are best solved when committed for the purpose of disentangling them, not when they are the actual deeds of others."[34] Scott Peeples makes a similarly apt comment: "Dupin's methods work only within the world of Poe's creation; it is no coincidence that in 'The Mystery of Marie Rogêt,' the only tale based on an actual unsolved case, Dupin fails to solve the mystery and Poe fails to write a compelling story."[35] Unable in the sequel to get the better of his readers and surpass his previous effort, it is therefore not surprising that Poe returns to a fictional world entirely of his own creation in the final Dupin tale.

The Purloined Letter

And what a return it is for Dupin *and* Poe. The detective not only thoroughly and conclusively drubs his opponent, revenging himself upon a formidable old rival who once treated him badly, but also pockets a substantial reward. Like the protagonist, his creator returns to top form in the finale, producing the most concise, ingenious, and satisfying installment of the series, regarded by many critics as his best detective story and one of the greatest tales of detection ever written. Knight, for example, states, "'The Purloined Letter' is not only the most famous of the Dupin stories and the most dramatically successful, it is also the most purely fantastic, the one where intellectual powers are realised in a quite fanciful environment."[36] Hoffman, similarly, states:

> Now, freed from the tyranny of facts which had hobbled him in "Marie Rogêt," Poe contrives an all but perfect plot. It goes beyond the demonstration of Dupin's superiority to the Prefect to embrace a much more interesting and significant theme: the identity of his mental operations—those of genius—with the workings of the mind of his real adversary, the criminal.[37]

Indeed, in a true masterstroke that has had profound implications for detection generally, Poe no longer pits Dupin against rival crime solvers who lack his analytical abilities; instead, he has him go head-to-head with "an unprincipled man of genius" (*CW*, III 993). David Reynolds distinguishes the final tale from its predecessors as follows: "His two previous detective stories had affirmed the power of the analytical mind but still had devoted much time to popular reportage of gory events. In 'The Purloined Letter' the emphasis is reversed: not only are there no gory events, but the crime is the bloodless one of letter stealing and the identity of the criminal is known from the start."[38] Perhaps in part because of his lack of success in the previous story, Poe outdoes himself in "Purloined," composing what amounts to a treatise on how to write detection and making it necessary for subsequent authors to keep pace with him by bringing innovations to the form.

In the first two tales, to which the narrator refers explicitly in the opening paragraph of "Purloined," Dupin uses ratiocination and imagination, aided in "Murders" by observation, to anticipate or reconstruct the thought processes of others, whether it be his crime-solving opponents (the narrator, the Prefect, and the journalists of Paris) or persons directly involved in the crimes (the ape's owner and Marie's betrayer). None of these people, however, possesses a mind to rival Dupin's. For this reason, although Poe's deceptiveness makes it all but impossible to predict his detective's solutions, there is never a doubt as to whether Dupin will win the contests. In the final story, however, the protagonist faces an opponent whose abilities and relish for competition bear a remarkable resemblance to his own, as indicated by the Minister D-----'s use of logical reasoning, creative thinking, and an eye for detail to get the better of both the Queen, another female victim (this time of theft and blackmail), and the Prefect G-----.[39] The latter confesses that the Minister "is more astute than" himself in the case of the stolen letter (*CW*, III 978), just as he had to admit Dupin's triumph over him in the first story. Finally, facing off against a worthy adversary in the trilogy's final installment, the hero savors his most satisfying victory.

Once again at a loss in an important case, the Prefect comes to Dupin, providing the facts of the theft of an intimate communication addressed to the Queen. Entering the royal apartment immediately following her failed attempt to hide the missive from the oblivious King, D----- observes the letter, instantly deduces the reason for her consternation, and conjures up a means of gaining an advantage over her that he can convert into political capital. After pretending to read a letter he has with him, he places it next to the Queen's and later snatches up hers rather than his own, knowing that she can make no objection in front of her husband. At the mercy of the Minister so long as he has the piece of paper, the Queen confides in G-----, offering him a huge reward for its recovery. D----- anticipates this move and assesses his opponents much more effectively than they assess him.

Dupin faults the Prefect for failing to size up his opponent's intellect accurately and adjusting his procedures accordingly. Using an analogy to the game of even and odd to explain how to best one's adversaries, Dupin cites the example of an eight-year-old boy who won all the marbles at his school because "he had some principle of guessing; and this lay in mere observation and admeasurement of the astuteness of his opponents" (*CW*, III 984). Violating this principle, G----- dismisses the Minister as a fool because he writes verse. Being "guilty of certain doggrel" himself (*CW*, III 979), Dupin knows better, asserting the superiority of the poetic imagination over mere mathematical calculation. Well acquainted with D-----, Dupin fashions a plan that ultimately results in the recovery of the letter, explaining to his companion that "if the Minister had been no more than a mathematician, the Prefect would have been under no necessity of giving me this check. I knew him, however, as both mathematician and poet, and my measures were adapted to his capacity . . . . I knew him as a courtier, too, and as a bold *intriguant*. Such a man, I considered, could not fail to be aware of ordinary policial modes of action" (*CW*, III 988). Knowing that G----- and his men will not rest until they find the hidden letter, he decides not to hide it at all. The more the police dig and probe and subdivide, the further they are from finding the letter, eventually becoming convinced that it is not in the Minister's hotel.

Underscoring the resemblance between himself and D-----, Dupin uses his ratiocination and imagination to formulate a hypothesis immediately after hearing the Prefect's recitation of the facts of the case. Just as he reasoned that the room in the Rue Morgue could not have been locked, he concludes that the letter has to be somewhere in the Minister's apartment, and, employing the schoolboy's principle, he projects himself into his adversary's head in order to determine its location, imagining what he himself would do to outwit the Prefect: "I saw, in fine, that he would be driven, as a matter of course, to *simplicity*" (*CW*, III 989), leaving the letter right out in the open yet in disguised form. To explain his theory, as well as the distinction between the mind of someone such as D----- and himself, on the one hand, and that of a person like the Prefect, on the other, Dupin makes reference to another game, one in which players challenge each other to find a word on a map: "A novice in the game generally seeks to embarrass his opponents by giving them the most minutely lettered names but the adept selects such words as stretch, in large characters, from one end of the chart to the other. These, like the over-largely lettered signs and placards of the street, escape observation by dint of being excessively obvious" (*CW*, III 989). Having relied on logical reasoning and creative thinking to develop a theory, Dupin uses his powers of observation to confirm its validity and resorts to masquerade to ensure his victory over D-----. Wearing green spectacles, as he did in "Mystery," Dupin pays a call on the Minister, feigning weak eyes so that he can carefully survey the apartment. At length he focuses upon a letter in a card rack, concluding that he has found what he has been seeking, even though it appears to differ substantially from G-----'s description: "the radicalness of these differences, which was excessive . . . , so inconsistent with the *true* methodical habits of D-----, and so suggestive of a design to deceive the beholder into an idea of the worthlessness of the document; these things, I say, were strongly corroborative of suspicion, in one who came with the intent to suspect" (*CW*, III 991). After committing the features of the disguised letter to memory so that he can make a counterfeit, Dupin deliberately leaves his snuff box behind, giving him an excuse to return the next day when he stages the more elaborate part of his masquerade. While a man he has hired creates a disturbance outside that distracts D-----, Dupin exchanges the Queen's letter for a copy of it he has made.

Worth much more to G----- than the hefty finder's fee he pays to Dupin, the letter itself, of course, serves as indisputable proof of the detective's victory over the Minister in the case of the purloined letter. However, because he and D----- have been competing for several years and he has vowed to get the upper hand, Dupin refuses to settle for anything less than a total victory over his rival, and this explains why he does not simply tell the Prefect where to find the letter. Like the detective, the criminal in "The Purloined Letter" possesses superior reasoning skills, a "lynx" eye, and a facile imagination, which enable him to blackmail the Queen successfully and outmaneuver the Prefect thoroughly. Yet D----- does not take into consideration the one man in Paris with both the ability and the well-established personal incentive to foil his plot, and consequently Dupin wins both the immediate and long-standing contests between them. According to Thoms, "Ultimately, of course, the Minister, who has incorporated the lady's [i.e., the Queen's] story into his own plot of blackmail, proves less masterful than Dupin, who absorbs the machinations of the Minister into his more encompassing counterplot."[40] Leaving the *facsimile* so that it appears that the letter is still in the apartment, Dupin sets his opponent up for a devastating reversal of fortune: "Being unaware that the letter is not in his possession, he will proceed with his exactions as if it was. Thus will he inevitably commit himself, at once, to his political destruction" (*CW*, III 993). To ensure that D----- will know who has so soundly beaten and thoroughly revenged himself upon him, Dupin inscribes a couplet from Crébillon's *Atrée* inside the phony letter: "—Un dessein si funeste,/S'il n'est digne d'Atrée, est digne de Thyeste" (*CW*, III 993). This reference to Atreus and Thyestes, mythological brothers who commit horrible crimes against each other, emphasizes the resemblance and the enmity that exist between Dupin and D-----.[41] It also suggests their moral equivalence.

Although the master criminal in "The Purloined Letter" possesses superior analytical ability, the detective comes out on top. Unlike Dupin, who has openly vowed to "remember" the "evil turn" his rival once did to him, D----- forgets about or discounts this warning—and pays the price for it. Despite the hero's uncanny knack for imaginatively projecting himself into the minds of others, including his opponents', he states that he cannot fully conjure the mental state of the Minister when he realizes he has been defeated—and by whom: "I confess, however, that I should like very well to know the precise character of his thoughts, when, being defied by her whom the Prefect terms 'a certain personage,' he is reduced to opening the letter which I left for him in the card-rack" (*CW*, III 993). Perhaps Dupin is incapable of imagining D-----'s chagrin because he cannot envision someone with a mind comparable to his own suffering such a humiliating defeat.

Given the extent to which self-interest motivates the detective, the nature of justice in "Purloined," as in "Murders" and "Mystery," especially for the victimized women, is dubious at best. David Van Leer asserts, "Dupin's solutions lack the moral dimension by which [mystery] fictions customarily celebrate the detective's ability to right wrongs or restructure a disordered society."[42] In addition to using his ratiocination to prove the innocence of his friend Le Bon (i.e., the good or good man), Dupin in the first tale establishes that no one— no human being—committed cold-blooded murder. As Hervey Allen remarks in his early biography of Poe, "The moral issue is entirely dodged by making the criminal an ape; thus a double horror was invoked without the necessity of blame."[43] Moreover, there is no condemnation of or punishment for the sailor, despite the fact that this man's negligence has led directly to the brutal deaths of two women. The sailor does not personally commit the killings of the mother and daughter, but he certainly bears responsibility for their slaughter by an exotic animal he brought from a colonial outpost to the metropolis. Rather than receiving a prison term or a fine or even a reprimand, however, he actually profits personally as a result of the notoriety the case attracts, selling the ape to the *Jardin des Plantes* for "a very large sum" (*CW*, II 568).[44]

Similarly, in "Mystery" Dupin does not begin his investigation because he wants to see justice done in the case of Marie Rogêt; lost in his esoteric studies, he has no idea that she is dead until the Prefect comes to him offering a reward. In addition, mirroring the first tale's silence on these matters, "Mystery" provides no details relating to such things as motive, moral responsibility, and punishment in connection with the death of the *grisette*, only a cryptic note assuring readers that "the result desired was brought to pass" (*CW*, III 772). As Laura Saltz puts it, "Despite the narrator's promises and Dupin's preternatural intelligence, the case remains unsolved. Though Dupin produces Marie's body as evidence of a crime, he leaves the nature of the crime, the possibility that she has been violated, and the identity of the culprit disturbingly obscure."[45] Van Leer, however, reading "against the grain," contends that the sequel exhibits more "intellectual honesty" than the stories that precede and follow it: "In attempting to solve a real-life crime, Poe faces directly in 'Mystery' the intellectual paradoxes of knowing reality that he skirts around in the more conventionally successful Dupin tales," adding that "current critical preference for the 'Murders' or 'Letter' over the 'Mystery' may mark not our admiration for the intricate philosophies of the former, but our fear of the social reality of the latter."[46]

In the third story, Dupin identifies himself not only as an enemy of D----- but also as a partisan of the Queen, yet, although he immediately suspects that the letter has been hidden in plain sight, he does not act promptly to extricate the "illustrious personage" from her predicament despite his professed loyalty to her. "If Dupin was primarily interested in quickly recovering the letter and thus quickly rescuing the royal lady from blackmail," Thoms remarks, "He would have volunteered to accompany the Prefect on one of his searches of the Minister's hotel."[47] Instead, the detective waits until the "enormous" reward has been doubled and G----- says he is prepared to pay 50,000 francs on the spot for the document before turning over, in dramatic fashion, the letter he has apparently had in his possession for some time. Moreover, no one—not the Queen (who, while she is victimized by the unscrupulous Minister, seeks to hide evidence of a presumably illicit relationship from the King), nor D-----, nor Dupin—has to face official retribution for his or her actions. According to Thoms, "In the Dupin stories the detective emerges not as the criminal's polar opposite but as an ambiguous figure who shares that transgressor's desire for control," ultimately seeking to incorporate "the criminal and his hidden story into [the detective's own] more comprehensive narrative."[48]

Like Dupin, Poe comes out victorious in the concluding installment of the series, successfully manipulating readers and topping what he had previously accomplished. He devises one of his most remarkable stratagems, hiding the solution out in the open (in the same manner that the Minister fools the Prefect) by having Dupin suggest to G----- near the beginning, "perhaps the mystery is a little *too* plain . . . [a] little *too* self-evident" (*CW*, III 975). A revealer and a creator of hoaxes, like Barnum, Poe not only devotes entire texts to unmasking or perpetrating frauds but also, as Scott Peeples points out, attempts to perform both actions in several of his writings, often with less-than-satisfactory results.[49] In "Purloined," however, he brilliantly pulls off this trick by having Dupin expose and duplicate the ruse concocted by D-----. Moreover, by devoting roughly half of the tale to the detective's explanation of how he undoes (but also redoes) what the Minister has done, Poe manages to approximate the feat attributed to the famous showman Barnum quoted earlier—humbugging readers and then telling them how he did so.

Incorporating a metafictional wrinkle into the genre, Poe also addresses the writing of detection itself. According to Irwin, "As Poe practices it, the detective story is a literary form closely aware of its own formal elements, its antecedents, its associations—indeed, so much so that it subtly thematizes these as part of the textual mystery that the reader must unravel in the tale."[50] In an oft-cited essay, Liahna (Babener) Armstrong astutely observes that the uncanny resemblance between D----- and Dupin—the fact that they have surnames beginning with *the same letter*, they write poetry, they steal *the same letter*, they are motivated by self-interest, and so forth—places the criminal and the detective on an equal moral plane, making them virtually interchangeable.[51] Yet she does not fully explore the implications of this insight. If the finale is read as a story about how authors project themselves into the minds of readers and, to paraphrase "Murders," seduce them "into error" or "miscalculation," then the significance of the crime solver being nearly identical with the criminal emerges, for writers of this type of fiction must both devise a problem or crime (like D-----) and offer a solution to it (like Dupin), weaving a tangled plot and then undoing it. In "The Blue Cross," which evokes "The Purloined Letter" in several ways, G. K. Chesterton draws attention to the metafictional thread Poe sews into the fabric of detection. The renowned Parisian sleuth Valentin, reflecting on his missed opportunities to capture his foil, the mastermind Flambeau, remarks, "The criminal is the creative artist; the detective only the critic."[52] However, by luring Flambeau into a clever trap and thereby accomplishing what the celebrated detective could not, the unassuming Father Brown, whom both Frenchmen underestimate, disproves Valentin's assertion. Suggesting that the writer of detection, similar to the truly analytical detective, must be both creative and resolvent, Chesterton's tale, like Poe's letter to Cooke, serves to underscore the fact that the hoaxer, debunker, cryptographer, and manipulator Poe creates adversarial characters such as Dupin and D----- so as to divert attention from the fact that he—the author—like Penelope, has woven a web in order to unravel it.

In addition to encoding a metafictional dimension into the detective form, Poe begins the practice of having later detective fictions refer to earlier ones. Perhaps one of the most elaborate chains of reference within the genre links Valerie Wilson Wesley's contemporary black, female private eye, Tamara Hayle and Poe's "Murders" by way of Dashiell Hammett's *The Maltese Falcon*. In a 2003 interview, Wesley reveals that she has Tamara drive a Volkswagen Jetta to acknowledge her debt to Sue Grafton, whose white, female, hard-boiled detective, Kinsey Milhone, drives a VW Beetle. Milhone herself is based in

Santa Teresa, the same southern California town where Ross Macdonald's series character, Lew Archer, operates. The name of Macdonald's detective, in turn, evokes Sam Spade's partner Miles Archer, who takes a bullet in the heart early in Hammett's classic hard-boiled novel, which itself evokes the first Dupin story in which the sailor who brings the ape from Asia to Paris works on a Maltese vessel.[53] Although the detectives themselves typically know nothing of such links, writers and often readers of detection have a keen awareness of them.

Poe employs three distinct detective plots in the Dupin tales: "Murders" turns out to be a missing animal mystery; despite Poe's equivocal revisions, "Mystery" remains a whodunit, as the narrator's reference to the "murder of Marie Rogêt" (*CW*, III 974) at the start of the final story confirms; and "Purloined" concerns the location of a stolen article. Poe tricks readers by changing the game on them, anticipating Raymond Chandler's observation in "Casual Notes on the Mystery Novel" that "the only reasonably honest and effective method of fooling the reader . . . is to make the reader exercize [*sic*] his mind about the wrong problem, to make him, as it were, solve a mystery (since he is almost sure to solve something) which will land him in a bypath because it is only tangential to the central problem."[54] Such narratives, as Chandler puts it in a 1949 letter, concern the search "not for a specific criminal, but a raison d'être, a meaning in character and relationship"—what "the hell" happened rather than who did it.[55] "The Murders in the Rue Morgue" appears to be a whodunit; however, Dupin eventually reveals that, despite Poe's misleading title, no murder has occurred because the killer is not human. Thus, in the Dupin trilogy, Poe introduces three major detective plots into modern detection that have been used, reused, and reimagined by subsequent writers: what we might call the whatwuzit of "Murders," the whodunit of "Marie Rogêt," and the whereisit of "The Purloined Letter."

In attempting to repeat but also outdo himself in the sequels to "Murders" through the use of self-referentiality, metafictionality, multiple plotlines, and various forms of competition, Poe ensures that authors of detective stories will compete with him—and one another—to bring innovations to the form, thereby creating the opportunity for these writers to pursue a variety of personal, artistic, moral, ideological, and political agendas. Some critics have characterized Poe as an antidemocratic Southern apologist and aesthete who takes pains to eliminate moral, social, and political considerations from his detective texts. Jon Thompson, for example, asserts, "If the conventions of detective fiction offer unique possibilities for exploring social and political relations, then, given Poe's role in the shaping of the genre, it is ironic that these sociopolitical concerns are marginalized" in the Dupin trilogy.[56] Nevertheless, as Maurice Lee aptly observes, "the Dupin stories introduce but do not exhaust the possibilities of detective fiction, offering later writers a generative model open to improvisation."[57] Indeed, by weaving subversion and authorial competition into the warp and woof of detection, Poe has made it possible for later writers to use the form covertly or overtly to address issues of gender, race, ethnicity, sexual orientation, and empire. The remarkably wide range of directions in which writers after Poe have taken the genre he founded serves to substantiate Raymond Chandler's assertion in "Casual Notes on the Mystery Novel" that detection is "a form which has never really been licked, and those who have prophesied its decline and fall have been wrong for that exact reason," to which he adds, "since its form has never been perfected, it has never become fixed. The academicians have never got their dead hands on it. It is still fluid, still too various for easy classification, still putting out shoots in all directions."[58]

Conceiving of detection in terms of competition between characters, between himself and his readers, and between the first Dupin story and its two sequels, Poe playfully incorporates character rivalry, authorial sleight of hand, and generic malleability into the form, key elements that in large measure have accounted for the longevity, popularity, and significance of not only classic but also hard-boiled detective fiction.[59] As with Barnum's notorious humbugs, people welcome the intellectual challenge Poe's detection presents, do not mind being tricked so long as the stratagems are clever, and delight in figuring out how they have been deceived. Although he would no doubt be shocked to learn what has happened to detection, Poe, who perpetrated "The Balloon Hoax" and greatly desired widespread recognition for his literary innovations, would likely take satisfaction in the fact that the way he launched the genre has made it necessary for subsequent authors not only to emulate but also to compete with him. Whether they be thoroughly conventional and highly conservative in the manner of Agatha Christie or boldly experimental, subversively parodic, and politically radical on the order of Chester Himes and Ishmael Reed, writers of detection follow Poe by depicting struggles for supremacy between characters and making references to games and other forms of competition while vying with him and other writers of detection to find new ways not simply to entertain readers but also to outwit, enlighten, edify, unsettle, and politicize them.

As the next two chapters will show, evidence of the influence of Poe's detective fiction on American narratives can be seen in texts by white male authors as early as 1850, as well as in antebellum and postbellum texts by white and African American women writers. Chapter 5 examines fictions by the canonical figures Hawthorne, Whitman, Melville, and Twain that incorporate elements of detection to serve moral, sociological, political, and comic ends. Chapter 6 devotes attention to Poe's other famous ratiocinative tale, "The Gold-Bug," which explicitly addresses the theme of race while adopting a neutral position on slavery and employing minstrel stereotypes so as to appeal to the widest possible audience. In her wildly popular novel *The Hidden Hand*, E. D. E. N. Southworth pursues a similar strategy. Responding to narratives such as those by Poe and Southworth, Harriet Jacobs prior to the Civil War and Pauline E. Hopkins during the post-Reconstruction era turn to detection to combat the racist ideology on which slavery and Jim Crow depend.

Varieties of Detection in Nathaniel Hawthorne's *The Scarlet Letter*, Walt Whitman's *Life and Adventures of Jack Engle*, Herman Melville's *Benito Cereno*, and Mark Twain's "The Stolen White Elephant"

I shall seek this man, as I have sought truth in books; as I have sought gold in alchemy. There is a sympathy that will make me conscious of him. I shall see him tremble. I shall feel myself shudder, suddenly and unawares. Sooner or later, he must needs be mine.

Nathaniel Hawthorne, *The Scarlet Letter*

That he was an unprincipled man, with boundless selfishness and avarice, seemed sure enough; but whether he was a cunning villain, or no, puzzled me to tell.

Walt Whitman, *Life and Adventures of Jack Engle: An Autobiography*

"What are you knotting there, my man?"
"The knot," was the brief reply, without looking up.
"So it seems; but what is it for?"
"For some one else to undo."

Herman Melville, *Benito Cereno*

Great is the detective! He may be a little slow in finding a little thing like a mislaid elephant,—he may hunt him all day and sleep with his rotting carcass all night for three weeks, but he will find him at last—if he can get the man who mislaid him to show him the place!

Mark Twain, "The Stolen White Elephant"

Three-quarters of a century have passed since Edmund Wilson published a trio of essays attacking detective fiction in the *New Yorker*, summed up by the question, "Who Cares Who Killed Roger Ackroyd?"[1] and, to this day, skepticism, if not hostility, still often greets the genre, which remains somewhat marginalized in American literary scholarship. Critics readily credit Poe with inventing modern detection and acknowledge that canonical writers, including William Faulkner, tried their hands at it, yet they tend to devote little attention to the form—and the strategies for reading it—except in essays and books devoted exclusively to the subject. However, if we take this remarkably malleable genre seriously, then we can see the role played by Poe's detection—and, more importantly, the different varieties of detection—in mid- to late nineteenth-century texts by canonical white males not normally associated with the form. Foremost among these are Nathaniel Hawthorne's *The Scarlet Letter*, Walt Whitman's recently recovered *Life and Adventures of Jack Engle*, Herman Melville's *Benito Cereno*, and Mark Twain's "The Stolen White Elephant."

Hawthorne, who told Poe in a June 17, 1846, letter that he "could never fail to recognize the force and originality" of his tales,[2] uses the word "detect" frequently in his most famous novel, particularly after Roger Chillingworth commits himself to solving the mystery of Pearl's paternity. Therefore, it is appropriate to regard this character as a kind of detective, as critics such as Richard Kopley and George Dekker have done, although a very different one from Poe's Dupin.[3] By no means a fully developed novel of detection as we understand it today, Whitman's *Jack Engle*, set in Lower Manhattan, nevertheless does include a crime-solving figure who matches wits with a swindling lawyer. It also echoes Poe's fabrication imagery in referring to the effort to "unravel" the "web of deviltry" of the criminal.[4] In Melville's novella, Amasa Delano's inability to recognize and draw proper conclusions from the clues before his eyes, that is, his role as the antithesis of Poe's Dupin, may not be immediately apparent; however, at *Benito Cereno*'s conclusion Delano's incompetence as a detective becomes clear. The retrospective narrative structure and the heterogeneous content of Melville's story also link it to detection; moreover, what might be called Delano's hyperrationality—as well as the Gothic terms used to express it—connects the novella to Poe. The author of several complete and fragmentary texts that utilize the conventions of detection, Mark Twain pointed out the "curious" nature of "a 'detective' story" and wondered whether there was "ever one the author needn't be ashamed of, except 'Murders in the Rue Morgue'" in an 1896 notebook entry.[5] Twain's statement reflects his mixed feelings toward the form and its founder. By singling out Poe's first ratiocinative tale as the only detective text its author need not feel sheepish about, rather than the three Dupin stories in aggregate, Twain suggests that "Marie Rogêt" and "Purloined"—and, by extension, all subsequent detective stories—fail to exhibit the originality of "Murders." Instead, they subvert, perform variations on, parody, and play with the form Poe invented in "Murders"—strategies that have characterized the genre from its inception and hold the key to not only its popularity but also its adaptability to a wide range of political, personal, and artistic purposes. The connections to and the divergences from Poe's ratiocinative tales in Hawthorne, Whitman, Melville, and Twain's texts serve to highlight not only the personal, aesthetic, and political concerns as well as the particular strengths of these writers but also the widespread influence of Poe and of detection from the late 1840s through the early 1880s.

Roger Chillingworth: Nathaniel Hawthorne's Malevolent, Deluded Detective

In *The Scarlet Letter*, the use of terminology typically associated with the detective form is not limited to "detect" and "detection," which appear throughout the novel; rather, the words "mystery," "solution," "clew," "investigation," "investigator," "case," and "crime" appear one or more times between Chapter IV, when Roger Chillingworth sets out to discover the identity of the man who impregnated Hester Prynne, and the conclusion of Chapter X, when he has his answer. Although readers know (or strongly suspect) that Arthur Dimmesdale fathered Pearl, this by no means diminishes the former Roger Prynne's role as a detective—albeit a fanatical, deluded, and malevolent one.[6] Hawthorne echoes Sir Thomas Browne's contention that even the most arcane mysteries can be deciphered ("What song the Syrens sang, or what name Achilles assumed when he hid himself among women, although puzzling questions, are not beyond *all* conjecture"), which Poe uses as the epigraph to "The Murders in the Rue Morgue" (*CW*, II 527), when Chillingworth tells Hester, "there are few things—whether in the outward world, or to a certain depth, in the invisible sphere of thought,—few things hidden from the man who devotes himself earnestly and unreservedly to the solution of a mystery."[7] Clearly the healer, herbalist, and erstwhile alchemist Chillingworth regards himself as someone capable of solving the most challenging enigmas. Yet, unlike Poe's Dupin, it is not solely through dispassionate analysis that the "Leech" believes he will find the man he seeks. As he tells his estranged wife in the first epigraph to this chapter, an inner sensibility relating to the sin that binds together the book's four main characters will guide him. Dupin does indeed solve mysteries for personal reasons—"amusement" and recompense to a man who once did him a "service" in "Murders," monetary gain in its two sequels, and revenge in "The Purloined Letter."[8] However, he never allows himself to be emotionally invested in, much less obsessed by, his cases in the way that Chillingworth does the search for Pearl's father in *The Scarlet Letter*.

Thus, whereas Poe conceives of detection as an intellectual duel between one or more sets of competitors, Hawthorne takes morality as his subject in his novel, thereby anticipating the defining aspect of G. K. Chesterton's Father Brown stories. Unlike conventional crime solvers, Brown does not necessarily seek to expose the wrongdoer and subject him or her to a public trial and community-mandated punishment. The same can be said of Chillingworth. However, in contrast to Chesterton's man of God, who strives to save the souls of those whose crimes he has detected, Hawthorne's "man of science" allows his search for the one who cuckolded him to devolve into an all-consuming personal vendetta. Chillingworth may believe he acts "with the severe and equal integrity of a judge, desirous only of truth" (81), yet, as Hawthorne's narrator notes, "as he proceeded, a terrible fascination, a kind of fierce, though calm, necessity seized the old man within its gripe, and never set him free again, until he had done all its bidding" (81). J. Gerald Kennedy's characterization of the narrator of Poe's "The Man of the Crowd" (1840) as a "deluded detective" aptly describes Chillingworth. According to Kennedy, "the psychological tension between the narrator's detached, analytical view of human experience and his mounting fascination with" the object of his inquiry functions as "the real conflict" in this tale by Poe, which critics have seen as an important precursor to the Dupin trilogy.[9] As evidenced by the regimen of private torture he imposes on Arthur Dimmesdale, however, Chillingworth is portrayed by Hawthorne as a much more sinister figure than the narrator of "The Man of the Crowd."

Brook Thomas notes that even though in Hawthorne's day "various states began applying the so-called unwritten law by which a husband who killed his wife's lover in the act of adultery was acquitted," *The Scarlet Letter* "generates little sympathy for Hester's husband."[10] Yet it is not simply that his status as a cuckold fails to touch readers; rather, his appearance, intentions, and actions thoroughly repulse them. At the moment in Chapter X when Chillingworth finally has ocular proof of Dimmesdale's guilt, Hawthorne's narrator explicitly compares him to the devil:

> With what a ghastly rapture, as it were, too mightily to be expressed only by the eye and features, and therefore bursting forth through the whole ugliness of his figure, and making itself riotously manifest by the extravagant gestures with

which he threw his arms towards the ceiling, and stamped his foot upon the floor! Had a man seen old Roger Chillingworth, at that moment of his ecstasy, he would have had no need to ask how Satan comports himself, when a precious human soul is lost to heaven, and won into his kingdom. (87)[11]

Here and elsewhere, the novel indicates that the physician is guilty of a greater moral crime than that committed by Hester and Dimmesdale in conceiving Pearl or by the Minister in failing to own up to what he has done, a sentiment that is expressed by Dimmesdale himself—first in Chapter XVII when he states, "We are not, Hester, the worst sinners in the world. There is one worse than even the polluted priest! That old man's revenge has been blacker than my sin. He has violated, in cold blood, the sanctity of a human heart" (118), and again in Chapter XXIII when he tells Chillingworth, "May God forgive thee! . . . Thou, too, hast deeply sinned!" (151). Critics have seen Dupin and D----- as morally equivalent rivals, and many writers of detection since Poe have depicted the crime solver and the criminal as doubles. Hawthorne, however, characterizes his obsessed detective as a far-greater wrongdoer than the man he pursues, showcasing his concern with morality.

John T. Irwin has convincingly argued that the myth of Theseus and the Minotaur informs Poe's conception of detection. In a somewhat similar manner, Hawthorne depicts Dimmesdale being stalked by the evil Chillingworth in a maze of the Minister's own making. Ultimately, however, in a scene that resonates with Poe's profoundly influential solution to the mystery in "The Purloined Letter," Dimmesdale manages to evade his tormentor's grasp not through concealment or flight but rather through public exposure. As Chillingworth states in the penultimate chapter, it is only on the hyper-obtrusive scaffold that his long-suffering victim could have eluded him. Dimmesdale's Market-Place confession can thus be compared to the stratagem used by D----- in outwitting the police prefect G----- (and by Poe himself in mystifying readers) in "The Purloined Letter." Analogous to the power that the purloined letter allows D----- to wield over the Queen, which would vanish if the missive were made public and the King thereby were to learn of its contents, Chillingworth's knowledge that the Minister fathered Pearl enables him to influence Dimmesdale malignly and mercilessly only so long as the girl's paternity remains a secret. Despite his desperate attempt to do so, Chillingworth cannot prevent the Minister from revealing the truth. Immediately following the confession, the physician ruefully says, "Had thou sought the whole earth over . . . there was no one place so secret,—no high place nor lowly place, where thou couldst have escaped me,—save on this very scaffold" (149); and, after Dimmesdale literally bares his breast to the crowd, his tormentor repeatedly states, "Thou hast escaped me!" (151). In contrast to Poe, who in "The Purloined Letter" portrays the brilliant sleuth Dupin vying with an equally gifted criminal in a story emphasizing intellectual competitiveness and cunning, Hawthorne in *The Scarlet Letter* uses a very different kind of detective as the villain of his morality play.

Successfully Combating Crime in Walt Whitman's *Jack Engle*

In announcing the recovery of the six-part serial novel *Life and Adventures of Jack Engle: An Autobiography* (1852), Zachary Turpin reminds us that before Walt Whitman brought out the first edition of *Leaves of Grass* in 1855 he published several works of fiction, which "appeared alongside Hawthorne's, Poe's, Cooper's, and Child's, in some of the premier literary magazines in the United States, including the *Democratic Review*, the *Columbian Lady's and Gentleman's Magazine*, the *American Review*, and the *Union Magazine*." Turpin asserts that the "multitudinous" *Jack Engle* "incorporates elements of nearly every genre of prose Whitman ever made use of: sentimentalism, sensationalism, adventure fiction, reform literature, parables, the picaresque, autobiography (supposedly), suspense fiction, place painting, revenge narrative, didactic moralism, detective fiction, early realist fiction, the essay, journalistic reportage."[12] Celebrating the vibrancy and diversity of New York City, the serial tells the sometimes desultory tale of an orphan who improbably finds both wealth and love. At the same time, it devotes many of its pages to the successful thwarting of a criminal intrigue.[13] Although a murder figures in the plot, the majority of the story concerns the contest between a corrupt Wall Street attorney, fittingly named Covert, and a trio of young people he attempts to cheat, namely, the protagonist Jack, the Quaker foundling Martha, and the Spanish singer Inez, who, aided by the lawyer's clerk-turned-detective Wigglesworth, work together to put a stop to Covert's embezzlement scheme.[14] In doing so, the novel implicitly evokes not only the nascent genre of crime fiction generally, as Turpin notes, but also Poe's detection specifically.

At the urging of his kindly foster father, twenty-year-old Jack studies law in Covert's office, where he quickly befriends the aged clerk Wigglesworth and the errand boy Nathaniel. Besides having a flirtatious relationship with Inez, who herself narrowly escapes being defrauded by Covert, Jack meets Martha, the lawyer's ward and would-be sexual prey, when he is summoned to his employer's house. Shortly thereafter, she sends Jack a plea for help at roughly the same time he learns from Wigglesworth that Covert, an "unprincipled man" from the beginning of his career, has evil designs on Martha and that he himself is a target of the attorney's "game of deceit and falsefacedness."[15] Marveling at the "wonderful power" of "the mind," Wigglesworth, in spite of poor health, undertakes a thorough investigation of his employer's machinations. He tells Jack, "I *resolved* to live until I had unravelled the web of deviltry which, as I have told you, I providentially got the clue of," and he does indeed amass a "chain of evidence against" Covert (313–14, 317). As Jack himself says about the clerk, "The old man had been indefatigable; and truly, as he said, for the last few months, had lived but for hardly any other purpose than to investigate and make plain the mystery" (315). The emphasis on the power of the intellect and the terms "clue," "evidence," "investigate," and "mystery" relate directly to the detective genre; moreover, the phrase "unprincipled man" evokes "The Purloined Letter," and the words "unravelled" and "web" echo Poe's ideas about detection as revealed in his August 9, 1846, letter about his ratiocinative tales.

Informed of the desperateness of the Martha's situation, Jack knows that to be successful in a battle of wits with Covert "subtlety must be opposed to subtlety" (321), and, in the middle of the night, he, Nathaniel, and Inez manage to relocate the Quaker girl from Covert's home in Lower Manhattan to a hiding place across the North (i.e., Hudson) River in Hoboken. Jack expresses admiration for the "sharpness" (321) of the clerk and Martha, who secure various documents proving the attorney's crimes: "For Covert had not all the cunning of the game on his side. Wigglesworth and the young Quakeress, during the three days past, had made some master-moves; and, deep as I knew the lawyer to be, it seemed, when I heard all[,] that they were likely to countermine him, . . . [thereby] digging the very ground from under his feet" (320–21). The term "master-moves" evokes game playing, which features prominently in the Dupin trilogy and subsequent detective stories.[16]

A handwritten statement that Jack quotes in full reveals that, in a fit of anger, Martha's affluent father killed an insolent tradesman, someone he had known since boyhood, who was none other than Jack's parent. Awaiting punishment while in prison, the unfortunate "murderer," as he refers to himself, composed a will that makes Martha his heir but also includes a generous legacy for his victim's only child. Covert, then a relatively young man, whom the prisoner engaged to represent him, concealed this document and gradually used illicit maneuvers to steal the money. Aided by their friends, the two orphans eventually foil the lawyer, who at the end of the novel becomes a "fox caught in a trap while he thought he had so nicely fixed traps for others" (348), and, after a "long life of lies and cheats for gain" (348), flees to a distant town in Canada. Meanwhile, the newly wealthy Jack and Martha, who have fallen in love, get married.

Unlike Dupin and William Legrand (the protagonist of "The Gold-Bug," to be discussed in Chapter 6) in Poe's ratiocinative tales, Wigglesworth plays a secondary role in Whitman's novel and lacks the brilliance of these men; nevertheless, in certain ways he bears a striking resemblance to them. First, just as Dupin (as well as Legrand) hails from an "excellent," "illustrious family" and yet "had been reduced to such poverty that the energy of his character succumbed beneath it" (*CW*, II 531), Wigglesworth, as Jack informs us, has not always led a penurious life: "For his family, particularly on the maternal side, was of considerable rank, reduced as the old man had become" (331). Second, similar to the claim of Dupin's companion in "The Murders in the Rue Morgue" (and the narrator's assertion in "The Gold-Bug" about Legrand) that his friend exhibits signs of "an excited, perhaps of a diseased intelligence" (*CW*, II 533), Jack initially thinks Wigglesworth crazed when the clerk unfolds Covert's scheme to him, stating bluntly, "Old man, . . . you are certainly out of your wits" (301). Third, similar to Dupin's duel with D----- in "The Purloined Letter," Wigglesworth relies on his extensive knowledge about the lawyer and his keen assessment of the man's intellect and character to get the better of his unscrupulous employer. Thus, featuring a detective figure who vows to "unravel" (301) a "web of villainy" (331), *Life and Adventures of Jack Engle* not only uses language associated with crime fiction broadly and that of Poe in particular[17] but also makes reference to games and hunting to describe the competition in cunning between the criminal Covert and the motley collection of New York types who constitute Jack and his circle of friends.

Amasa Delano: Herman Melville's Anti-Dupin

If Poe's interest in detection is primarily intellectual and aesthetic, Hawthorne's largely moral and psychological, and Whitman's mostly atmospheric, adding intrigue and suspense to his portrayal of life in New York City, Melville's in *Benito Cereno* serves a sociopolitical purpose, anticipating the narratives of Harriet Jacobs and Pauline Hopkins to be discussed in Chapter 6. The novella's initial publication, as Andrew Delbanco reminds us, was in *Putnam's*, "a partisan magazine committed to the anti-slavery cause."[18] In its far-from-straightforward structure, incorporation of documentary evidence, and depiction of a person confronting a puzzling mystery, the novella draws on the detective form. Yet in contrast to Poe's brilliant Dupin—or Hawthorne's single-minded Chillingworth and Whitman's dogged Wigglesworth for that matter—Melville's detective figure, Captain Amasa Delano of Massachusetts, utterly fails to read correctly the ample clues before his eyes because of his mental limitations, naiveté, and race prejudice.[19] Although Delano's innocence and obtuseness save him from death at the hands of the black mutineers, as Cereno notes in the coda, the narrative ominously and presciently predicts that a terrible reckoning lies ahead for Northern whites precisely because of their willful ignorance about race and slavery.

Confirming Kevin J. Hayes's observation that the structure of *Benito Cereno* "recalls Poe's detective stories,"[20] Melville explicitly calls attention to the novella's idiosyncratic organizational scheme near the end when the narrator states, "Hitherto the nature of this narrative, besides rendering the intricacies in the beginning unavoidable, has more or less required that many things, instead of being set down in the order of occurrence, should be retrospectively, or irregularly given."[21] The novella, in other words, resembles tales of detection, which are written backward in order to produce a specific effect, as Poe indicates in his aforementioned letter to Cooke. Moreover, similar to the first Dupin tale, in which newspaper accounts of the killings are quoted at length, and especially "The Mystery of Marie Rogêt," in which the detective solves the case using only textual evidence, much of which appears in the story verbatim or in summarized form, Melville devotes almost one-fifth of the story to (selectively edited) testimony given in court in connection with the events that occurred on the *San Dominick*. However, Melville uses this information to provide the solution to the mystery instead of presenting such raw data to set up the problem and to provide clues to its solution, as Poe does.

From the start, Melville's narrator stresses Delano's cognitive and temperamental limitations, describing him as a "blunt-thinking American" (57) of "a singularly undistrustful good nature" (47), who is "incapable of sounding . . . wickedness" (112). Throughout the long day he spends on the *San Dominick*, Delano misses the indications that a slave mutiny has taken place, including the decay and disorder of the ship, Cereno's odd behavior, the lack of white officers aboard the vessel, and the inappropriate attire of the surviving

Spaniards. Moreover, at the end he concedes to Cereno that "acuteness might have cost me my life" (115). As Delbanco observes, "In Amasa Delano, Melville created a character whom we recognize as an ancestor of those callow Americans who walk through the novels of Henry James mistaking malice for charm, botching uncomprehended situations with the unintended consequences of their good intentions."[22] In "The Murders in the Rue Morgue" and his letter to Cooke, Poe compares the solving of a mystery to the disentangling of a snarled thread. Melville incorporates this imagery into the plot of *Benito Cereno* through the exchange between Delano and a Spanish sailor, which serves as the third epigraph to this chapter, and the latter's act of tossing the complicated knot he has been tying at Delano and urging him to "Undo it, cut it quick" (76). However, the dull American captain, "knot in hand and knot in head" (76), as Melville's narrator refers to him, proves totally unequal to the task of unravelling the riddle before his eyes.[23]

The hyperrational Amasa Delano in "Benito Cereno," similar to the narrator of Poe's "The Fall of the House of Usher" (1839), denies the evidence of unsettling and untoward occurrences provided by his senses because it contradicts his preconceived notions about certain people and the nature of reality itself. The two terms conflict: whereas to be rational means to be "reasonable" or "judicious" and requires the elimination of emotion, to be hyper means to be "extreme" or "excessive" and has everything to do with emotion. Poe's narrator would have us believe that he is documenting the mental decline of Roderick Usher—his nervous agitation, his conviction that fear will be his undoing, his bizarre paintings and musical compositions, his assertions that the house is alive, his mad hilarity on the night of the storm, and his death of fright in the embrace of his bloody, and, finally, deceased sister. Prior to the climactic moment, however, the narrator has admitted that, in spite of his rationalist pose, both the gloomy mansion and Roderick's mental state have unsettled him: "It was no wonder his condition terrified—that it affected me. I felt creeping upon me, by slow yet certain degrees, the wild influences of his own fantastic yet impressive superstitions" (*CW*, II 411). Precisely because he adopts such a similarly hyperrationalist pose, Delano ultimately finds himself compromised vis-à-vis the very people about whose lack of rationality he earlier expressed such confidence, namely the Africans on the *San Dominick*. When, finally, the "scales [have] dropped from his eyes" (99), the Yankee captain realizes that he has been duped by an elaborate charade perpetrated by people he considered intellectually incapable of subterfuge. Delano not only repeatedly suppresses his intimations of highly sophisticated cunning among the blacks (just as Poe's narrator vehemently rejects the possibility of uncanny phenomena in the Usher mansion despite what his senses tell him), but also, in doing so, uses—or, more precisely, causes Melville's slippery narrator to use—terminology that explicitly evokes Gothic fiction—and that of Poe in particular.[24]

In adopting the role of the hyperrationalist vis-à-vis what he assumes to be the superstitious and/or mentally unbalanced Cereno, Delano dismisses his own fears—couched in Poe-like language—as irrational. Cereno swoons in response to Delano's offhand, hypothetical remark about the owner of the *San Dominick*'s slaves, Alexandro Aranda—"Were your friend's remains now on board this ship, Don Benito, not thus strangely would the mention of his name affect you" (61). Convinced there is no danger, Delano speculates that his Spanish counterpart must be "the victim of that sad superstition which associates goblins with the deserted body of man, as ghosts with an abandoned house. How unlike are we made! What to me, in like case, would have been a solemn satisfaction, the bare suggestion, even, terrifies the Spaniard into this trance" (61). Dismissing the possibility of anything sinister taking place on board the ship, just as he denies the existence of evil in the world, the hyperrationalist Delano is blissfully unaware that beneath a covering of canvas—that is, hidden in plain sight—Aranda's skeleton has been affixed to the prow by the African mutineers in order to terrify the remaining Spanish slavers into submission to their will.

As his misgivings grow in response to the incongruous things he observes during the long day he spends aboard the *San Dominick*, Delano's decidedly Gothic suspicions become focused on Cereno, about whom he begins "to feel a ghostly dread" such that he regards "the dark Spaniard himself [as] the central hobgoblin of all" (68–69). Yet, despite the ample evidence and his own inklings that everyone on the ship is engaging in a carefully orchestrated masquerade, Delano refuses to believe that a plot of some kind threatens his life. He compares what he terms his superstitious fears to a recurring fever that he must vigilantly attempt to fight off:

> Ah, thought he—gravely enough—this is like the ague: because it went off, it follows not that it won't come back.
>
> Though ashamed of his relapse, he could not altogether subdue it; and so, exerting his good nature to the utmost, insensibly he came to a compromise.
>
> Yes, this is a strange craft; strange history, too, and strange folks on board. But—nothing more. (78)

Echoing the speaker of "The Raven" (who, at the end of the poem's first, third, fourth, and sixth stanzas, denies that anything material is knocking at his chamber door with the words "nothing more"), the hyperrationalist Delano concedes the oddity of it all but will not allow himself to regard his fears, which he elsewhere terms "phantoms," as having a legitimate basis in reality.

Melville makes clear that Delano's incomprehension derives not simply from his mental limitations and sanguine temperament but also from his prejudice against blacks. Building on Toni Morrison, Greg Grandin refers to Delano's "republican racism": "In the United States, at least, one response to the challenge that slavery posed to the American promise of self-creation was to make a fetish out of the ideal of freedom, to measure that ideal not in the degree of dependencies and enthrallments all humans find themselves in by dint of being human, but in opposition to history's most brutal expression of bondage."[25] Offering ready assistance to a slave ship in distress—but not to a group of enslaved Africans fighting for their freedom—and considering scenes of black subservience "pleasing" but the sight of two Africans pushing a European a "spectacle of disorder" (70), Delano fails to interpret correctly what is happening on the *San Dominick* because he regards whites as intellectually superior to blacks and slavery as an acceptable practice. Confident that the whites are "the shrewder race" and the blacks are "stupid" (75), Delano never once allows the possibility that the slave Babo has taken command to cross his mind. According to Laurie Robertson-Lorant,

> Melville builds suspense by limiting his third-person narrative to Delano's point of view until the point where Delano himself realizes with a shock that the Africans have taken over the ship and slaughtered most of the whites, and that Babo has woven an elaborate web of deception from the American's own prejudices. By the end of the story, Melville has drawn readers who adopt Delano's view of the *San Dominick* into the same entangling web.[26]

Robertson-Lorant deftly draws on the imagery of tangling and disentangling from Melville's novella, as well as echoes Poe's language in "Murders" and his letter to Cooke, in this passage. By using elements of detection, Melville shocks those readers who fail to unravel the ample clues of a slave rebellion into acknowledging their own "republican racism."

As the court documents incorporated into Melville's text reveal, Babo relies on Delano and the white sailors' ideas about race to make the show he is directing convincing.[27] In the novella's coda, we are told that Cereno remains haunted by

"The negro" (116) until his early death, having had to alter his notions about the intellectual capabilities of black people (and his own status as someone supposedly innately superior to them) because of Babo, "whose brain, not body, had schemed and led the revolt" (102). However, the end of the story ominously indicates that Delano has not been similarly transformed, despite having seen the truth. Ultimately, then, *Benito Cereno*, which Eric Sundquist appropriately terms the "most troubled and explosive tale of America's antebellum destiny," suggests that Northern whites who share Delano's beliefs about race and slavery may, in an eerie anticipation of the Civil War, be likely to face a harrowing experience of their own.[28] To evoke these looming horrors, Melville not only draws upon the language and the delusional characters of Gothic fiction, echoing, in particular, Poe's "The Fall of the House of Usher" but also creates an anti-Dupin in Delano.

Mark Twain's Purloined Critter

When I was in sixth grade over forty-five years ago, a thin paperback entitled *101 Elephant Jokes* was all the rage. The book included the following absurd sequence of riddles:

> Q: Where do you find an elephant?
>
> A: Elephants are so darn big you rarely ever lose one.
>
> Q: What is the difference between an elephant and a plum?
>
> A: Their color.
>
> Q: What did Tarzan say when he saw the elephants coming?
>
> A: Here come the elephants!
>
> Q: What did Jane say?
>
> A: Here come the plums! (She was colorblind.)[29]

Why did so many of us laugh at such nonsense? The answer is simple: elephants are enormous and for this reason enormously comical. Thus, the notion of losing something so big—or confusing it with something so small as a piece of fruit— tickles the funny bone. It is precisely this type of joke, which children instantly grasp, that serves as the preposterous premise of Mark Twain's "The Stolen White Elephant," a story that has baffled critics. It is not so much that they do not get the joke; rather, they look for more than (or some deeper significance to) this humor. Recognizing the comic potential of not only lost elephants but also pompous, bumbling, greedy sleuths, Twain in "The Stolen White Elephant" created a wickedly funny detective story. Because many scholars dismiss detective fiction on account of its supposedly formulaic nature, they often fail to treat it as a subject worthy of serious investigation. Although such critics as Howard G. Baetzhold, Virginia Hale, Roy Madison Underwood, Jr., R. Jeff Banks, and Lillian S. Robinson have noted—quite correctly—that Twain lampoons the Pinkertons, the New York City Police, and dime novel detectives in his story,[30] none has taken the genre seriously enough to recognize that Twain explicitly and implicitly spoofs the man who established the basic components of the modern detective story: Edgar Allan Poe.

By singling out Poe's first ratiocinative tale as the only detective text its author need not be ashamed of, rather than the trilogy as a whole, Twain's 1896 notebook entry quoted earlier suggests that even Poe's other Dupin stories do not match the originality of "Murders." Instead, what they—and subsequent detective stories—do is rework the form Poe invented in the first tale by means of subversion, variation, and parody. Seventeen years earlier, Twain expressed a similar sentiment in a January 21, 1879, letter he wrote from Munich to William Dean Howells that refers directly to "The Stolen White Elephant":

> My book is half finished; I wish to heaven it was done. I have given up writing a detective novel—can't write a novel, for I lack the faculty; but when the detectives were nosing around after Stewart's loud remains, I threw a chapter into my present book in which I have very extravagantly burlesqued the detective business—if it is possible to burlesque that business extravagantly.[31]

In 1882, when the story finally appeared in print (in the collection *The Stolen White Elephant, etc*), it included the following facetious footnote: "Left out of A Tramp Abroad, because it was feared that some of the particulars had been exaggerated, and that others were not true. Before these suspicions had been proven groundless, the book had gone to press. —M. T."[32] By expressing doubt as to whether "it is possible to burlesque that business extravagantly," Twain's letter wryly suggests that detectives are already caricatures and thus, by extension, that narratives about them have a built-in element of parody. Although he was unquestionably one of the most important nineteenth-century American authors to write detective fiction, his uneasiness with the form reflects a critical bias against the genre that continues to exist today. Ronald Thomas aptly states that for Twain detection "was a form with which he remained fascinated throughout his entire career . . . , however uneasily."[33] Perhaps Walter Mosley has come the closest to summing up Twain's relationship with this type of writing by referring to his detective texts as "a mixed bag" and asserting that he "runs roughshod over the conventions of the genre, when he is not spoofing them outrageously (but not always successfully)."[34]

Twain was attracted to detection, as the relatively large number of published and incomplete texts he wrote that are wholly or partially devoted to the form indicates, but he clearly found it problematic. He produced inferior detective stories, including "Simon Wheeler, Detective" and *Tom Sawyer, Detective*, the failure of which Allan Gribben attributes to Twain's "incongruous humor," "cumbersome plot[s]," and "preferred settings of small towns and rural farms."[35] However, he also penned a few texts in which detective elements are subordinate yet nevertheless significantly contribute to the efficacy of the whole, such as the delightful "Facts Concerning the Recent Carnival of Crime in Connecticut" (1876) and the underrated, politically engaged *Pudd'nhead Wilson* (1894). In addition, although Twain certainly seems more comfortable sending up the genre than writing it more or less straight, even here the results are uneven. His parody of Arthur Conan Doyle, "A Double-Barreled Detective Story" (1902) is meandering and only intermittently entertaining. Gribben asserts that Twain "sadly botched" this "Sherlock Holmes parody,"[36] an assessment echoed by Richard Kellogg, who terms it "rambling and confusing," and W. Keith Kraus, who states that it is "the author's failure to make his parts work together that has relegated the story to literary obscurity."[37]

In contrast, Bret Harte's concise and hilarious "The Stolen Cigar Case" (1902) has long been among the most celebrated Holmes parodies. Some of Harte's early fame rested on a series of send-ups of writers such as Charles Dickens, Victor Hugo, Charlotte Brontë, and Wilkie Collins, which he called *Condensed Novels*. At the end of his life, he wrote a second series that included the Doyle spoof. Rejecting the sycophantic narrator's commonsense suggestions for finding a missing cigar case, the bumbling Hemlock Jones (whose skills as a detective are limited to deducing the fact that it's raining from a wet overcoat and a dripping umbrella) suspects his friend of purloining the case, dons preposterous disguises (including that of a minstrel) to shadow him, and openly accuses the narrator of theft. Similar to the letter in Poe's third Dupin story, which Harte sends up, the supposedly stolen case has been in one of the celebrated detective's drawers the whole time. In addition to its ridiculous characters and the spot-on spoofing of Doyle's language, the humor in the story derives in part from a category mistake, namely Jones's confusing a whereisit for a whodunit.

Like Harte in "The Stolen Cigar Case," Twain gets things right in "The Stolen White Elephant," a brilliant, funny parody not only of real-life detectives and those appearing in dime novels but also, and more importantly, of Poe's detective fiction. In this 4500-word story, Twain, like Poe, evokes the theme of empire. The unnamed narrator tells how he, an Anglo-Indian colonial agent, was charged with transporting the eponymous Jumbo, a present from the King of Siam to the Queen of England, from Thailand to Great Britain. During a stop in the United States to rest the animal, the narrator learns that the elephant has gone missing from its cage in Jersey City. He immediately enlists the services of the renowned Chief Inspector Blunt of the New York City Police force, a man in whom he has complete faith. Blunt fruitlessly dispatches hundreds of detectives to locate Jumbo, personally reviewing the conflicting and often preposterous telegraph reports they send to him. The narrator follows Blunt's advice to the letter—or, more precisely, to the penny—offering a reward of $25,000 for the elephant and then doubling, trebling, and quadrupling that amount, which the detectives eventually keep, as well as reimbursing them for their copious expenses, totaling an additional $42,000. Neither the revelation that Blunt's two main suspects are long dead nor the discovery of the body of the deceased Jumbo in the sleeping quarters of the detectives fails to shake the narrator's admiration for the chief inspector or his profession.

Oddly, Poe has not figured in critical discussions of "The Stolen White Elephant." In his 1997 book on Twain, Peter Messent uses the story as the basis for his reading of the author's work generally, arguing that this short story has to be more than just a parody of detective fiction. Because what is obvious and what is hidden are rarely clear in Twain's fiction, the lost or stolen elephant must mean something, according to Messent, who suggests that it may be an allegorical figure for "the comic principle itself, with Twain representing comedy as a potentially anarchic force; a threat to the established social order and all the codes and conventions on which it depends."[38] Messent, tellingly, finds "The Stolen White Elephant" problematic because he regards parody and detection as irreconcilable:

> Twain's comedy might be explained as operating precisely in the gap between his story's two narrative strands. The reader is aware of all the incongruities of the tale which render its status as a detective story absurd. Yet, he or she is none the less involuntarily caught within the fictional system which has been engaged; is made to follow the detective story through to its frustrating—as far as the conventions of the genre are concerned—conclusion. . . . We end up looking

for readerly satisfaction in a form of narrative that has already been subjected to parody and which we have been thus warned not to take seriously. These two readerly responses cannot be squared.[39]

Dissenting strongly from Messent, I contend that parody, whether covert or overt, has been an essential element of detective fiction from the beginning and that, in "The Stolen White Elephant," Twain the humorist merely makes hilariously explicit something—that is, parody—that is implicit in all detective fiction, particularly American detection, following Poe's "Murders."

Baetzhold, Hale, Underwood, Banks, and Robinson have established that in "The Stolen White Elephant" Twain lampoons the detective profession, specifically the Pinkertons and the New York Police Department, which had bungled a famous body snatching case. However, in doing so, these critics have overlooked the specific literary texts to which Twain's story responds. Twain constructs "The Stolen White Elephant" so that he can burlesque detective plotlines and conventions pioneered by Poe, most significantly the stolen-property tale initiated in "The Purloined Letter" and the missing animal mystery first seen in "The Murders in the Rue Morgue." In addition, Twain alludes to the convention of the locked room first seen in "Murders," the technique of armchair detection employed by Dupin in "The Mystery of Marie Rogêt," the use of cryptography to solve a mystery first seen in "The Gold-Bug," and even one of the most prominent theories about Poe's death.

To my knowledge, no scholar has regarded "The Stolen White Elephant" as a parody of Poe's detective fiction. Baetzhold has pointed out the similarities between specific plot details in the story and the theft of the body of the multimillionaire Alexander Turney Stewart from his tomb in New York City, first reported in newspapers on November 8, 1878, just two months before Twain started work on his tale, citing the aforementioned letter to Howells in which Twain makes the connection between the story and the case explicit. Two years after Stewart's death, construction began on a special mausoleum in Garden City, Long Island, to hold his remains; however, grave robbers intervened to make the transfer impossible. Despite the acting police commissioner's confident declaration that the body would quickly be recovered, the efforts of countless public and private detectives (including the Pinkertons), considerable press coverage, and a reward of $50,000, the case dragged on well into the 1880s and was never satisfactorily resolved.

Baetzhold and others have also noted the unmistakable references to the Pinkerton detective agency and its trademark single open eye, the basis for the expression "private eye," which appeared on the backs of a series of popular books ghostwritten for Allan Pinkerton and reputedly based on the exploits of his agency. In Twain's tale, as the days go by with the elephant still at large, the fawning narrator laments that the newspapers mock the detectives by printing "all sorts of ridiculous pictures of the detective badge." "You have seen the badge printed in gold on the back of detective novels, no doubt," he continues; "It is a wide-staring eye, with the legend, 'WE NEVER SLEEP.' When detectives called for a drink, the would-be facetious barkeeper resurrected an obsolete form of expression and said, 'Will you have an eye-opener?'"[40] As Robinson notes, Twain's gullible civil servant "is the classic unreliable narrator, not because of any premediated falsification, but because his point of view is so uncritical."[41] This, of course, links him to Poe's likewise unnamed narrator in the Dupin tales, whom Poe uses to manipulate readers. The exorbitant cost of Blunt's operation and his emphasis on shadowing the elephant also serve to travesty Pinkerton's procedures. Baetzhold concludes his essay with the assertion that "out of a combination of the death of a 'Siamese God' [as the white elephants of Thailand were believed to be], Pinkerton's detective tales, and a sensational unsolved grave-robbery, Mark Twain wove his elaborate burlesque of detectives and their methods."[42] Without denying the presence of these factors, I contend that there is far more at work in Twain's story and that to appreciate Twain's humor fully his sending up of Poe must be recognized.

References to at least four of Poe's detective stories occur in "The Stolen White Elephant," but the links to "The Purloined Letter" predominate. Rather than a pilfered letter whose whereabouts are unknown, Twain humorously writes about a purloined critter, an article of stolen property so large it should be impossible to hide. Resembling the police prefect G-----, the bumbling, ineffective Inspector Blunt contrasts with the brilliant amateur Dupin. On a few occasions, however, Blunt's antics parody those of Poe's detective, and the resolution to Twain's story clearly spoofs Dupin's solution to the mystery in "The Purloined Letter." Although the scope of their investigations could not be more different, Poe's G----- and Twain's Blunt proceed more or less geographically. G----- divides the Minister D-----'s apartment and grounds into squares and carefully examines each one— without success. Likewise, in hunting the elephant, Blunt sends detectives out broadcast, north to Canada, west to Ohio, south to Washington, D.C. Although several of Blunt's detectives see—or think they see—the elephant, none succeeds in recovering him. Similarly, the conclusion of Twain's story, in which Blunt trips over the dead elephant, burlesques the Minister D-----'s method of concealment, about which Dupin quickly formulates a theory that he then sets out to confirm. Poe's sleuth explains that to hide something effectively, it must be positioned so conspicuously as to escape notice, exemplifying his point by referring to a game involving the names of places printed on a map. The letter is right in front of G----- and his men all the time, but they miss it because they expect it to be hidden. Likewise, Blunt and his men absurdly manage to miss the gargantuan Jumbo, who dies within their sleeping quarters. The sole unflattering newspaper account of the chief inspector's blundering discovery of the elephant, which serves as the final epigraph to this chapter, lampoons the solution to "The Purloined Letter."

Blunt's actions also spoof Dupin at times. In "The Purloined Letter," G----- reasons inductively, gathering facts first and then basing his conclusions on them. Because his searches fail to locate the letter, he surmises that it must not be in D-----'s apartment. In contrast, Dupin devises a theory that satisfactorily accounts for the situation and the principals involved—reasoning that the letter must be in D-----'s apartment and in a place so obvious that G----- has missed it. Then he proceeds to find evidence to confirm it—paying a visit to D-----'s apartment, where he spies the disguised letter in a conspicuous place. In a parody of eccentric, ratiocinative crime solvers such as Dupin, Blunt spends six or seven minutes silently contemplating the facts of the case the narrator has just presented and then declares: "Now let us proceed to business—and systematically. Nothing can be accomplished in this trade of mine without strict and minute method" (10). As Robinson points out, Twain's story "takes off from (and on) the popular notion of the brilliant detective whose reasoning powers far surpass those of ordinary, commonsensical mortals."[43] Revealing the detectives' relentless pursuit of fame and glory, the narrator reports that, despite Blunt's expressed wish for secrecy when they first meet, the

> next morning it was all in the newspapers, in the minutest detail. It even had additions—consisting of Detective This, Detective That, and Detective The Other's "Theory" as to how the robbery was done, who the robbers were, and whither they had flown with their booty. . . . The eleven theories all named the supposed robbers, but no two named the same robbers; the total number of suspected persons was thirty-seven. The various newspaper accounts all closed with the most important opinion of all—that of Chief Inspector Blunt. (17–18)

Jumbo's disappearance, according to Blunt, is the work of two men—later revealed to be long deceased—who are also suspected of stealing "the stove out of the detective headquarters on a bitter night last winter" (18). The crowning comic twist Twain gives to "The Purloined Letter" lies in the fact that despite Blunt's assertions (and unlike the Minister D-----, who unquestionably filches the letter), no one ever steals Jumbo; he simply breaks free and goes on a rampage. What this means, of course, is that Blunt and his detectives are not simply bumblers but thieves themselves, hoodwinking the narrator out of his life savings. As Mosley notes, Twain's story "shows us that the law can be more corrupt than it is misguided and still hold us in thrall to its uniform."[44]

Twain has fun with not only Poe's third Dupin story but also the first. Like the orangutan in "Murders in the Rue Morgue," Jumbo, a beast of incredible strength being transported from Asia to Europe, escapes from his owner and kills people. In contrast to Poe's story, however, there is no doubt as to who or what is responsible for the deaths that occur in "The Stolen White Elephant." Unlike Blunt, who revels in the publicity that Jumbo's rampage generates, the narrator of Twain's story, to a much greater extent than the sailor who brought the ape from the East Indies to Paris in "Murders," experiences great regret for what his animal has done: "There was no joy for me. I felt as if I had committed all those red crimes, and the elephant was only my irresponsible agent" (28). He sadly provides a long list of Jumbo's victims, which, in a nod to the means by which Poe's orangutan gains entrance to the house where he kills the two women, includes "a lightning-rod agent" (28).

Twain's most obvious reference to "Murders" occurs when he burlesques the device of the locked room, which Poe originates in that story. In the initial Dupin tale, the Paris police are baffled because the crimes were committed despite the fact that the doors of the victims' bedroom were locked and the windows apparently nailed shut. Theorizing that the assailant could not have been human from the facts of the case he has read in the newspapers and his firsthand observation of the apartment, Dupin concludes that an ape must be responsible and places an advertisement in the papers stating that he has found such a creature to prove his theory, which, of course, is quickly confirmed. In Twain's story, although all the evidence suggests that the immensely powerful Jumbo has simply broken out of his cage, Blunt and the men under him reason quite differently. In recounting the detectives' widely divergent theories about the elephant's disappearance printed in the newspapers, the narrator states:

> No two theories were alike; or even much resembled each other, save in one striking particular, and in that one all the eleven theories were absolutely agreed. That was, that although the rear of the building was torn out and the only door

remained locked, the elephant had not been removed through the rent, but by
some other (undiscovered) outlet. All agreed that the robbers had made that
rent only to mislead the detectives. (17)

Here and elsewhere, the sleuths implausibly assert that an elaborate conspiracy
has taken place.

Although Twain's parody focuses primarily on "The Purloined Letter" and
"The Murders in the Rue Morgue," "The Stolen White Elephant" also refers to two
other detective stories by Poe and even his mysterious death. Most of the second
section of Twain's story comprises telegraph messages Blunt receives from the
detectives in pursuit of Jumbo. In a parody of the motif of armchair detection
first used by Dupin in "The Mystery of Marie Rogêt," Blunt sifts through the
dispatches sent to him by his detectives. Unlike Dupin, however, who simply
by carefully reading the accounts of the case reported in the papers succeeds in
solving the mystery, Blunt fails to notice the contradictions in the messages he
reads and reaches absurd conclusions. In one instance, the detective Darley—
the name of the illustrator of Poe's "The Gold-Bug" in 1843 (see Chapter 3)—
informs his superior: "Shadowed the tracks three miles westward. Large, deep,
and ragged. Have just met a farmer who says they are not elephant tracks. Says
they are holes where he dug up saplings for shade trees when ground was frozen
last winter" (21).[45] In response, Blunt asserts once more that there is a vast
conspiracy afoot—"Aha! a confederate of the thieves! The thing grows warm"—
and commands his agent to "arrest the man and force him to name his pals.
Continue to follow the tracks—to the Pacific, if necessary" (21–22).

In an obvious parody of "The Gold-Bug," Blunt attempts to arrange a meeting
with the "thief" by running the following gobbledygook advertisement in
the newspapers: "A.—xwblv. 242 N. Tjnd—fz328wming. Ozpo—; 2 mo. ogw.
Mum" (32). For Peter Messent, who does not choose to take Twain's parody
seriously, Blunt's message (which contains the letter sequence *po*) remains
"impenetrable," epitomizing what he and other critics have found unsettling
about the story. Describing "The Stolen White Elephant" as "pointedly pointless,"
Messent asserts:

Though the specific comic techniques Twain uses can be identified, the story as
a whole, like so much of Twain's work, seems not quite to add up. The reader is
left with a peculiar sense of not having got the joke. This sense of puzzlement,
the struggle to interpret satisfactorily a problematic text, is (self-reflexively)
signalled as a subject of narrative concern when Inspector Blunt . . . places
an advertisement in the morning papers to open negotiations with the thief.

His message remains a form of gibberish for both the narrator and the reader (though their response to it implicitly differs). Shared codes break down as both are left on the outside, as it were; the point of the communication completely blunted.[46]

Messent correctly identifies the "self-reflexive" character of Twain's story; however, he fails to see how this relates to detective fiction's inherently parodic nature. Consequently, he does not perceive the connection between Blunt's ad and "The Gold-Bug."[47]

Finally, Twain appears to spoof a prevalent theory put forward to explain what happened to Poe shortly before his death in Baltimore in 1849, by having his narrator report that "in one place [Jumbo] had 'interfered with an election and killed five repeaters'" (28). This statement echoes several biographers' accounts of what may have occurred with Poe, such as the following:

There was an election on Wednesday, October 3rd, for Members of Congress and House of Delegates, and the fact that Poe was found in or near a polling place has given rise to vivid pictures, all problematical, of his having been drugged, taken from one polling place to another to be voted as a "repeater," and then abandoned when his usefulness was over. There is no doubt that such practices were frequent in those days, but that Poe was made a victim of them has not been fully established.[48]

On March 27, 1881, over a year before Twain's story saw print, Edward Spencer proposed this theory to explain Poe's demise in the *New York Herald*, emphasizing Poe's Whig sympathies and the proximity of the Whig "coop" for repeaters to the polling place (actually a tavern called Gunner's Hall) where Poe was found insensible;[49] however, the controversy over what precisely happened had been raging for several years—and has continued to this day.

Uncovering the extent of Twain's spoofing of Poe in "The Stolen White Elephant" amounts to much more than antiquarian literary detective work because so much of Twain's humor derives from a series of category mistakes committed by Blunt that correspond to the specific detective plotlines and conventions at which Twain pokes fun. At first, the chief inspector absurdly treats the exaggeratedly conspicuous Jumbo—nineteen feet tall, forty-eight feet long, and fitted with a carrier that can accommodate fifteen people—as a missing person, asking the animal's caretaker about any minute distinguishing characteristics he might have, such as scars. However, very soon—and even before the elephant destroys property and kills people—Blunt, rather than treating Jumbo as missing, describes him as a "criminal" (similar to the police with the orangutan in "Murders") and directs several detectives to "shadow" him (though at one point the elephant begins to follow them). At still other times, Blunt refers to Jumbo as a piece of "property" (similar to the queen's missive in "The Purloined Letter") with which certain "thieves" have absconded. This is especially true at the conclusion of the story when Blunt, after literally tripping over Jumbo's rotting body, triumphantly declares, "Our noble profession is vindicated. Here is your elephant" (33). The chief inspector claims success because the narrator's "stolen" property has been recovered even though the process has reduced the narrator to bankruptcy, destroyed his reputation, and failed to prevent the deaths of countless people and the prized animal.

An awareness of Twain's parodic intentions with regard to Poe helps readers to appreciate the story's humor and grasp its punch line fully. Messent, however, claims that the conclusion of "The Stolen White Elephant" serves as a microcosm of the conflict between parody and detection that he sees throughout the story:

> Blunt places his coded advertisement, the meaning of which remains obscure. He then leaves his client . . . supposedly to meet with the criminals at midnight. Both client and reader are left ignorant of what then occurs and are left to puzzle over a series of questions. *Are* there any criminals actually involved? Does a meeting take place? Is the detective duping his client? Finally Blunt literally stumbles over the rotting corpse of the stolen elephant—if it ever *was* stolen—with no further detail given of the clues or information which led him there. The detective is then celebrated as a hero for recovering the elephant, the death of which renders that act of recovery pointless. These joint strands of the narrative operate in antithetical relationship to that logical clarity with which detective stories, and their closures, are conventionally associated.[50]

Like Blunt and G-----, Messent overlooks what lies right before his eyes, namely that this ending, like the incongruity of a lost or stolen elephant, *is* funny, and that the way in which it culminates Twain's parody of Poe's detective stories intensifies the humor. Moreover, uncovering the full extent of Twain's send-up of the writer who did more than anyone else to found modern detective fiction undermines Messent's assertions about the "undecidability" of "The Stolen White Elephant." Acknowledgment of Twain's devilishly funny spoof of Poe's detective fiction serves as a challenge to critics who search for a hidden meaning beneath the parody and assert that Twain's story fails artistically and/or lacks resolution.[51]

Twain's awareness of Poe commenced long before he composed "The Stolen White Elephant." In the mid-1860s, Twain wrote a parody of "The Raven" titled

"The Mysterious Chinaman," and before 1875, according to Franklin R. Rogers, Twain began working on "Simon Wheeler, Detective."[52] Moreover, as Gribben reports in "'That Pair of Spiritual Derelicts': The Poe-Twain Relationship," scholars have pointed out connections between "The Gold-Bug" and *The Adventures of Tom Sawyer*, and between "William Wilson" and "The Facts Concerning the Recent Carnival of Crime in Connecticut," an inventory Gribben himself expands by linking *The Narrative of Arthur Gordon Pym* to *Adventures of Huckleberry Finn*, "Some Words with a Mummy" to several of Twain's sketches, and "Thou Art the Man" to *Pudd'nhead Wilson*. Meanwhile, R. Kent Rasmussen notes the mention of "The Bells" in *A Tramp Abroad* and hears echoes of Poe in *Life on the Mississippi*; Jack Scherting connects "The Cask of Amontillado" and "The Man That Corrupted Hadleyburg"; Steven E. Kemper compares "A Descent into the Maelstrom" and "The Invalid's Story"; and J. R. Hammond, like Gribben, sees links between Poe's humorous writings, especially "Some Words with a Mummy," and "The Facts Concerning the Recent Carnival of Crime in Connecticut," "How I Edited an Agricultural Paper," and "Curing a Cold."[53] I contend that we must place "The Stolen White Elephant" at the top of this list, recognizing in it not only Twain's thorough familiarity with and elaborate parody of Poe's detective fiction but also his keen insight into the intrinsically self-reflexive and parodic nature of the genre initiated in the Dupin stories. In doing so, he makes explicit what is implicit in all detective writing and, as a skilled humorist, takes things to exaggeratedly absurd levels in order to achieve well-aimed and well-executed comic effects.

Amenable to a range of purposes, detective fiction has appealed to a wide variety of writers since its inception. As several critics, including Catherine Ross Nickerson, Kathleen Gregory Klein, Stephen Soitos, and Frankie Y. Bailey, have asserted, by the turn of the twentieth century, women and African American authors embraced detection as a means to address issues of gender and race.[54] However, as this chapter has shown, the process of using elements of the malleable form Poe created for a specific moral, political, or artistic program began much earlier. Between the early 1850s and the early 1880s, such major nineteenth-century American writers as Hawthorne, Whitman, Melville, and Twain reworked and responded to the genre launched by Poe through their depictions of obsessive, deluded, malign, dimwitted, prejudiced, corrupt, and/or cozening detective figures.

Madness, Mystification, and "Average Racism" in "The Gold-Bug," E. D. E. N. Southworth's *The Hidden Hand*, Harriet Jacobs's *Incidents in the Life of a Slave Girl*, and Pauline Hopkins's *Hagar's Daughter*

Why, to be frank, I felt somewhat annoyed by your evident suspicions touching my sanity, and so resolved to punish you quietly, in my own way, by a little bit of sober mystification.

Poe, "The Gold-Bug"

"This convict, as you are aware, is a man of consummate cunning. . . ."
"Ah, but . . . his cunning was no match for mine, you know!" said Capitola, smiling.

E. D. E. N. Southworth, *The Hidden Hand*

I knew his cunning nature too well not to perceive that this was a trap laid for me. . . . I resolved to match my cunning against his cunning.

Harriet Jacobs, *Incidents in the Life of a Slave Girl*

It's as sure as preaching that somebody who knows something must take hold of Miss Jewel's case or that son of Sodom will carry his point. . . . I'll see if this one little black girl can't get the best of as mean a set of villains as ever was born. . . .

Pauline Hopkins, *Hagar's Daughter: A Story of Southern Caste Prejudice*

A century separates the manumitted slave Jupiter, who does not know his left from his right in "The Gold-Bug," and the black "day houseman" Sam in Cornell Woolrich's "It Had to Be Murder" (1942), the source for Alfred Hitchcock's celebrated 1954 film *Rear Window*. Yet these characters resemble each other in striking ways. Each is a superstitious, dialect-speaking, older African American male ordered, without explanation, to undertake a dangerous ascent in the seemingly whimsical pursuit of the solution to a mystery by his incapacitated white employer—the putatively insane William Legrand in Poe's story and the cast-ridden Jeff (Hal Jeffries) in Woolrich's. Significantly, Jeff's servant, who would be transmogrified into the wealthy socialite Lisa Fremont played by Grace Kelly in *Rear Window*, bears the same name as the ex-slave in Thomas Nelson Page's influential plantation story "Marse Chan" (1884). Such continuity in the portrayal of black characters in fiction by white American authors makes all the more noteworthy mid-nineteenth- and turn-of-the-twentieth-century black texts that not only denounce slavery and depict its horrors but also counter-discursively respond to the pervasive marginalization and stereotyping of African Americans in literary and popular culture.

In "The Gold-Bug," Poe explicitly introduces the theme of race into detective fiction. Apart from the sensation created by "The Raven" in 1845, he achieved the most notoriety during his lifetime with this ratiocinative tale about a coded map leading to pirate treasure, which won the first prize of $100 in a contest sponsored by the *Dollar Newspaper* of Philadelphia. After first appearing in that publication in June 1843, it was reprinted later that year and often thereafter in American newspapers (without any additional compensation for Poe). A pirated version was brought out in England in 1846 or 1847, and French, German, and Russian translations of the story were published before 1850.[1] An immediate and sustained international success, "The Gold-Bug," as Burton Pollin has established in *Images of Poe's Works*, has been illustrated more frequently than any other Poe text by a wide margin.[2]

Similar to Dupin, Legrand hails from a once wealthy family (of French descent), possesses extraordinary analytical skills, lives a secluded life with another man, and has the story of his resolution of an arcane problem told by an unnamed male friend who fears for his sanity. Moreover, each resorts to mystification to get the better of other people. Just as Dupin employs disguise and masquerade to defeat D-----, Legrand feigns madness by insisting on carrying the golden scarab during the search for Captain Kidd's treasure and commanding Jupiter to drop it through the eye of the skull so as to "punish" the narrator for his doubts about Legrand's sanity, as he puts it in a statement near the end of the story that serves as the first epigraph to this chapter. Moreover, just as Poe humbugs readers in the Dupin trilogy, he leads readers of "The Gold-Bug" to believe that the insect has some sort of occult power. A review of his *Tales* in the October 1845 issue of the *Aristidean* that Thomas Mabbott, G. R. Thompson, and other scholars contend was largely or wholly written by Poe himself declares:

> The bug, which gives the title to the story, is used only in the way of mystification,
> having throughout a seeming and no real connection to the subject. Its purpose

is to seduce the reader into the idea of supernatural machinery, and to keep him so mystified until the last moment. The ingenuity of the story cannot be surpassed. Perhaps it is the most *ingenious* story that MR. POE has written.[3]

Ten months later, Poe again addressed the ingeniousness of his ratiocinative tales in his aforementioned letter to Philip Pendleton Cooke.

Despite the many similarities between them, one thing in particular distinguishes Dupin from Legrand. Whereas the former isolates himself in Paris with a white companion, the latter lives at a distance from other people with an older black servant on South Carolina's Sullivan's Island, which was for decades the primary depot for slaves arriving in North America from Africa and the West Indies.[4] Through the relationship between the devoutly loyal and at times comically obtuse ex-slave Jupiter and the eccentric sleuth Legrand, the tale, as Toni Morrison remarks in *Playing in the Dark: Whiteness and the Literary Imagination* (1992), reveals much about attitudes toward and depictions of race in texts by nineteenth-century white American writers, with Poe standing out, in Morrison's estimation, as the most significant of them all.[5]

Although both were raised in the South, critics have long situated Poe and E. D. E. N. Southworth (1819–99) on opposite sides of the debates over slavery that dominated antebellum political discourse. Poe worked as an assistant to the editor of the *Southern Literary Messenger* in the mid-1830s, a period during which apologies for slavery occasionally appeared in the journal. Moreover, in some of his writings, he attacked abolitionists as extremists, and, although he lamented the misfortunes occasioned by slavery, he never advocated its gradual much less its immediate elimination.[6] In contrast, Southworth, a slave owner herself, as Paul Christian Jones has revealed, published her early work in antislavery newspapers, publicly denounced the peculiar institution, supported the Union during the Civil War, and had close friends who were abolitionists.[7] However, her wildly popular novel *The Hidden Hand*, first serialized in 1859, pursues a neutral policy on slavery and uses caricatured racial representations similar to "The Gold-Bug," published sixteen years earlier. To avoid offending white readers in either the North or the South and thus appeal to the widest possible national audience, Southworth chose to adopt the deliberately apolitical strategy of the *New York Ledger* in which her novel appeared three times between 1859 and 1883 before it was finally published in book form in 1888. In the narrative, she never mentions the word "slavery" in connection with Southern black bondmen and women; moreover, like Poe, she employs clichéd, minstrel show figures reflecting what Terrence Whalen terms the "average racism" of Americans

North and South during the nineteenth century (and beyond).[8] Because of the long-term popularity and unique publication history of *The Hidden Hand*, black women authors signified on (i.e., counter-discursively wrote back to) it during both the late antebellum period—Harriet Jacobs in *Incidents in the Life of a Slave Girl* (1861)—and the post-Reconstruction era—Pauline Hopkins in *Hagar's Daughter: A Story of Southern Caste Prejudice* (1901–02).[9]

Whereas Poe in "The Gold-Bug," as noted earlier, portrays Legrand as an alleged lunatic who confines himself in an isolated cabin on a Southern island, Southworth, Jacobs, and Hopkins depict supposed madwomen in Southern attics. In *The Hidden Hand*, following the murder of her husband, Capitola Le Noir *mère* is imprisoned and declared insane by her brother-in-law Captain (later Colonel) Gabriel Le Noir. In *Incidents*, in order to extricate herself and her children from slavery, Linda Brent chooses to conceal herself for nearly seven years rather than remain Dr. Flint's slave; however, in stark contrast to Legrand's (Spartan but otherwise comfortable) self-imposed exile, her confinement takes place in a cramped and vermin-infested crawlspace that takes a significant toll on her physically, emotionally, and psychologically. In Hopkins's novel, Hagar Sargeant, like the elder Capitola, is held captive and pronounced mentally unsound by her brother-in-law St. Clair Enson after a disfigured dead body has been deemed to be that of her husband. Without question, Charlotte Brontë's *Jane Eyre* (1847), in which Rochester locks up his first wife Bertha Mason in a room on the third floor of Thornfield Hall, serves as a key intertext for each of these women-authored narratives.

In *Incidents*, Jacobs creates a hybrid text that, as critics have noted, draws on and repurposes elements of the African American male slave narrative, Gothic fiction, and the Anglo American female seduction novel. Her biographer Jean Fagan Yellin states, "Very helpful were the books in [her employer Nathaniel Parker Willis's] library that taught her the conventions of fiction—works like *Uncle Tom's* Cabin, with Cassy's desperate drama of sexual slavery, and *Jane Eyre*, with its story of a woman's struggle for autonomy."[10] However, scholars for the most part have failed to acknowledge that she also reworks aspects of detective fiction in presenting the struggle between Linda and her master. Jacobs does so as part of a larger strategy to rebut caricatured depictions of US blacks in white-authored texts, including "The Gold-Bug" and *The Hidden Hand*. Hopkins likewise turns to detection in the latter chapters of *Hagar's Daughter* to challenge the stereotyped portrayals of African Americans in popular white fiction of her own era, *The Hidden Hand* among them. In doing so, she builds on the project she began with "Talma Gordon" (1900), widely recognized as the first African American detective and mystery story, a multilayered reimagining of "The Gold-Bug" that, as I have discussed elsewhere,[11] exposes and excoriates not only the racist ideology at the heart of slavery and Jim Crow America but also, as Hopkins stresses in this fiction published during the Philippine-American War, Western imperialism.

Uniting a Divided Country by Means of "Average Racism" in "The Gold-Bug" and *The Hidden Hand*

Literary historians identify Page's "Marse Chan: A Tale of Old Virginia," published in the April 1884 issue of *Century Magazine*, as a pivotal text of the plantation school. Yet key features of such writing appear in antebellum stories, including not only "The Gold-Bug" and *The Hidden Hand* but also *Swallow Barn; Or, A Sojourn in the Old Dominion* (1832) by Poe's early mentor/patron and longtime correspondent John Pendleton Kennedy, whose second novel, *Horse-Shoe Robinson*, published in 1835, the young author reviewed.[12] Morrison states in reference to Poe, "We can look to 'The Gold-Bug' . . . for samples of the desperate need of this writer with pretensions to the planter class for the literary techniques of 'othering' so common to American literature: . . . strategies employed to secure his characters' (and his readers') identity."[13] The association between the loyalty of Legrand's Newfoundland and that of Jupiter anticipates a statement about Northern white racial attitudes in *Benito Cereno*, as well as the connection made between Marse Chan's dog and his former slave Sam in Page's story. Melville's narrator states of the naïve, self-satisfied, racially biased Yankee sea captain Amasa Delano, "In fact, like most men of a good, blithe heart, Captain Delano took to negroes, not philanthropically, but genially, just as other men to Newfoundland dogs" (84). "Marse Chan" illustrates the supposedly dependent nature of blacks through the figure of Sam, whose current occupation seems to consist largely of looking after his deceased master's pet. Page not only depicts Sam lifting fence rails for the aged canine and admitting to spoiling him with "sweet 'taters," but concludes the story by having Sam ask his wife "have Marse Chan's dawg got home?"[14] Clearly the point is to equate Sam and the hound as loyal, subservient beings lost without their master.

However, we fix its origins, plantation literature typically features nostalgia for the antebellum slavocracy (specifically a quasi-familial but rigidly stratified relationship among slaves and their owners), chivalrous white Southern males and virtuous white Southern women, and faithful blacks who speak in an exaggerated dialect. Postbellum fictions, such as Page's, portray former slaves pining for a return to the days when their masters cared for them and depict a dysfunctional society resulting from the devastation of the Civil War and the depredations of Reconstruction. As "Marse Chan" begins, not only is the title character gone but his whole class has died out, his parents having passed within a year of his death and his lifelong love interest Anne having succumbed to a combination of fever contracted while working as a nurse and a broken heart. Set in 1872, Page's narrative clearly implies that had the war never taken place beautiful, orderly plantations would still be intact, honorable and principled men and women like Marse Chan and Anne would be in charge, and blacks such as Sam would have whites to provide them with direction and a purpose in life.

The brilliance and iconoclasm of *Playing in the Dark* sparked considerable critical interest in Poe, slavery, and racial representations. The most important of the responses to Morrison's book was J. Gerald Kennedy and Liliane Weissberg's collection *Romancing the Shadow: Poe and Race* (2001), which helped to clear the air by addressing some long-standing controversies and has focused much of the subsequent scholarship on the topic. In the collection's first and arguably most significant essay, "Average Racism: Poe, Slavery, and the Wages of Literary Nationalism," reprinted from his 1999 monograph *Edgar Allan Poe and the Masses*, Whalen asserts that throughout the writer's career and especially between August 1835 and January 1837 when he was employed at the *Southern Literary Messenger* Poe was not a free agent when it came to political issues— slavery being the foremost among them. As Whalen explains in a key passage, the impoverished Poe made use of "a deliberate strategy designed to unify sections divided by slavery":

> To understand the complex relation between race and literature, . . . it is also necessary to account for the pressures of literary nationalism and the national literary market because these pressures put constraints on commercial writers in all regions and contributed to the always unfinished formation of what might be called average racism. For Poe and other antebellum writers, average racism was not a sociological measurement of actual beliefs but rather a strategic construction designed to overcome political dissension in the emerging mass audience. In other words, publishers and commercial writers were seeking a form of racism acceptable to white readers who were otherwise divided over the more precise issue of slavery.[15]

Noting that "The Gold-Bug" is one of only two stories that Poe set in an identifiably Southern location and dismissing as absurd the claim in the unsigned *Aristidean* review of his *Tales* that Jupiter "is drawn accurately," Whalen asserts that Poe, who saw how slavery divided Northern and Southern readers, "shrewdly tries to have it both ways": "On the one hand, he exploits conventions about the intimate, loyal bonds between white masters and black servants. On the other hand, he attempts to evade any outcry over such a portrayal by making Jupiter free. . . . In other words, Poe capitalizes on the average racism of his audience while neutralizing the sectional conflict over slavery" (32). White American writers after Poe, both before and following the Civil War, employed this strategy, which undoubtedly contributed to the decades-long popularity of *The Hidden Hand*.

Since the critical rediscovery of Southworth in the 1970s, there has been no clear consensus on her position in regard to slavery in her best-known novel, with some people viewing it as subtly abolitionist, others reading it as supportive of the Southern slave system, and still others regarding it as apolitical by design. Although they acknowledge that the novel may not appear that way today, Nina Baym and Paul Christian Jones contend it was in fact antislavery, the former characterizing it as "highly critical of the southern ideology and implicitly favorable to northern values" and the latter asserting that Southworth uses conventions of the plantation novel "to challenge the slave system rather than defend it." In contrast, Michelle Ann Abate, who credits Southworth with launching American tomboyism in the novel, argues that it functions as "a eugenic strategy, intended to bolster the health" of white Southern Womanhood imperiled by frailty. Adopting a third position, Christopher Looby describes Southworth's serial as a "fictional correlate of [*New York Ledger* editor Robert] Bonner's determined political nonpartisanship and antisectionalism."[16]

In contrast, scholars have been in near-total agreement about the book's racial representations, which have been characterized as "offensive," "cultural schlock," "racist," "patronizing," "demeaning," "stereotyped," and "straight off the minstrel stage."[17] Applying the notion of "average racism" that Whalen discusses in connection with Poe to *The Hidden Hand* helps to clarify matters somewhat. The novel reflects the conventional beliefs about race held by white American society North and South in the 1840s and 1850s. It employs minstrel stereotypes in its depiction of black characters that were familiar to and readily accepted by the vast majority of antebellum readers, using the superstition and ignorance, comical foolishness, extreme cowardice, and exaggeratedly nonstandard speech of enslaved characters to highlight the brilliance, clear-headedness, bravery, eloquence, and, above all, freedom of the adolescent protagonist Capitola. Familiar and acceptable to white readers above and below the Mason-Dixon Line, including many abolitionists who worked tirelessly to bring an end to slavery but not necessarily to provide African Americans with equal rights, such "average racism" did not offend Southworth's antislavery Northern readers whom she placates by never once in her lengthy novel employing the words "slave" or "slavery" in relation to black characters actually in bondage but often using these terms metaphorically in connection with white characters in desperate situations.

Like Poe and other nineteenth-century white American writers, as Beth L. Lueck observes, Southworth "uses Gothic conventions to express cultural concerns about race," typically making "southern plantations the locus for her meditations."[18] In her first two long fictional narratives, *Retribution* (1849) and *Hickory Hall* (1850), published in the abolitionist newspaper the *National Era* (where Harriet Beecher Stowe's *Uncle Tom's Cabin* first appeared in 1851 and 1852), Southworth, according to Lueck, locates the "real horror" in slaveholders and a system of sexual exploitation resulting in miscegenation "rather than projecting evil onto the black bodies of her slave characters, the more typical pattern in [white] American literature."[19] However, in *The Hidden Hand*, initially serialized two years before the attack on Fort Sumter, she conforms to Robert Bonner's policy of neutrality vis-à-vis slavery and of "average racism" at the *New York Ledger*. On the one hand, characters with "black" in their names, the protagonist Capitola Le Noir (aka Capitola Black) and the notorious thief Black Donald, are white.[20] Although the bold protagonist and the audacious criminal often don disguises, even in the case of the latter impersonating black people, they are not mixed-race characters passing for white.[21] Moreover, the true identities that eventually come to light have nothing to do with African ancestry—revealed to be an heiress, Capitola inherits the Le Noir estate including its slaves; Marah Rocke turns out to be the long-suffering, unjustly abandoned wife of "Old Hurricane" Ira Warfield; and her son Traverse proves to be none other than the rightful successor to Old Hurricane's plantation (and its slaves). On the other hand, with the exception of the mulatta midwife Nancy Grewell, who rescues the infant Capitola and dies early in the story, and Black Donald's mixed-race henchman "Stealthy Steve," the novel's African American characters are well-worn racial stereotypes: Warfield's fretful valet Wool, Capitola's credulous waiting maid Pitapat, and the mysterious free black witch/conjure woman known as Old Hat. Like Whitman in *Jack Engle*, published seven years earlier, Southworth evinces a fondness for symbolic character names in *The Hidden Hand*. Those of Wool and Pitapat, however, serve to reinforce the novel's racial stereotyping.

In *Retribution* and *Hickory Hill*, Southworth anticipates, as Lueck argues, Harriet Jacobs's reversal of the white Gothic in *Incidents in the Life of a Slave Girl*, by portraying slave masters and mistresses rather than people of African descent as evil. However, in her most famous novel, she reverts to conventional racial representations, using the superstition, timidity, foolishness, butchered English, exaggerated gestures, and physical awkwardness of her black characters to highlight not only Capitola's admirable traits (rationality, bravery, intelligence, eloquence, and grace) but also her social, class, legal, and intellectual standing as an independent young white woman and Southern heiress. Moreover, just as Poe obscures Jupiter's de facto status, Southworth, conforming to Bonner's suggestions or dictates, whitewashes the de jure status of her black characters. Although he has been "manumitted," Jupiter continues faithfully to serve "Massa Will." Meanwhile, even though Warfield clearly owns Wool and Pitapat and may treat or dispose of them as he chooses, Southworth never explicitly refers to them as chattel.

Herein lies the key difference between white writers, even those personally opposed to slavery such as Southworth, and black authors like Jacobs and Hopkins: for the latter, the slave system does not engender racism; rather, the racist ideology, that is, the "average racism," subscribed to by the vast majority of white people North and South makes possible and perpetuates the slave system and Jim Crow in the United States. By taking a neutral stance on slavery while employing minstrel caricature, literary texts such as "The Gold-Bug" and *The Hidden Hand* reinforce the nation's racial hierarchy before and after the Civil War. In responding to these white-authored publications, Jacobs and Hopkins draw on elements from multiple genres, including Gothic fiction and detection.

Hiding in Plain Sight and Reversing the Rendering of Black and White Speech in *Incidents in the Life of a Slave Girl*

In addition to evoking conventions of Gothic writing to depict Dr. Flint (based on Dr. James Norcom) as villainous, Jacobs uses elements derived from Poe's detection and Christian principles rooted in scripture to present the pseudonymous Linda Brent as both intellectually and morally superior to her master. She also combats "average racism" by reversing the ways in which authors typically render the spoken language of whites and African Americans. One of the explicit aims of her narrative is to rebut the inaccurate depictions of Southern slavery and people of African descent appearing in print. Jacobs no doubt sought to repudiate these portrayals in popular texts such as "The Gold-Bug" and especially, given its recent runaway success, *The Hidden Hand*, although she does not mention them by name.

Just as Poe, as far as we know, never met Melville (or Hawthorne, for that matter, although they corresponded), it is unlikely that he had a personal encounter with Harriet Jacobs, even though they shared an employer in the writer and editor Nathaniel Parker Willis. Jacobs worked for Willis as a nanny on three separate occasions. In 1842 and 1843, she lived with the family at the lavish Astor House hotel, which Poe would later frequently visit, near New York's City Hall Park; she accompanied Willis to Great Britain in 1845 and 1846, caring for his daughter Imogen following the death of his English wife Mary Stace Willis; and, after Willis remarried and started a new family, Jacobs served as a live-in caregiver for him in Manhattan and at Idlewild, his estate overlooking the Hudson River, in the 1850s and early 1860s, the period during which she composed *Incidents*.[22] Willis employed Poe at the New York *Evening Mirror* from the fall of 1844 to the spring of 1845 and wrote favorably about him following his untimely demise in 1849. He also introduced him to the poet Fanny Osgood at the Astor House in early March 1845 (*PL*, 511). Jacobs makes no explicit reference to Poe in her slave narrative or her correspondence, yet her subversive use of dialect, depiction of the battle of wits and wills between Linda Brent and Dr. Flint, and description of her hyper-obtrusive hiding place as a "living grave" in *Incidents in the Life of a Slave Girl* can all plausibly be seen as implicit responses to Poe's fiction, to which she almost certainly had access in Willis's residences.

Incidents in the Life of a Slave Girl concerns, among other things, the politics of slavery in the antebellum United States and a "competition in cunning" between the slave girl and her master. Similar to the contest of wits between Dupin and the Minister D----- in "The Purloined Letter," the moral and intellectual struggle between Linda and Flint dominates the narrative. In terms of their status in society and access to power, the middle-aged, affluent, white, male slaveholder and physician and the young, black, bondwoman could not differ more starkly. Nevertheless, the latter at times describes the contest between them as nearly a fair fight because of her higher moral purpose and tremendous volition: "My master had power and law on his side; I had determined will. There is might in each."[23] As critics such as Yellin, Henry Louis Gates, Jr., and Valerie Smith have pointed out, in writing *Incidents* Jacobs revises African American and Anglo American literary forms, such as the slave narrative, the seduction novel, and the Gothic.[24] Yet critics have failed to acknowledge that Jacobs turns to another Anglo American genre, namely detective fiction, in portraying Linda's battle with Flint. G-----'s prejudices cause him to underestimate and thus be outwitted by D----- in "The Purloined Letter," and racism causes the whites generally, and Amasa Delano in particular, to underestimate Babo in *Benito Cereno*. Similarly, Flint, whose obsessiveness and malignity link him to Hawthorne's deluded detective Chillingworth in *The Scarlet Letter*, repeatedly underestimates Linda's cunning, and thus she consistently outmaneuvers him.

At key moments, Linda gambles with her own life—something which, it is worth noting, she does not legally own—to get the better of Flint. As the tenth chapter, "A Perilous Passage in the Slave Girl's Life," reveals, Linda enters into a sexual relationship with a white man, Mr. Sands, which ultimately results in two children, in order to escape her master's long-held fixation with making her his concubine. In Chapter 17, to prevent her children from being broken in on the Flint plantation, Linda runs away. Unable to reach the free states, she uses a stratagem that to some extent recalls the one used by D----- in outwitting the police prefect G----- (and by Poe himself in mystifying readers) in "The Purloined Letter." She secretes herself in a place that Flint not only passes by multiple times each day but also occasionally visits and thus somewhere he would never think to look for her. In Poe's story, D----- leaves the letter out in the open, but in disguised form; moreover, Poe has Dupin reveal the solution to the mystery at the start of the story, concealing it as inconsequential banter between the detective and the Prefect. In the second half of the story, Dupin explains that to hide something effectively, it must be positioned so conspicuously as to escape notice, exemplifying his point by referring to a game requiring players to locate the names of places on a map, in which an experienced competitor selects a word composed of large letters that stretch across the page because people will miss it, instead of choosing the most inconspicuous word, the way a beginner does. Although Linda does not quite openly conceal herself as the Minister does the altered letter, she does take refuge in a cramped crawlspace in her grandmother's house a mere two hundred yards from Flint's home rather than some out-of-the-way location.[25]

Linda manages to transform this constricted and precarious hiding spot from a place of seeming limitation, danger, and weakness into a site of possibility, safety, and empowerment. Her "loophole of retreat," as she calls it—a phrase she derived from William Cowper, perhaps via Lydia Maria Child, but makes completely and uniquely her own[26]—enables her to become, like Ralph Ellison's invisible man in fiction and the little-known Mary Elizabeth Bowser in real life, a spy in enemy territory.[27] Jacobs depicts Linda in her hiding place assembling and drawing on an intelligence network that includes family members—particularly her aunt Nancy who works in the Flint household— and other blacks in the community to monitor and thus be able to counter her master's actions. She uses "the loophole of retreat" not only as the name for the cramped crawl space, at once coffin-like and womb-like, where Linda spends nearly seven years but also as the title of a chapter she places dead center in the narrative.[28] As Michelle Burnham explains, "loophole" has both a legal/textual and a military/spatial denotation; in other words, the term has both a figurative meaning and a literal one. Legal or textual loopholes, as Burnham suggests, are inherent in all laws, providing a means by which to evade responsibility, penalty, or punishment, but within a fortress, a loophole is a small opening through which to observe or shoot at an enemy without being seen or vulnerable to return fire.[29] This latter type of loophole serves both a defensive and an offensive function, something which is clearly reflected in *Incidents*. Linda often describes her struggle against Dr. Flint, in which her crawlspace plays a pivotal role, in military terms such as "battle" and "war."[30] After failing to escape to the North, she enters the loophole to avoid being returned to slavery and her master's control. Once there, however, she uses it to spy on Flint, gather intelligence about his movements, and send him fictionalized letters that convince him she is living in the North.

In the twenty-fifth chapter, titled "Competition in Cunning," Jacobs portrays Linda's success in tricking Flint into believing that she has reached the North by means of letters written to him from her loophole describing her supposed life in free territory, which she addresses and arranges to have sent to him from the North. To make them credible, she inserts realistic details, such as New York City street names, which she has culled from a pro-slavery Northern newspaper: "Early the next morning I seated myself near the little aperture to examine the newspaper. It was a piece of the New York Herald; and, for once, the paper that systematically abuses the colored people was made to render them service" (164). Her ploy succeeds so well that Flint, convinced that Linda resides in the North, has, as she puts it, "no suspicion of my being any where in the vicinity" (168). Thus, *Incidents in the Life of a Slave Girl* incorporates the competition that characterizes detective stories, evoking the rivalry between the canny detective Dupin and the master criminal D----- in Poe's "The Purloined Letter" in order to portray vividly the battle not simply of wits and wills but also of moral and political positions between the wily bondwoman Linda and her devious but consistently overmatched owner Dr. Flint.

Perhaps not entirely coincidentally (see Morrison's linking of Gothic fiction and the depiction of Africanist characters in white American fiction in *Playing in the Dark*), at roughly the same time that Jacobs was immured in her loophole—1835 to 1842—Poe was writing almost obsessively about people being buried alive. In Chapter 28, Jacobs, as she does elsewhere in the narrative, endeavors to rebut inaccurate portrayals of slavery that have appeared in print, including those by Northerners who travel to the South and recount their experiences. The last chapter before she decides to leave the loophole and escape the South, "Aunt Nancy" describes the funeral of her deceased mother's twin sister. Although the Flints do not pay for the ceremony, they conspicuously attend it, whereas the concealed fugitive Linda cannot do so without risking capture and reenslavement. In describing the proceedings, Linda exposes the fraudulent nature of any sentimentality slaveholders may appear to express toward those they hold in bondage:

> It was talked of by the slaves as a mighty grand funeral. Northern travellers, passing through the place, might have described this tribute of respect to the humble dead as a beautiful feature in the "patriarchal institution;" a touching proof of the attachment between slaveholders and their servants; and tender-hearted Mrs. Flint would have confirmed this impression, with handkerchief at her eyes. *We* could have told them a different story. We could have given them a chapter of wrongs and sufferings, that would have touched their hearts, if they *had* any hearts to feel for the colored people. We could have told them how the poor old slave-mother had toiled, year after year, to earn eight hundred dollars to buy her son Phillip's right to his own earnings; and how that same Phillip paid the expenses of the funeral, which they regarded as doing so much credit to the master. (188)

Dripping with sarcasm, these lines not only make plain the hypocrisy of the Flints, who worked Aunt Nancy to death, but also call into question the sincerity and morality of Northern readers who buy into such maudlin claptrap. The remainder of the passage concerns Linda herself:

> We could also have told them of a poor, blighted young creature, shut up in *a living grave* for years, to avoid the tortures that would be inflicted on her, if she ventured to come out and look on the face of her departed friend. All this, and much more, I thought of, as I sat at my loophole, waiting for the family to return from the grave; sometimes weeping, sometimes falling asleep, dreaming strange dreams of the dead and the living. (my emphasis, 188)

Significantly, although Linda has deliberately and sanely chosen live burial in her loophole over enslavement and sexual exploitation, nineteenth-century American society, maddened by the profits accruing from slavery and pervaded with a racial prejudice that deems her less than human, designates Linda as the criminal and the Flints as upstanding citizens.

Jacobs thus depicts Linda as not only intellectually superior to Dr. Flint but also as more morally advanced than whites South and North who subscribe to the racist ideology that supports slavery. However, her critique of American society and her response to texts such as "The Gold-Bug" and *The Hidden Hand* go far beyond this. Unlike most slave narratives, which conclude shortly after the narrator reaches the North and freedom, Jacobs devotes twelve of the forty-one chapters of *Incidents* to Linda's time in the North because what she experiences there is not freedom. In this section of the book, Jacobs chides her target audience, Northern white women, for, at best, countenancing and, at worst, participating in the segregation, prejudice, and discrimination directed against black people in the so-called free states. She uses Linda's employer in New York City to deliver a powerful condemnation of the North's complicity in slavery generally and its acquiescence to the national Fugitive Slave Law that was part of the Compromise of 1850 in particular: "Shame on my country that it *is* so! I am ready to incur the penalty. I will go to the state's prison, rather than have any poor victim torn from *my* house, to be carried back to slavery" (249). By vowing to accept the penalty for breaking the law rather than abet the slave system in any way, the second Mrs. Bruce (based on Cornelia Grinnell Willis) serves as a role model for the white Northern women who constitute the narrative's primary audience.[31]

Jacobs's strategic rendering of the language spoken by white and black characters serves as another means by which she responds to the "average racism" of the antebellum North and South reflected in fictions such as Poe's and Southworth's. Jupiter, Wool, and Pitapat consistently use a nonstandard English larded with solecisms and malapropisms whose incorrectness, ridiculousness, and graphic portrayal on the page make them appear inferior to, foolish in comparison with, and categorically different from the white characters. In Chapter XII of *Incidents*, Jacobs radically reverses the typical portrayal of white and black speech in American literature by having first Linda and then her grandmother employ standard English while a group of uneducated poor whites speak in a comically exaggerated dialect. Residing in her grandmother's (Aunt Martha's) house at this point in the narrative but not yet in hiding, Linda carefully observes these white men who have been organized into a ragtag militia to terrorize the black population of Edenton, North Carolina, in the wake of Nat Turner's rebellion in 1831. When she moves to take a box of coins found by one of the men, who are supposedly looking for evidence of insurrection, he says, "What d'ye foller us fur? D'ye s'pose white folks is come to steal?" In reply, Linda states, "You have come to search; but you have searched that box, and I will take it, if you please" (83). Shortly thereafter a similar exchange occurs: on opening a trunk full of bedding and linens, a man asks, "Where'd the damned niggers git all dis sheet an' table clarf," to which Aunt Martha responds, "You may be sure we didn't pilfer 'em from *your* houses" (84). The contrast continues and intensifies on the discovery of some letters written to Linda. Unable to read, the men believe they have found something incriminating: "We's got 'em! We's got 'em! Dis 'ere yaller gal's got letters!" (84). Interrogated by the group's captain, an especially cruel slave owner, Linda, stunningly, flaunts her literacy (and the power it confers on her) in the presence of these uneducated white men, stating, "most of my letters are from white people. Some request me to burn them after they are read, and some I destroy without reading" (84). Once again, her use of proper English contrasts with the blatantly backward language used by these illiterates. Moreover, her mastery of the printed word, which she later uses in her successful efforts to outsmart Flint, places her in a different intellectual class from the white "soldiers" who assume they are superior to her simply because of their race.

From a strictly legal point of view, Linda, like Poe's D-----, is the criminal who steals property (i.e., herself) and conceals it from the owner; however, because Flint, an incompetent detective (similar to Melville's Delano), does not judge his opponent accurately, he, in sharp contrast to Dupin, fails to recover the "stolen" property. From Jacobs's moral point of view, however, Flint is the criminal who has stolen Linda's liberty, while she, like Dupin, steals her property (i.e., herself) back and hides it (to prevent recapture). In the conclusion to Poe's trilogy,

Dupin (re)steals, reproduces, and replaces the letter D----- has purloined. In *Incidents*, Linda lifts (steals) information from a pro-slavery newspaper to create her bogus letter, which Flint, who receives it from the North, tries to reproduce and replace with a counterfeit of his own; however, because he underestimates Linda's wiliness, never suspecting her original ruse, she once again gets the better of him. Thus, like Poe's detective before her, Linda comes out on top, winning the "competition in cunning" not only with Flint specifically but also with the slavocracy and the "average racism" on which this reprehensible system rests.

Countering the Unexpiated National Sin of "Average Racism" in *Hagar's Daughter*

Writing during the post-Reconstruction period, Hopkins emphasizes that the race prejudice that enabled slavery has not diminished despite the demise of the peculiar institution. Thus, in *Hagar's Daughter*, pointedly subtitled *A Story of Southern Caste Prejudice*, she portrays both the ante- and postbellum eras to demonstrate the perpetuation of the racist ideology undergirding slavery, using many of the same conventions of sensationalism and the Gothic as Southworth while signifying on *The Hidden Hand* itself in the process. Moreover, similar to Jacobs, she turns strategically to elements of detection first seen in Poe and depicts the speech of her black characters in a nuanced manner.

Beginning with Hazel Carby in 1988, several critics have noted, analyzed, and commented on Hopkins's blending and subversion of popular literary genres and types in her three novels serialized in the *Colored American Magazine* between 1901 and 1903, especially the first of these, *Hagar's Daughter*.[32] Catherine Ross Nickerson, Jill Bergman, Carol Allen, and especially Eugenia DeLamotte have thoroughly and insightfully addressed Hopkins's innovative use of the Gothic in her novel. Yet no one, as far as I know, has discussed it in connection with the trope of the Madwoman in the Attic, first seen in Charlotte Brontë's *Jane Eyre* and employed in different forms in Southworth's *The Hidden Hand* and Jacobs's *Incidents*.[33] Hopkins in her novel portrays Hagar Sargeant Enson, recently exposed as one-sixteenth black and a slave, as a version of the supposedly insane imprisoned woman. However, rather than merely serving as a sinister *Doppelgänger* for the heroine and then dying in dramatic fashion, as Bertha Mason does in Brontë's novel, Hagar improbably survives (similar to Capitola's mother in *The Hidden Hand*), by leaping with her baby girl into the Potomac

River (in a scene reminiscent of William Wells Brown's *Clotel*). Moreover, in the later chapters, she serves as a forerunner for Jewel Bowen, the novel's titular heroine, underscoring the unbroken chain of white Southern perfidy.[34] In Hopkins's serial, following the revelation of Hagar's African ancestry and her slave status, which makes it necessary for her husband Ellis Enson to purchase her and his child from the man who owns them, Hagar retires to what was once her room, studies her white face in a mirror, which she then smashes to pieces, and, in an echo of Brontë's Bertha, "laugh[s] a dreadful laugh: first silently; then in a whisper; then in a peal that clashed through the quiet house," causing the household slaves Aunt Henny and her daughter Marthy to say to each other, "Missee Hagar done gone mad!"[35] Like her daughter twenty years later, the young mother remains shut up in this room in Enson Hall for one month.

St. Clair, Ellis's ne'er-do-well younger brother, takes legal possession not only of the Enson estate but also of his sister-in-law and his infant niece after the authorities rule that a corpse found in the vicinity is that of Ellis and the cause of death is suicide. Exiting the bedroom where she has been confined, Hagar defiantly bursts in on St. Clair and the slave trader Walker in Chapter VII, and once again Hopkins's language recalls Brontë's. In Chapter XXV of *Jane Eyre*, on the night before Jane is to be married, Bertha Mason, whom Rochester has imprisoned on the third floor, escapes her jailer Grace Poole and enters Jane's room. Described as "a woman, tall and large, with thick and dark hair hanging down her back" and "rolling," "bloodshot" eyes, who resembles "the foul German spectre—the Vampyre," she tries on and rips up Jane's wedding veil.[36] Hopkins portrays Hagar at the moment of her intrusion as follows: "Her dark eyes shown like stars, . . . her long hair hung in a straggling mass, rough and unkept, about her shoulders and over her somber dress. A more startled apparition could not well be imagined" (69). Hagar proceeds to accuse St. Clair of murdering his brother, to which he replies, "Mad woman! You are mad I say, trouble has turned your brain!" (70). When she responds by characterizing him as "Selfish, devilish, cruel" and pronounces a curse upon him, St. Clair declares, "This is too much for any man to stand from a nigger wench" (70), and he instructs Walker to sell her and her child at the Washington slave market.

Far from the ravings of a lunatic, however, Hagar's claim that her husband has been murdered, if not literally true as in the case of the elder Capitola in *The Hidden Hand*, is figuratively accurate. Before Ellis Enson was able to carry out his plan to move to Europe with Hagar and their baby, St. Clair incapacitated and exiled but did not kill his elder brother, dressing up a corpse with a disfiguring gunshot wound in Ellis's clothing and placing his brother's gun next to the body. Yet, prior to this St. Clair had effectively put an end to Ellis's life by shattering his happiness through the exposure of Hagar's mixed blood. In Chapter VIII, after being sold by Walker in nation's capital, Hagar makes a desperate dash for liberty, fleeing to Long Bridge linking Washington, D.C., and Virginia. With slave catchers approaching her from both sides, she "raise[s] her tearful, imploring eyes to heaven as if seeking for mercy and compassion, and with one bound spr[ings] over the railing of the bridge, and s[inks] beneath the waters of the Potomac river" (75). However, unlike Bertha Mason, who leaps to her death in the fire she sets that destroys Thornfield Hall and causes Rochester to be maimed and blinded, Hagar survives, as does her infant daughter, who proves to be the novel's main character.

Stressing the tenacious persistence of not only Southern rapacity but also a national "average racism," Hopkins portrays Jewel being kidnapped in Washington, taken to Maryland, and held prisoner for "four weeks" (214) in the same edifice (Enson Hall) and on the orders of the same man who imprisoned Hagar and then sold the mother and infant child into slavery two decades (and twenty chapters) earlier. The initial portion of *Hagar's Daughter* depicts the Enson estate as a seeming Eden, apparently immune to the horrors of slavery. It becomes clear that Hopkins does this so as to heighten the shock when the return of the scapegrace St. Clair and the declaration of his loathsome companion Walker that he owns Hagar obliterates this false paradise. A score of years later, the Enson Hall that serves as Jewel's prison resembles, as DeLamotte and others have noted, a Gothic haunted house, as seen in the following passage from Chapter XXVIII:

> When Jewel came to herself she was lying on an old-fashioned canopied bed with a coverlet thrown over her. The room was evidently, originally designed for a studio, and was lighted by a skylight: even now a flood of sunlight streamed from above, making more dingy and faded by comparison the appearance of the dusty canvases and once luxurious furniture scattered about the apartment. Evidences of decay were everywhere: a broken easel leant against the wall, and on a table odds and ends of tubes, brushes and other artistic paraphernalia were heaped in a disorderly mass. There was also a couch and easy chairs in faded brocade. (212)

With its long-abandoned art supplies, which once belonged to Hagar, and pervasive decrepitude, Jewel's prison eerily anticipates the Gothic habitations in William Faulkner's texts.

In the later chapters of the serial, the exterior of Enson Hall likewise evokes the Gothic decay so often seen in Poe's tales. Here, however, its terrors are inextricable from its traumatic slave history, as indicated by this passage from the start of Chapter XXX:

> Enson Hall reminded one of an ancient ruin. The main body of the stately dwelling was standing, but scarcely a vestige of the once beautiful outbuildings remained; the cabins in the slave quarters stood like skeletons beneath the nodding leaves and beckoning arms of the grand old beeches. War and desolation had done their best to reduce the stately pile to a wreck. It bore, too, an uncanny reputation. The Negroes declared that the beautiful woods and the lonely avenues were haunted after nightfall. It had grown a tradition that the ghost of Ellis Enson "walked," accompanied by a lady who bore an infant in her arms. (228)

As Carol Allen remarks, "By turning Enson Hall into a gothic place of horrors, Hopkins reverses the ideological postulations of [plantation] writers . . . [who] fabricate a romantic antebellum south. Hopkins' scene highlights that no safe romantic place exists in the history of slavery, as the 'big house' will be forever shadowed by the skeleton cabins."[37] A passageway Jewel discovers behind the torn canvas of one of Hagar's old pictures enables her to move around Enson Hall via back stairways once utilized by bondmen and women. Leaving the room that has been her jail cell, as her mother did two decades previously to confront St. Clair, Jewel explores the slave quarters of the house that was once her parents'. In doing so, she comes upon Aunt Henny, another captive of General Benson (aka St. Clair Enson), but also the "mammy" who raised Hagar on the adjoining Sargeant estate that became part of the Enson patrimony when Ellis and Hagar were married and was also taken over by St. Clair when his brother appeared to have killed himself.

Hopkins's use of dialect and portrayal of black characters varies in the ante- and postbellum sections of the narrative. The speech and demeanor of the African Americans in the former resemble to a certain extent the black dialogue and minstrel types employed by Poe and Southworth. However, in the latter, Hopkins presents a new generation of African Americans who have the ability to alternate between standard English and the dialect of their parents and grandparents, the foremost among these being Venus Johnson. At times she speaks in black vernacular while at others she uses colorful standard English, as she does in the passage that serves as the final epigraph to this chapter in which she, like Linda, not only asserts her intellectual and moral superiority to execrable white Southerners but also announces her bold determination to resist them by any means necessary. She does so by becoming a detective, making her the first African American female sleuth in fiction. As part of her investigative work, she wears male clothes and exhibits cunning and courage, similar to Capitola and Linda before her.

By disentangling the racially and politically convoluted case that Chief Henson, head of the federal government's investigative agency, has been unable to—in his own words, echoing Poe—"unravel," Venus demonstrates her analytical preeminence. Her race, gender, and youth may make Venus an unconventional detective, but her methods resemble those of Poe's Dupin: she reaches conclusions based on evidence and formulates a theory to account for a seemingly insoluble problem. Whereas Benson's new name, bogus title, and ingratiating charm fool other characters (including his own brother, the nation's top law enforcement officer), Venus sees him for what he is based in part on his treatment of her as a sexually vulnerable black maid. In response to Henson's question, "You do not like General Benson, I see," Venus replies, "Like him! who could, the sly old villain. He's mighty shrewd, and [foxy]. . . . He tries to be mighty sweet to me, but I like a gentleman to stay where he belongs and not be loving servant girls on the sly" (226). Hearkening back to Poe's emphasis on competition in the trilogy, Venus (similar to Linda vis-à-vis Flint) bravely decides to take Benson on one-on-one despite his powerful position, telling Henson, "I just made up my mind that it was Venus for General Benson, and that I'd got to cook his goose or he'd cook mine" (226). Following Venus's rescue of her grandmother and Jewel, Henny's testimony during Cuthbert Sumner's trial that Benson killed Elsie Bradford triggers additional revelations, namely that the "General" is really St. Clair Enson, that Henson is really Ellis Enson, that Estelle Bowen is really Hagar Sargeant, and, sometime later, that Jewel is really Hagar's daughter. Although Hopkins finesses some of the problems facing the US black writer of detection by waiting until the last third of her serial to turn to the genre, she refuses to suggest that Venus's solution of the mystery resolves all of the many crimes depicted in the novel, especially those related to racial intolerance.

The exposure of a previous wife in the person of Bertha Mason Rochester spares Jane a life of concubinage, a fate that looms over both Hagar and Jewel when their ancestries are revealed in scenes that occur more than twenty years apart. The ending of Hopkins's novel makes clear, however, that it is not the existence of a small percentage of African blood in the veins of the wife that prevents the continuation of the marriage between Jewel Bowen and Cuthbert Sumner; rather, it is the existence of prejudice against color in the mind of the Northerner Sumner, one more manifestation of the "average racism" pervading the country, that precludes the possibility of matrimonial bliss. Keenly aware of her husband's race prejudice, Jewel leaves the United States for Europe with her newfound and newly reunited parents. When, many months later, Sumner comes to regret his decision not to remain at the side of his wife, who secretly married and stood by him when he was accused of murder, he returns to the Gothic Enson estate, where, on his way to the mansion, he chances to walk through the graveyard and comes on the tombstone of Jewel, who died of Roman Fever while abroad.

The conclusion of *Hagar's Daughter* indicates that, just as Rochester cannot undo his marriage to Bertha Mason or successfully keep it a secret, the United States cannot deny or cover up the legacies of slavery during the post-Reconstruction era, which include the widespread presence of people of mixed-race ancestry (as a result of sexual exploitation), the continued discrimination against people of African descent, and the unchecked greed and immorality of unrepentant Southerners in positions of power. Falling face down on Jewel's grave, Sumner wonders what he has done to deserve such punishment, only to come to the realization that, as Hopkins's narrator states, "the sin is the nation's. It must be washed out. The plans of the Father are not changed in the nineteenth century; they are shown us in different forms. The idolatry of the Moloch of Slavery must be purged from the land and his actual sinlessness was but a meet offering to appease the wrath of a righteous God" (284). The humbling and physical diminishment of Rochester effected by Bertha Mason, coupled with Bertha's death, make the marriage of Jane and Rochester possible at the conclusion of Brontë's novel. In contrast, *Hagar's Daughter* does not end happily because during the post-Reconstruction era the sins of the past have neither been fully acknowledged nor expiated.

Poe's "The Gold-Bug" explicitly introduces the theme of race into detective fiction. In doing so, it takes a neutral position on slavery while trading in racial stereotypes reflective of the "average racism" of whites North and South during the antebellum period. Outspoken in her opposition to slavery, unlike Poe, Southworth nevertheless adopts his pragmatic strategy in *The Hidden Hand*, deliberately avoiding the words "slave" and "slavery" in connection with her black characters in bondage while depicting them in a blatantly caricatured manner. Pointedly responding to these texts and others that whitewash slavery and reduce African Americans to blackface, Jacobs in *Incidents in the Life of a Slave Girl*, published just prior to the Civil War, and Hopkins in her early twentieth-century serial *Hagar's Daughter* expose the cruelties of slavery and rebut the racist ideology that undergirds it and Jim Crow. Among the multiple genres, including the Gothic, that they draw on to accomplish this, detection plays an indispensable role, enabling them to portray US blacks occupying the moral and, to use Poe's language, the analytical high ground vis-à-vis evil Southerners and the prejudiced Northerners who enable them.

Southworth, Jacobs, and Hopkins stress the cunning of a young female character vis-à-vis one or more powerful and unscrupulous Southern white men. In *The Hidden Hand*, Capitola repeatedly outmaneuvers her guardian Ira "Hurricane" Warfield, her rapacious uncle and repugnant cousin Gabriel and Craven Le Noir, and the notorious criminal Black Donald and his henchmen. In *Incidents*, Linda consistently outwits her master Dr. Flint and succeeds in gaining freedom for herself, her daughter, and her son. Similarly, in *Hagar's Daughter*, Venus devises and implements a stratagem that thwarts the scheme of General Benson and thereby liberates her grandmother and her white mistress. Each of these young women not only resorts to cross dressing and other subterfuges but also exhibits extraordinary bravery to come out on top. However, as unconventional as Capitola's exploits may have been to nineteenth-century audiences, they in no way alter the status quo, as indicated by her becoming the mistress of a large estate with many slaves at the end of Southworth's novel, a conclusion that normalizes the social order. In contrast, Linda not only liberates her children and herself but also lays bare the depravity of the slavocracy and the "average racism" North and South that perpetuates it. Although her ancestry, sex, age, and circumstances differ radically from those of Dupin and Legrand, the lineage of Venus Johnson, the first African American woman detective, can nevertheless be traced back to Poe. Like those of Linda before her, Venus's actions during the post-Reconstruction era help to unmask, although they cannot put an end to, the persistent presence of treasonous Southerners and race prejudice in the United States in the decades following the Civil War.

Coda
"A Crime of Dark Dye": Misreading Poe's Criticism

I have read your occasional notices of my productions with great interest—not so much because your judgment was, upon the whole, favorable, as because it seemed to be given in earnest. I care for nothing but the truth; and shall always much more readily accept a harsh truth, in regards to my writings, than a sugared falsehood.

Nathaniel Hawthorne to E. A. Poe, June 17, 1846

There was but little literary criticism in the United States at the time Hawthorne's early works were published; but among the reviewers Edgar Poe perhaps held the scales the highest. He at any rate rattled them the loudest, and pretended, more than any one else, to conduct the weighing-process on scientific principles. Very remarkable was this process of Edgar Poe's and very extraordinary were his principles; but he had the advantage of being a man of genius, and his intelligence was frequently great.

Henry James, *Hawthorne*

In *Edgar Allan Poe and His Nineteenth-Century American Counterparts*, I have striven to separate the man from the mystifications by emphasizing Poe's multidimensionality through the focus on nonfiction in Part 1 and detection in Part 2; by devoting attention to his career as a magazinist in Chapters 1, 2, and 3; and by spelling out the deliberate design, careful craftsmanship, and immediate and long-term impact of his ratiocinative tales in Chapters 4, 5, and 6. In this Coda, I turn to Poe's critical assessments of Nathaniel Hawthorne in which he expresses some of his most influential statements about literary technique. Over the last several years, scholars have made considerable progress in addressing the misconception that Poe's fictional characters are reflections of himself. Ironically, however, this has not happened in connection with criticism addressing Poe's Hawthorne reviews, wherein he anticipates Henry James's stress on the craft of writing. Just as James, in "The Art of Fiction," insists that readers grant authors their "données" and then judge them on how well or poorly the conceptions behind their literary texts have been executed,[1] Poe states in his May 1842 review of *Twice-Told Tales*, "The true critic will but demand that the design intended be accomplished, to the fullest extent, by the means most advantageously applicable" (299). Nowhere is the bias against Poe the critic more pronounced than in the responses to his statements about "The Minister's Black Veil." Almost without exception, scholars have misidentified the woman who, according to Poe, falls victim to "a crime of dark dye" in Hawthorne's story. Largely resulting from their false assumptions about Poe, these (mis)readings vividly illustrate that his criticism, like his creative writing, needs to be read and evaluated apart from the myths that cling to his life and work.

Poe reviewed the expanded second edition of *Twice-Told Tales* in the April and May 1842 issues of *Graham's Magazine*, for which he served as an editor, chief reviewer, and frequent contributor. Uncharacteristically, Poe lavishes praise on Hawthorne, asserting that "As Americans we feel proud of the book," that his style is "purity itself," that "high imagination gleams from every page" of the collection, and that "Mr. Hawthorne is a man of truest genius."[2] Known for his slashing exposés of writers' weaknesses, Poe confines his reservations about the book to what he terms "trivial exceptions," stating, "There is, perhaps, a somewhat too general or prevalent tone—a tone of melancholy and mysticism. The subjects are insufficiently varied. There is not so much of versatility evinced as we might well be warranted in expecting from the high powers of Mr. Hawthorne" (300). More important, these reviews serve as the occasion for some of Poe's best-known critical pronouncements. He contends that to create the most powerful poems and stories writers should avoid compositions of "extreme brevity" and those of such length that "their perusal cannot be completed in one sitting" (298); moreover, an author must "conceive a certain unique or single effect" to be produced by a literary text, and every word of it should contribute to this "pre-established design" (299). A half-decade later, the November 1847 issue of *Godey's Lady's Book* included Poe's long-delayed combined review of *Twice-Told Tales* and *Mosses from an Old Manse*, which at times echoes but at others widely diverges from what he said about Hawthorne five years earlier.[3]

"The Minister's Black Veil" concerns Mr. Hooper, the soft-spoken, thirty-year-old, early 1700s New England pastor who puts a piece of black crape over most of his face one day, never satisfactorily explains his reasons for doing so, and refuses to remove it for the rest of his life.[4] In the May 1842 review, Poe states:

> "The Minister's Black Veil" is a masterly composition of which the sole defect is that to the rabble its exquisite skill will be *caviare*. The *obvious* meaning of this article will be found to smother its insinuated one. The *moral* put into the mouth of the dying minister will be supposed to convey the *true* import of the narrative; and that a crime of dark dye, (having reference to the "young lady") has been committed, is a point which only minds congenial with that of the author will perceive. (299)

For over sixty-five years, critics have identified the "young lady" that Poe refers to as the woman for whom Reverend Hooper performs a funeral ceremony early in the story, and several of them have commented on how wrong Poe gets things, attributing his supposed misreading to his macabre sensibility. However, these critics have almost universally failed to notice that the story includes another woman, also referred to as a "young lady," who is none other than Elizabeth, Hooper's "plighted wife," from whom he separates himself by donning the black veil.[5]

The misreading of Poe's comments or, more precisely, the ready acceptance of this misreading, apparently dates from a short 1952 essay in which Gilbert Voigt writes about critics who identify the "young lady" to whom Poe refers as the person at whose funeral Hooper presides. Voigt cites "three features of the tale" that support such an interpretation: the suggestion that Hooper feared the decedent's glance, an eyewitness's assertion that the corpse shuddered as Hooper bent over it, and the "fancy" of a married couple that they saw Hooper and the girl's spirit walking hand in hand. Voigt divides critics of the story into two camps. The first, which he affiliates with Poe's supposed reading, "attribute[s] to the minister some unnamed crime," while an opposing group of critics holds that "the veil has no reference to any particular crime or sin on the part of the minister."[6] In a 1962 essay, E. Earle Stibitz expands the number of interpretations of Hawthorne's story to three. One, which he connects to Poe, asserts that the veil "indicates some specific crime by Mr. Hopper"; the second sees it "as a device chosen by the minister to dramatize" people's inability to share their "inner heart" and "private guilt" with others; and the "third view holds that there is something fundamentally wrong in the minister's wearing of the veil."[7] Since that time, dozens of critics, whether or not they agree with the interpretation that Voigt and Stibitz connect with Poe, have assumed that the "young lady" referred to in his May 1842 review is the one who has died early in the story.

Over the years, scholars have claimed that Poe approaches Hawthorne's tale as either a detective story to be unraveled or a ghost story in which supernatural phenomena occur. Leland Person, for example, says, "Edgar Allan Poe thought he had solved the mystery [behind Hawthorne's tale]," a contention that Eamonn Dunne echoes.[8] Many scholars, utilizing a variety of critical perspectives, believe that Poe, as they read him, got things right—that Hooper has done something untoward to the dead young woman. Judy McCarthy remarks, "Poe, in his review of this story, asserted that Hooper had committed a 'crime of dark dye' against the dead girl; most of the critics agree with this reading, if not in letter, in spirit."[9] Many others, however, have accused Poe of badly misreading the tale, with some of them going so far as to ridicule him in the process.

Whether they agree with it or not, the majority of these readings of Poe's supposed interpretation assume that the "crime of dark dye" perpetrated by Hooper is a carnal one. H. J. Lang claims that Poe believed "Hawthorne's insinuations made it abundantly clear where to look for a sin: in the sexual sphere."[10] Gender critics concur, namely Cynthia Jordan, whose feminist essay focuses on the underlying "woman's" or "second" story of Hawthorne's tale, and David Leverenz, who argues, "Mr. Hooper's accusation of universal guilt veils a secret crime. Presumably he had impregnated and then killed the young lady whose corpse was said to shudder as he leaned over the body and hastily caught back his veil."[11] Other scholars associating Poe's reading with one or more sexual crimes committed by Hooper include Carl Ostrowski and Paul Emmett. The former asserts that Hooper hides his face to cover the ravages of syphilis with which he infected the "young lady," a suicide, and the latter discusses several possible crimes committed by Hooper in a lengthy Freudian reading.[12] Moreover, a footnote to Lydia G. Fash's 2013 essay, stating, "Edgar Allan Poe suggested that the cause of the veil is a sexual transgression,"[13] indicates that such readings of Poe's statements about Hawthorne's story continue to this day.

Some of those who find fault with the interpretation of the story they attribute to Poe offer suggestions for why he went so far astray. Believing Hawthorne's story concerns symbolism rather than Hooper's illicit acts, W. B. Carnochan says that Poe "is happy in the discovery of the concealed evidence, from which he infers a romantic solution more congenial to his taste than the merely generalized didacticism of the 'moral' that the minister pronounces at his death." He adds that a minor character's fancy that she saw the spirit of the deceased "young lady" walking with Hooper is what gave "Poe the lead he was looking for."[14] Similarly, D. A. Miller states that the May 1842 review "too aggressively projects onto Hawthorne's story Poe's own imaginary world of lost Lenores and missing Marie Rogêts."[15] George E. Haggerty contends, "For Poe, the minister's relationship with the 'young lady,' so obviously hinted at the beginning of the tale, is the key to its meaning," but he "is wrong to feel so secure" in such a reading. Haggerty criticizes Poe for failing to distinguish his own sense of the Gothic, which resembles Ann Radcliffe's, from that of Hawthorne, who relies on "a more general ambiguity of interpretation, which . . . heightens the Gothic power of his tale."[16] Noted Poe scholar G. R. Thompson makes an excellent distinction between a Poesque tale and a Hawthornesque sketch in an essay about Poe's three Hawthorne reviews. In the process, he reaffirms the significance of Poe's critical assessments and their profound and long-standing influence on short story criticism and American literary criticism as a whole. Nevertheless, he asserts, "Poe missed the point of Hawthorne's volumes [of short fiction]," to which he adds, echoing many other critics, "just as he missed the point of 'The Minister's Black Veil.'"[17]

The most condemnatory response to Poe's supposed misreading of Hawthorne's story that I have encountered is that of Joel Porte. He declares:

> Edgar Allan Poe, trying to be clever but not being quite clever enough suggested that the "exquisite skill" of the tale would be caviar to the general [public] because they would fail to perceive "the *true* import of the narrative . . . that a crime of dark dye (having reference to the 'young lady') has been committed." That is only one of the easier traps Hawthorne has set for the reader's imagination, for although Poe's reading is not necessarily wrong, it is surely inadequate and might well have provoked Hawthorne's smile from beneath his own veil. If the minister were, indeed, punishing himself so rigorously and unremittingly for the crime of fornication (or did Poe characteristically think of murder rather than sex?), it would be hard to understand why that odd smile so frequently plays about Hooper's mouth.[18]

Tellingly, Porte does not just accuse Poe of attempting to be ingenious and falling short of the mark; he also suggests that Poe cannot do anything—imagine a fictional scenario, compose a poem, or, in this case, write a book review—without revealing a habitual obsession with homicide. Part, but by no means all, of the problem may rest with the words "dark dye" that Poe uses to characterize Hooper's transgression. Richard Kopley has noted that the phrase has "a long and interesting background . . . going back to 1600" and thus it "seems a time-honored intensifier."[19] Although critics assume they know what "a crime of dark dye" refers to, Poe's phrase, unique as it is memorable, has no obvious, intrinsic, or concrete meaning. In fact, in *Squire Trevlyn's Heir: A Novel of Domestic Life*

(1864)—the only other text I know of in which it appears in full—Mrs. Henry (Ellen) Wood uses it in connection with neither a sex crime nor a murder but the burning of a hayrick.

Poe's reference to "The Minister's Black Veil" in his discussion of another story in his May 1842 review may have suggested to critics that he believes something supernatural happens during the funeral. He finds "The Old White Maid," an inconclusive tale about a young man who dies mysteriously and the two women who love him, "objectionable, even more than the 'Minister's Black Veil,' on the score of its mysticism" (299). Although the use of the word "mysticism" may seem to indicate that he believes the young woman's body does flinch as the minister leans over her, thereby revealing, in keeping with folk belief, that Hooper had a hand in her death, Poe was very particular at times in his criticism about this term, using it in the sense of a hidden meaning rather than something occult. In his January 1840 *Burton's Gentleman's Magazine* review of Thomas Moore's *Alciphron*, he states, "The term *mystic* is here employed in the sense of Augustus William Schlegel, and of most other German critics. It is applied by them to that class of composition in which there lies beneath the transparent upper current of meaning, an under or *suggestive* one."[20] This definition corresponds nearly exactly with not only what he goes on to say in the May 1842 review about "The Old White Maid"—"Even with the thoughtful and analytic [reader], there will be much trouble in penetrating its entire import" (299)—but also what he asserts about "The Minister's Black Veil," that is, "The *obvious* meaning of this article will be found to smother its insinuated one." In other words, Poe approves of such "mystic" tales so long as they provide sufficient evidence for the acute reader to fathom the hidden meaning that the less sophisticated reader misses, which he contends is the case in "The Minister's Black Veil" but not in "The Old White Maid."

I agree with several critics, most of whom do not mention Poe, who hold that by choosing to wear the black veil Hooper acts in at best a willful and at worst a delusional and even a solipsistic manner. As I believe Poe perceptively recognized, as revealed in his comments on the story, Hawthorne does indeed suggest that Hooper, like Aylmer in "The Birth-mark," commits a serious crime by sacrificing the actual—a lifetime with a loving woman (as well as a long-term interpersonal relationship with his parishioners) in this world—for an ideal, namely a supposed union without any veils in the next world. Those who assume Poe is referring to the deceased "young lady" rather than Elizabeth appear to have been seduced into this misreading because they, as amply illustrated by the passages by Porte and others quoted earlier, presume that Poe could only read (or misread) things in one way—a twisted, Gothic one.

Such critics assume that Poe was more concerned about reading a literary text in a way that suited his own predilections (or, as Porte would have it, his own obsessions) than in the way that the author conceived of it and intended it to be read. By using the word "congenial" in his assertion that Poe "infers a romantic solution more congenial to his taste than the merely generalized didacticism of the 'moral' that the minister pronounces at his death,"[21] Carnochan appears to believe that Poe refers to himself when he says that "only minds congenial with that of the author will perceive" that a "crime of dark dye" has been committed. However, because Poe uses the first-person plural elsewhere in the review—for example, "As Americans we feel proud of this book"—the "author" to whom he refers has to be Hawthorne and not himself. To ignore the "mystic" purpose, in the Schlegelian sense, behind Hawthorne's tale, clearly indicated by it being subtitled "A Parable," and to read it instead as a tale of detection or a ghost story, Poe would have had to abandon his critical principles totally, something he would not and did not do.

The efforts of scholars to demystify Poe's life and his creative works as well as to chart his response to and influence on his counterparts, to which I have attempted to contribute in the two major sections of this book, have been underway for some time and have borne considerable fruit. However, these endeavors need to be continued and must, as I have made an effort to show in this Coda, be extended to his critical writings, especially his famous reviews of Nathaniel Hawthorne, as the nearly monolithic misreading of Poe's statements about "The Minister's Black Veil" vividly illustrates. Poe was a renowned, incisive, prolific, and, for the most part, principled critic who knew that Hawthorne's intentions were to craft a moral tale of great psychological depth about alienation and delusion—something that is demonstrated by Poe's statements about the tale so long as they are read in the light of his critical theories and his critical practice rather than the persistent myths about him.

Notes

Introduction: Dreams and Mystifications of Poe

1 On its page devoted to the poem, the indispensable website of the Edgar Allan Poe Society of Baltimore (www.eapoe.org), maintained and regularly augmented by Jeffrey Savoye, makes it easy for readers to compare the different versions of "A Dream within a Dream" (the first of which dates from 1827) and to see its evolution: https://www.eapoe.org/works/info/pp017.htm.

2 *The Collected Works of Edgar Allan Poe*, 3 vols, ed. Thomas Ollive Mabbott (Cambridge: Harvard University Press, 1969–78), vol. I, 451–52. (Hereafter cited in the text as *CW*.)

3 Kenneth Silverman, *Edgar A. Poe: Mournful and Never-ending Remembrance* (New York: HarperCollins, 1991), 402. Silverman also connects the "Golden grains of sand" in the poem's second stanza with the California Gold Rush, a subject that he and other critics see Poe addressing in his later poem "Eldorado," which will be discussed in Chapter 1.

4 Joseph Jay Rubin, however, asserts, "After the loss of the *Democrat*, Whitman worked that autumn for Nat[thaniel Parker] Willis, who added a daily evening edition to his weekly *Mirror*. Touched by a visit in September by the long-suffering Mrs. Clemm, Willis had hired her son-in-law, Poe. Whitman saw his colleague often, since Poe attended to his duties faithfully at a corner desk, and both frequented the oyster cellar conducted in the heart of the Ann Street printing district by a Washingtonian famous for terrapin stew," *The Historic Whitman* (University Park: Pennsylvania State University Press, 1973), 111. Kenneth Silverman likewise raises the possibility of an 1844 encounter: "If Poe worked in the [*Mirror*] office in October, he may well have met Whitman, who served on the staff for a few weeks that month," *Edgar A. Poe*, 486. Yet, there really is not enough evidence to see Poe and Whitman as "colleagues" at the *Mirror*, the way that Rubin suggests they were, as the younger man likely submitted material to the *Mirror* rather than actually working there. In a April 27, 2013, response to a query I posted on the Poe Studies Association's listserv, Adam Bradford stated that Rubin apparently believes "Whitman wrote for the *Mirror* in late 1844 because of a note he left in an unpublished manuscript entitled 'Autobiographical Data' that says: 'From the middle to the latter part of Oct. 1844 I was in *New Mirror*.' This is Whitman's sole comment on the work he did for

Willis at the time. Whitman wrote casually on a piece by piece basis for most of the papers his work appeared in during the mid-1840s (as he would for Poe in the *Broadway Journal* in Nov. of 1845), and he never mentions having the kind of desk job in the paper's office that Poe had. As a result, his statement that 'I was in *New Mirror*' has seemed to most Whitman scholars like an admission that his work appeared in the paper, not an assertion that he worked in the office." Rubin also contends that Whitman attended Poe's lecture on "The Poets and Poetry of America" at the New York Society Library in late February 1845 during the period when "The Raven" was causing a sensation. He envisions Whitman taking the ferry to Manhattan to attend the lecture, in which he believes the aspiring poet would have had a keen interest. Writing the day before the talk in the Friday, February 27, 1845, issue of the *Evening Mirror*, Willis predicted that "those who would witness a fine carving" of "the critical blade of Mr. Poe" would be there, Dwight R. Thomas and David K. Jackson, *The Poe Log: A Documentary Life of Edgar Allan Poe, 1809–1849* (Boston: G. K. Hall & Co., 1987), 507. (Hereafter cited in the text as *PL*.) Whitman's presence among the roughly two hundred people in attendance is certainly plausible. However, as with a possible meeting between the two men in the offices of the *Mirror*, Whitman does not mention the lecture in his reminiscences of Poe.

5   Walt Whitman, *Specimen Days & Collect* (Philadelphia: Rees Welsh & Co., 1882), 17.

6   Whitman, *Specimen Days & Collect*. On another occasion, in January 1889, Whitman said the following about the meeting with Poe: "I have seen Poe—met him: he impressed me very favorably: was dark, quiet, handsome—Southern from top to toe: languid, tired out, it is true, but altogether ingratiating. . . . We had only a brief visit: he was frankly conciliatory: I left him with no doubts left, if I ever had any," Horace Traubel, *Intimate with Walt: Selections from Whitman's Conversations with Horace Traubel, 1888–1892*, ed. Gary Schmidgall (Iowa City: University of Iowa Press, 2001), 204. For a recent discussion of Poe's experiences in Manhattan in 1844 and 1845 that includes the meeting with Whitman, see Fran Leadon, *Broadway: A History of New York in Thirteen Miles* (New York: W. W. Norton, 2018), 241–48.

7   Adam Bradford opens *Communities of Death: Whitman, Poe, and the American Culture of Mourning* (Columbia: University of Missouri Press, 2014) by imagining Whitman's journey from Brooklyn to the newly relocated office of the *Broadway Journal* and his conversation with Poe (1–4). As part of his thesis that the contrast between Poe's and Whitman's response to death was instrumental in enabling the latter to define himself as an artist, Bradford analyzes the statements Whitman made about Poe from 1875 to the end of his life at considerable length, stating

in connection with them, "He repeatedly testified to the oddly recuperative potential of Poe's Gothic and macabre literature and claimed it played a central role in spurring him to produce the rather remarkably transcendent *Leaves of Grass*" (6).

8 Adam Bradford devotes the Conclusion (185–201) of *Communities of Death* to Whitman's participation in the ceremony commemorating the reinternment of Poe, suggesting, among other things, that it may have inspired Whitman to purchase an elaborate tomb for himself and plan his own funeral.

9 In May 1888, while recollecting the ado created by "The Raven," Whitman again described how over time his attitude toward Poe's poetry became more positive: "Do I like Poe? At the start, for many years, not: but three or four years ago I got to reading him again, reading and liking, until at last—yes, now—I feel almost convinced that he is a star of considerable magnitude, if not a sun, in the literary firmament. Poe was morbid, shadowy, lugubrious—he seemed to suggest dark nights, horrors, spectralities—I could not originally stomach him at all. But today I see more of him than that—much more. If that was all there was to him he would have died long ago. I was a young man of about thirty, living in New York, when 'The Raven' appeared—created its stir: everybody was excited about it—every reading body: somehow it did not enthuse me," Horace Traubel, *With Whitman in Camden (March 28–July 14, 1888)* (New York: D. Appleton & Co., 1908), 138–39.

10 Walt Whitman, "How I Made a Book," in *Democratic Vistas, and Other Papers* (London: Walter Scott, 1888), 131.

11 "Walt Whitman at the Poe Funeral," [Washington] *Evening Star*, November 18, 1875, 2.

12 Fernando González-Moreno and Margarita Rigal-Aragón, *The Portrayal of the Grotesque in Stoddard's and Quantin's Illustrated Editions of Edgar Allan Poe (1884)* (Lewiston, NY: Edwin Mellen, 2017), 51.

13 The story of Poe's adventures in Greece and St. Petersburg, whose origins may date as far back as 1827 (see Silverman, *Edgar A. Poe*, 38), appeared in Rufus Griswold's *Poets and Poetry of America* (Philadelphia: Carey and Hart, 1842), 387, and was frequently repeated in print thereafter. See also the section of the Edgar Allan Poe Society of Baltimore's website devoted to *Edgar Allan Poe, Drugs, and Alcohol*, www.eapoe.org/geninfo/poealchl.htm.

14 Fernando González-Moreno and Margarita Rigal-Aragón, "Poe and the Art of Painting: Tales to Be Seen—The First Spanish Illustrated Edition," *Edgar Allan Poe Review* 19, no. 1 (Spring 2018): 24.

15 See, for example, James Gargano's influential essay "The Question of Poe's Narrators," *College English* 25, no. 3 (December 1963): 177–81.

Chapter 1

1 See note 3 of the Introduction.

2 *The Collected Letters of Edgar Allan Poe*, 2 vols, 3rd ed., ed. John Ward Ostrom, Burton R. Pollin, and Jeffrey A. Savoye (New York: Gordian Press, 2008), vol. I, 264. (Hereafter cited in the text as *CL*.)

3 Looking ahead to another Benjamin (Walter), rather than back to Franklin, Betsy Erkkilä reads several of Poe's tales and poems as conservative critiques of Jacksonian democracy and mob rule. See Erkkilä, "Perverting the American Renaissance: Poe, Democracy, and Critical Theory," in *Poe and the Remapping of Antebellum Print Culture*, ed. J. Gerald Kennedy and Jerome McGann (Baton Rouge: Louisiana State University Press, 2012), 65–100.

4 J. A. Leo Lemay argues that Franklin's *Autobiography* "was the main satiric context for Poe's 'The Business Man,'" particularly the 1845 version of the story published in the *Broadway Journal*, "Poe's 'The Business Man': Its Contexts and Satire of Franklin's *Autobiography*," *Poe Studies* 15, no. 2 (December 1982): 29.

5 *Autobiography of Benjamin Franklin*, ed. John Bigelow (Philadelphia: J. P. Lippincott, 1868), 168. (Subsequent citations from this edition will be listed in the text.)

6 In "Rip Van Winkle," Washington Irving, with a humorous nod to Franklin, refers to the title character and his cohorts who sit around the local tavern discussing month-old news as a "junto."

7 For information on the *Folio Club*, see Alexander Hammond, "A Reconstruction of Poe's 1833 *Tales of the Folio Club*: Preliminary Notes," *Poe Studies* 5 (1972): 25–32 and "Edgar Allan Poe's *The Tales of the Folio Club*: The Evolution of a Lost Book," in *Poe at Work: Seven Textual Studies*, ed. Benjamin Franklin Fisher (Baltimore: The Edgar Allan Poe Society of Baltimore, 1978), 13–43. See also J. Gerald Kennedy, "Inventing the Literati: Poe's Remapping of Antebellum Print Culture," in *Poe and the Remapping of Antebellum Print Culture*, 18–21.

8 Heinz Tschachler, *The Monetary Imagination of Edgar Allan Poe: Banking, Currency and the World of Politics in the Writings* (Jefferson: McFarland, 2013), 22.

9 Arthur Hobson Quinn, *Edgar Allan Poe: A Critical Biography* (Baltimore: Johns Hopkins University Press, 1998), 267.

10 Bruce I. Weiner, *The Most Noble of Professions: Poe and the Poverty of Authorship* (Baltimore: The Edgar Allan Poe Society of Baltimore, 1987), 6; Tschachler, *The Monetary Imagination*, 43.

11 The preceding summary of Poe's life draws on the biographies by Quinn, Silverman, and Jeffrey Meyers, *Edgar Allan Poe: His Life and Legacy* (New York: Cooper Square, 2000), as well as *The Poe Log*.

12 At the end of a 2011 essay addressing Poe's penury, Gavin Jones refers to *Poor Richard's Almanac*: "Max Weber famously turned to Benjamin Franklin's maxims to

discover the ethos of capitalism in its purest form. Yet the maxim is an inherently reversible form, each maxim always implying its equal and opposite maxim." In other words, those who fail to heed Poor Richard's advice risk dire consequences. Retiring early and rising early make "a man healthy, wealthy, and wise," according to the 1735 edition of the *Almanac*, but this famous proverb suggests, alternatively, that burning the midnight oil and lying abed until mid-morning damage a person physically, monetarily, and mentally.

13 Meyers, *Edgar Allan Poe*, 91.

14 Hammond, "Edgar Allan Poe's *The Tales of the Folio Club*," 14.

15 For a discussion of Poe's considerable knowledge about the technology and techniques of book publishing, including his enthusiasm for anastatic printing, see Chapter One, "The Writer of a Visual Era," in *The Portrayal of the Grotesque*, 11–47.

16 Leon Jackson, "'The Italics Are Mine': Edgar Allan Poe and the Semiotics of Print," in *Illuminating Texts: Typography and Literary Imagination*, ed. Paul C. Gutjar and Megan L. Benton (Amherst: University of Massachusetts Press, 2001), 156.

17 R. T. P. Allen, "Edgar Allan Poe," *Scribner's Monthly*, November 1875, 143.

18 This is not to be confused with Matthew Arnold's use of the term in "The Function of Criticism at the Present Time."

19 "Our Amateur Poets. No. I: Flaccus," *Graham's Magazine*, March 1843, 195.

Chapter 2

1 Kevin J. Hayes, *Poe and the Printed Word* (New York: Cambridge University Press, 2004), 56.

2 Poe states in Part III of *Doings in Gotham* (May 25, 1844), "Business has experienced a thorough revival, and 'all goes merry as a marriage bell'" (3), indicating that, after seven years, New York had finally emerged from the doldrums caused by the Panic of 1837.

3 J. Gerald Kennedy, "'A Mania for Composition': Poe's Annus Mirabilis and the Violence of Nation-building," *American Literary History* 17, no. 1 (2005): 1–35.

4 In a May 4, 1845, letter to Frederick W. Thomas, in which he says about the state of his finances "The Devil himself was never so poor," Poe proposes writing "a series of letters—say one a week" on "the literary gossip of New-York" (*CL*, I 550).

5 Between *Doings* and the *Literati*, Poe began another nonfiction series: *Marginalia* (seventeen installments, November 1844 through September 1849 in the *Democratic Review, Godey's Lady's Book, Graham's Magazine*, and the *Southern Literary Messenger*), supposedly random and disconnected responses to passages in books. In the opening article of *Marginalia*, he emphasizes that these "scribblings," as he calls them, appear inside of a book but outside of the text on the margins.

Thus, the book itself provides both the text and the context for each musing, although Poe often does not identify into which books he supposedly inscribed these jottings, thereby taking them out of their text and context. "Marginalia," *United States Magazine and Democratic Review*, November 1844, 485.

6   "Some Secrets of the Magazine Prison-House," *Broadway Journal*, February 15, 1845, 103.

7   "Marginal Notes.—No. II," *Godey's Lady's Book*, September 1845, 121.

8   Scott Peeples, "'To Reproduce a City': New York Letters and the Urban American Renaissance," in *Poe and the Remapping of Antebellum Print Culture*, 118. A page-three item dated April 2, 1845, appearing under the heading New York Correspondence, that was published in the April 5, 1845, issue of the (Washington, DC) *Weekly National Intelligencer* serves to confirm this entanglement, as it anticipates not only the objections to a production of a play by Sophocles that Poe would elaborate in "The Antigone at Palmo's," *Broadway Journal*, April 12, 1845, 236–37, but also some of the statements about alternative names for the United States in Poe's *Marginalia* (Item 184), *Graham's Magazine*, December 1845, 312. There is nothing specifically connecting the writer (or, more likely, writers) of the New York Correspondence pieces in the *Weekly Intelligencer* in the first half of 1845 to Poe, but they do echo subjects of concern to him, several of which he addressed in the *New York Mirror* and the *Broadway Journal*.

9   For a recent discussion of Poe's 1844 series, see Roger Forclaz, "Poe's *Doings in Gotham*: A Note on Charles Sealsfield," *Edgar Allan Poe Review* 19, no. 1 (Spring 2018): 107–12.

10   *Doings in Gotham, Columbia Spy*, May 18, 1844, 3.

11   Ibid.

12   Peeples, "'To Reproduce a City,'" 111.

13   *Doings in Gotham, Columbia Spy*, May 18, 1844, 3.

14   *Doings in Gotham, Columbia Spy*, June 15, 1844, 3; *Columbia Spy*, June 29, 1844, 3; and *Columbia Spy*, June 1, 1844, 3.

15   *Doings in Gotham, Columbia Spy*, June 1, 1844, 3.

16   *Doings in Gotham, Columbia Spy*, May 27, 1844, 3.

17   *Doings in Gotham, Columbia Spy*, June 29, 1844, 3.

18   Rufus W. Griswold, "Curiosities of American Literature," in *Curiosities of Literature, and the Literary Character Illustrated, with Curiosities of American Literature*, ed. I. C. D'Israeli (New York: D. Appleton & Co., 1846), 13. Ha(w)thorne (1731–96) engaged the British off the coast of Portugal in 1777.

19   Bradstreet's first book of poems appeared in London in 1650. An expanded collection of her poems was published posthumously in Boston in 1678.

20   This comes from "To the Reader," a Preface dated November 1843, Griswold, "Curiosities of American Literature," 2.

21 For an overview of the relationship between the two men, see the "Edgar Allan Poe and Rufus Wilmot Griswold" page of the E. A. Poe Society of Baltimore's website, http://www.eapoe.org/geninfo/poegrisw.htm.

22 *Doings in Gotham, Columbia Spy*, July 6, 1844, 3.

23 *Doings in Gotham, Columbia Spy*, May 18, 1844, 3.

24 *Doings in Gotham, Columbia Spy*, June 8, 1844, 3.

25 *Doings in Gotham, Columbia Spy*, May 18, 1844, 3.

26 *Doings in Gotham, Columbia Spy*, June 29, 1844, 3.

27 *Doings in Gotham, Columbia Spy*, June 8, 1844, 3.

28 Ibid.

29 *The Literati of New York City* [Part 1], *Godey's Lady's Book*, May 1846, 195.

30 Ibid.

31 "Why Have the New Yorkers No Review?" *Evening Mirror*, January 8, 1845, 2.

32 Kennedy, "Introduction," in *Poe and the Remapping of Antebellum Print Culture*, 9.

33 Kennedy, "Inventing the Literati," 13.

34 *The Literati of New York City* [Part 1], 194.

35 Edgar A. Poe, "Literary Criticism," *Godey's Lady's Book*, April 1845, 182.

36 *The Literati of New York City* [Part 1], 194.

37 Ibid.

38 Ibid., 194–95.

39 "Some Secrets of the Magazine Prison-House," 104.

40 *The Literati of New York City* [Part 1], 195.

41 *The Literati of New York City* [Part 3], *Godey's Lady's Book*, July 1846, 16.

42 Ibid., 18.

43 Ibid.

44 *The Literati of New York City* [Part 6], *Godey's Lady's Book*, October 1846, 157–58.

45 *The Literati of New York City* [Part 4], *Godey's Lady's Book*, August 1846, 72.

46 Poe also mentions Griswold in the Elizabeth Bogart section of Part 5 of the *Literati*, *Godey's Lady's Book*, September 1846, 130.

47 Joseph Schick, "The Origin of 'The Cask of Amontillado,'" *American Literature* 6 (March 1934): 18–21.

48 J. T. Headley, *Letters from Italy* (London: Wiley and Putnam, 1845), 194.

49 See, for example, Simonetta Berbeglia, "'L'uomo murato' in San Lorenzo nei racconti dei viaggiatori stranieri," *Memorie Valdarnesi* 172 (2007): 147–56; *L'enigma della "mummia,"* Valdarnotizie.com, July 6, 2011, http://www.valdarnotizie. com/attualita/lenigma-della-mummia; and *La leggenda dell'uomo murato a San Giovanni*, YouTube video, March 30, 2010, https://www.youtube.com/watch?v=BA_ B3W9HI7s. I am not the first person to connect *l'uomo murato* to "The Cask of Amontillado." Simonetta Berbeglia does so in passing in a 2010 article concerning a lost poem that Robert Browning wrote about Wally in the 1840s or 1850s,

"A Skeleton in the Wall: Robert Browning's Italian Story," *Journal of Browning Studies* 1 (February 2010): 70–79, 104.

50 *Handbook for Travellers in Central Italy* (London: John Murray, 1843), 206; Octavian Blewitt, *Handbook for Travellers in Central Italy*, 2nd ed. (London: John Murray, 1850), 236–37.

51 J. T. Headley, *Italy and the Italians: In a Series of Letters* (New York: I. S. Platt, 1844).

52 This issue also contained an address Cornelius Matthews delivered on June 30 that was entitled and served as the manifesto for "Young America," a nationalistic literary movement with which Headley and Evert Duyckinck were closely affiliated.

53 "Letter to the Editor," *New York Daily Tribune*, November 11, 1847, 2; Joy Bayless, *Rufus Wilmot Griswold* (Nashville: Vanderbilt University Press, 1949), 132–36.

54 Writers' Program of the Works Projects Administration in the State of New York, *New York: A Guide to the Empire State* (New York: Oxford University Press, 1940), 147.

55 For Poe's relationship with Young America, see note 13 in Chapter 3.

56 Edgar Allan Poe, review of *Letters from Italy*, by Joel T. Headley, *Broadway Journal*, August 9, 1845, 75.

57 "City Items," *New York Daily Tribune*, May 1, 1846, 2; [Margaret Fuller] "Headley's Napoleon," *New York Daily Tribune*, May 1, 1846, 1.

58 "Vermont University Commencement—Rev. J. T. Headley's Address," *New York Daily Tribune*, August 8, 1846, 1.

59 "Poe on Headley and Channing: Joel T. Headley," *Southern Literary Messenger*, October 1850, 610.

60 "Poe on Headley and Channing: Joel T. Headley," 608.

61 "Text: Edgar Allan Poe, 'The Living Writers of America,' (A), Manuscript, 1846–47," E. A. Poe Society of Baltimore, http://www.eapoe.org/works/misc/livingw.htm.

62 Francis B. Dedmond, "'The Cask of Amontillado' and the War of the Literati," *Modern Language Notes* 15 (1954): 137–46.

63 According to Yonjae Jung, "the vengeful Montresor represents Poe himself; Fortunato can be seen as Poe's antagonist whom he both envied and despised in the bleak literary scene" of the antebellum era, "Poe's Magazinist Career and 'The Cask of Amontillado,'" *American Studies in Scandinavia* 46, no. 2 (2014): 70.

64 The latter group, which includes James Gargano, Daniel Hoffman, J. Gerald Kennedy, myself, and many others, note that Montresor (1) is a premeditated murderer who provides no justification for his crime, (2) undermines his claims for self-possession by admitting to hesitating and trembling during the live burial of Fortunato, (3) dubiously asserts that a physical cause (nitre, a substance used to mummify bodies) made his "heart" grow sick as he completes the deed, and (4) presumably confesses all of this to a priest—the "You" of the opening paragraph— as he lies on his deathbed—likely much more concerned about whether he will rest in peace than the man he entombed fifty years earlier.

Chapter 3

1 An earlier version of this chapter was written with Travis Montgomery, who has graciously allowed me to include previously published material in this book, for which I am deeply grateful. It is an expansion and a commingling of two papers, "Scribblers and Scriveners: Poe, Melville, and Antebellum Literary New York" (Gruesser) and "Inside the Prison House: Melville's 'Bartleby, the Scrivener,' the New York Magazine World, and the Example of Poe" (Montgomery), which were part of the "Poe and New York City II" panel at the 2015 International Edgar Allan Poe Conference in New York City. The authors' fellow panelist was Margarida Vale de Gato, whose paper about connections between "Bartleby" and "The Raven" was titled "'Still more a fixture than before': Poe and Melville Working in Close(d) Chambers." I would like to express my thanks to Margarida and to Hershel Parker for their helpful suggestions.

2 Herman Melville to Nathaniel Hawthorne, "Pittsfield [June 1?] 1851," in *Correspondence*, ed. Lynn Horth (rev. and aug, from *The Letters of Herman Melville*, ed. Merrell R. Davis and William H. Gilman), vol. 14 of *The Writings of Herman Melville* (Evanston and Chicago: Northwestern University Press and the Newberry Library, 1993), 191.

3 James C. Wilson, "'Bartleby': The Walls of Wall Street," *Arizona Quarterly* 37, no. 4 (1981): 335; Andrew Delbanco, *Melville: His World and Work* (New York: Vintage Books, 2006), 7.

4 Dan McCall, *The Silence of Bartleby* (Ithaca: Cornell University Press, 1989), 32.

5 Wilson, "'Bartleby,'" 335.

6 Leo Marx, "Melville's Parable of the Walls," *Sewanee Review* 61, no. 4 (1953): 603–04.

7 Laurie Robertson-Lorant, *Melville: A Biography* (Amherst: University of Massachusetts Press, 1998), 335; Delbanco, *Melville*, 219.

8 McCall, *The Silence of Bartleby*, 13.

9 *Literary World*, December 3, 1853, 295; reprinted in *Bartleby the Inscrutable: A Collection of Commentary on Herman Melville's Tale "Bartleby the Scrivener,"* ed. M. Thomas Inge (Hamden: Archon, 1979), 32; review of *The Piazza Tales*, by Herman Melville, *Democratic Review* 38, no. 2 (September 1856): 172.

10 Perry Miller, *The Raven and the Whale: The War of Words and Wits in the Era of Poe and Melville* (New York: Harcourt and Brace, 1956).

11 Harry Levin, *The Power of Blackness: Hawthorne, Poe, Melville* (New York: Alfred A. Knopf, 1958), 187.

12 James L. Colwell and Gary Spitzer, "'Bartleby' and 'The Raven': Parallels of the Irrational," *Georgia Review* 23, no. 1 (1969): 43.

13 R. Bruce Bickley, Jr., *The Method of Melville's Short Fiction* (Durham: Duke University Press, 1975), 30; Daniel A. Wells, "'Bartleby the Scrivener,' Poe, and the

Duyckinck Circle," *ESQ* 21, no. 1 (1975): 35–39. For Poe's complicated relationship with Young America, a nationalist group associated with Duyckinck, see Claude Richard, "Poe and 'Young America,'" *Studies in Bibliography* 21 (1968): 25–58; and Meredith L. McGill, "Poe, Literary Nationalism, and Authorial Identity," in *The American Face of Edgar Allan Poe*, ed. Shawn Rosenheim and Stephen Rachman (Baltimore: Johns Hopkins University Press, 1995), 271–304.

14 Hershel Parker, *Herman Melville: A Biography, Vol. 2: 1851–1891* (Baltimore: Johns Hopkins University Press, 2002), 176.

15 Mildred Travis, "The Idea of Poe in *Pierre*," *ESQ* 50, supplement (1968): 59–62; Harrison Hayford, "Poe in *The Confidence-Man*," *Nineteenth-Century Fiction* 14, no. 3 (1959): 207–18.

16 Herman Melville, "Hawthorne and His Mosses, by a Virginian Spending July in Vermont," in *The Piazza Tales and Other Prose Pieces, 1839–1860*, ed. Harrison Hayford, Alma A. MacDougall, G. Thomas Tanselle et al., in vol. 9 of *The Writings of Herman Melville* (Evanston and Chicago: Northwestern University Press and the Newberry Library, 1987), 243; Edgar Allan Poe, "Tale Writing—Nathaniel Hawthorne," *Godey's Lady's Book*, November 1847, 256.

17 William E. Engel, *Early Modern Poetics in Melville and Poe: Memory, Melancholy, and the Emblematic Tradition* (Farnham: Ashgate, 2012), 3; see also William Gowans, "[Reminiscences of Edgar A. Poe]," *Catalogue of American Books*, no. 28 (1870): 11; and Hayes, *Poe and the Printed Word*, 46, 84.

18 Hershel Parker, *Herman Melville: A Biography, Vol. 1: 1819–1851* (Baltimore: Johns Hopkins University Press, 1996), 433.

19 Charles Frederick Briggs to James Russell Lowell, March 8, 1845; *PL* 514.

20 Ezra Greenspan, *George Palmer Putnam: Representative American Publisher* (University Park: Pennsylvania State University Press, 2000), 287, 311, 314.

21 Charles Frederick Briggs, "From 'The Personality of Poe' (1877)," in *Poe in His Own Time: A Biographical Chronicle of His Life, Drawn from Recollections, Interviews, and Memoirs by Family, Friends, and Associates*, ed. Benjamin F. Fisher (Iowa City: University of Iowa Press, 2010), 297. Some of Briggs's contemporaries also observed the gray hue of the eyes of Poe. For a list of portraitists and writers who identified Poe's eyes as "grey," see the "Edgar Allan Poe's Appearance, Etc." page on the Edgar Allan Poe Society of Baltimore website, http://www.eapoe.org/geninfo/poeapprn.htm.

22 Herman Melville, "Bartleby, the Scrivener: A Story of Wall-Street," in *The Piazza Tales and Other Prose Pieces, 1839–1860*, 19, 27, 32. (Subsequent citations will be listed in the text.)

23 Hayes, *Poe and the Printed Word*, 96; *PL* 417.

24 Hershel Parker, *Herman Melville: A Biography, Vol. 2: 1851–1891*, 173; *Melville Biography: An Inside Narrative* (Evanston: Northwestern University Press, 2013), 154; and *Herman Melville: A Biography, Vol. 2: 1851–1891*, 176.

25 Rufus W. Griswold, "'Death of Edgar Allan Poe,' in *New York Daily Tribune* (1849)," in *Poe in His Own Time*, 73. Melville may have read the longer version of this biographical notice that Griswold included in his edition of Poe's writings. According to Merton M. Sealts, Jr., Melville presented a set of Poe's works to his wife Elizabeth in 1861, and this set, now lost, was an 1859 printing of Griswold's edition. See entry 404a in *Melville's Reading: A Check-list of Books Owned and Borrowed* (Madison: University of Wisconsin Press, 1966), 86. Melville's decision to make a gift of these books indicates familiarity with their contents.

26 Nathaniel Parker Willis, "'Death of Edgar A. Poe' (1850)," in *Poe in His Own Time*, 94–95.

27 Willis, "Death of Edgar A. Poe," 94.

28 The initial productivity of Bartleby resembles the creative surge Poe experienced from 1844 to 1846, a time that Scott Peeples calls "the pivotal, hectic period in Manhattan," during which "Poe published fifteen new stories—more than any comparable period of his career—but also contributed dozens of reviews, editorials, notices, and announcements to the *Evening Mirror* and the *Broadway Journal.*" See Peeples, "'To Reproduce a City." For another account of Poe's creative activity during this period, with a focus on 1844, see Kennedy, "'A Mania for Composition.'"

29 According to Sidney P. Moss, Poe left the *Mirror* in March 1845, *Poe's Major Crisis: His Libel Suit and New York's Literary World* (Durham: Duke University Press, 1970), 128. For information on Poe's professional labors as well as his comings and goings between October 1844 and March 1845, the period during which he worked at the *Evening Mirror*, see *PL*, chap. 7 (393–480) and chap. 8 (483–608).

30 Wells, "'Bartleby,'" 35.

31 Willis, "Death of Edgar A. Poe," 94.

32 Nathaniel Parker Willis to George Pope Morris, 1859, quoted in John H. Ingram, *Life and Letters of Edgar Allan Poe*, ed. G. T. Bettany (London: Ward, Lock, and Bowden, 1891), 210.

33 In a May 29, 1829, letter to his foster father John Allan, Poe declared, "I have long given up *Byron* as a model" (*CL*, I 30). That statement was somewhat premature, if not disingenuous, for the (in)famous British poet remained, as many critics have observed, an influence on not only Poe's writings but also accounts of his life that he gave to others.

34 Robert Weisbuch, *Atlantic Double-Cross: American Literature and British Influence in the Age of Emerson* (Chicago: University of Chicago Press, 1986), 43.

35 Willis, "Death of Edgar A. Poe," 96.

36 Wells, in "'Bartleby,'" makes a similar claim, but he associates the lawyer with Evert Duyckinck, "an unpaid agent," who "was indeed a 'conveyancer' of sorts" (36).

37 Although Willis typically expressed favorable views of Poe, defending his ill-fated fellow writer against detractors such as Griswold, Poe apparently

harbored ambivalent feelings about the well-to-do editor. In "Poe's 'Quiz on Willis,'" *American Literature* 5, no. 1 (1933): 55–62, Kenneth L. Daughrity makes a case for reading "The Duc De L'Omelette," an early Poe tale, as an extended joke at the expense of Willis, who had a foppish turn. Perhaps the story was the result of Poe's frustrations about struggling for financial security in a publishing world that rewarded writers he considered undeserving of the celebrity they enjoyed. This satirical effort may have involved some personal score settling, for, in 1829, Willis had rejected the poem "Fairyland," which Poe submitted to the *American Monthly Magazine*. See Richard Benton, "Willis— and Poe," review of *Nathaniel P. Willis*, by Cortland P. Auser, *Poe Studies* 4, no. 2 (1971): 56. As noted in Chapter 2, Poe wrote about Willis in *Doings of Gotham* (1844) and in *The Literati of New York City* (1846). For Poe's interactions with and responses to Willis, see Sidney P. Moss, *Poe's Literary Battles: The Critic in the Context of His Literary Milieu* (Carbondale: Southern Illinois University Press, 1963).

38 Scott Peeples, "'The *Mere* Man of Letters Must Ever Be a Cipher': Poe and N. P. Willis," *ESQ* 46, no. 3 (2000): 125, 130.

39 In addition to Charles Sellers's *The Market Revolution: Jacksonian America, 1815–1846* (New York: Oxford University Press, 1991), important studies of the period include Harry L. Watson's *Liberty and Power: The Politics of Jacksonian America*, rev. ed. (New York: Hill and Wang, 2006); and Sean Wilentz's *The Rise of American Democracy: Jefferson to Lincoln* (New York: Norton, 2005).

40 Walter Benjamin, "Theses on the Philosophy of History," in *Illuminations: Essays and Reflections*, trans. Harry Zohn, ed. Hannah Arendt (New York: Schocken Books, 2007), 257–58. Significantly, in "Perverting the American Renaissance," Betsy Erkkilä indicates that Benjamin's vision corresponds to the "view of history" advanced "in [Poe's] three angelic dialogues" (88).

41 At least one other critic has linked Melville's tale to Poe's "The Cask of Amontillado," noting that "Bartleby" shares the thematic preoccupation with confinement that pervades "Cask." See A. W. Plumstead, "Bartleby: Melville's Venture into a New Genre," in *Melville Annual 1965: A Symposium; Bartleby the Scrivener*, ed. Howard P. Vincent (Kent: Kent State University Press, 1966), 87. Plumstead does not, however, offer much commentary on this insight, saying nothing about the death of Adams, which recalls the murder of Fortunato in Poe's tale.

42 McCall, *Silence of Bartleby*, 26.

43 Melville's epilogue, with its references to undelivered missives, may allude to a tale in which Poe had memorably written about letters. The transmission of messages and the failure thereof have been subjects of enduring fascination for

commentators on "The Purloined Letter" (1844), among them Jacques Lacan and Jacques Derrida, who famously differed over the former's contention that letters always arrive at their destinations.

44 See Jonathan Elmer, "'Bartleby,' Empson, and Pastoral Pleasures," *J19* 2, no. 1 (2014): 26, 27.

Chapter 4

1 Neil Harris, *Humbug: The Art of P. T. Barnum* (Boston: Little, Brown and Co., 1973), 62. (Subsequent citations to this book will be listed in the text.)

2 Harris connects Dupin's relish for problem solving to this operational aesthetic, Ibid., 85. For a discussion of Poe and "The Barnumesque Object," see Jonathan Elmer, *Reading the Social Limit: Affect, Mass Culture, and Edgar Allan Poe* (Stanford: Stanford University Press, 1995), 182–223. For a reading of Poe's writings, including his detective fiction, in connection with competition, game playing, and revenge, see Scott Peeples, *Edgar Allan Poe Revisited* (New York: Twayne, 1998), 106–32. For promotional material relating to the Feejee Mermaid and the Great Buffalo Hunt, as well as contemporary reactions to these spectacles, see James Cook, *The Colossal P. T. Barnum Reader: Nothing Else Like It in the Universe* (Urbana: University of Illinois Press, 2005), 109–12 and 185–90. For a discussion of hoaxing in Poe, see Lynda Walsh, "What Is a Hoax?: Redefining Poe's *Jeux de Esprit* and His Relationship with His Readership," *Text, Practice, and Performance* 4 (2002): 103–20.

3 Harris, *Humbug*, 77.

4 Thus, in the Dupin tales, Poe employs *Agon, Alea,* and *Mimicry,* three of the four categories of play delineated by Roger Caillois in *Man, Play, and Games* (Urbana: University of Illinois Press, 2001), 14–26. Although I do not refer specifically to game theory in the text of this chapter, John von Neumann and Oskar Morgenstern's groundbreaking book on the subject, *Theory of Games and Economic Behavior* (Princeton: Princeton University Press, 1944), provides a wealth of information about and useful terminology relating to games. The unique position they assign to poker within their theory (because of the role played by bluffing in this game), for example, can be usefully applied to hard-boiled fiction. On the subject of game theory, see also Morton Davis, *Game Theory: A Nontechnical Introduction* (New York: Basic Books, 1970). For a discussion of the connection between anthropological and psychological studies of play and Poe's Dupin stories, see Leroy L. Panek, "Play and Games: An Approach to Poe's Detective Tales," *Poe Studies* 10 (Dec. 1977): 39–41.

5 Peter Thoms, "Poe's Dupin and the Power of Detection," in *The Cambridge Companion to Edgar Allan Poe*, ed. Kevin Hayes (Cambridge: Cambridge University Press, 2002), 135; Burton R. Pollin, "Poe's 'The Murders in the Rue Morgue': The Ingenious Web Unravelled," *Studies in the American Renaissance* 1 (1977): 254.

6 Daniel Hoffman, *Poe Poe Poe Poe Poe Poe Poe* (New York: Doubleday, 1972), 114.

7 Ronald Thomas remarks, "it is fitting that a story credited with launching a new literary genre about the cryptic unreadability of crime should begin by instructing the reader how this new kind of story should be read," *Detective Fiction and the Rise of Forensic Science* (New York: Cambridge University Press, 2003), 44.

8 Maurice S. Lee, "Edgar Allan Poe (1809–1849)," in *A Companion to Crime Fiction*, ed. Charles J. Rzepka and Lee Horsley (Malden: Wiley, 2010), 372. On the subject of women and violence in Poe's fiction, see Leland Person, "Poe and Nineteenth-Century Gender Constructions," in *A Historical Guide to Edgar Allan Poe*, ed. J. Gerald Kennedy (New York: Oxford University Press, 2001), 129–65.

9 John T. Irwin, "A Clew to a Clue: Locked Rooms and Labyrinths in Poe and Borges," in *The American Face of Edgar Allan Poe*, 147.

10 Thomas, *Detective Fiction*, 47.

11 Irwin, "A Clew," 147.

12 Ibid., 147–48.

13 In the first printing of the story, Dupin claims to have found the hair of the ape intermixed with "the tresses remaining upon the head of Madame L'Espanaye"; however, in later versions, he asserts that he extracted it from the dead woman's fingers, which seems less plausible, as the police would almost certainly have examined her hands.

14 Thomas, *Detective Fiction*, 47.

15 As Christopher Rollason observes, "The sailor's presence in 'the Indian Archipelago' (modern Indonesia) is not fortuitous, but dictated by European economic interests: he is French, the 'Maltese vessel' hails from a British colony, and Borneo was colonized by the British and Dutch. The murders are ultimately a consequence of European colonialism," "The Detective Myth in Edgar Allan Poe's Dupin Trilogy," in *American Crime Fiction: Studies in the Genre*, ed. Brian Docherty (New York: St. Martin's, 1988), 10. Stanley Orr goes further, regarding the sailor as the first of a long series of "defective" Westerners who appear in detective fiction. In "Murders" and other texts, including the Orientalist novellas in which Sherlock Holmes first saw print, according to Orr, "a weak and irresponsible colonial adventurer introduces an exotic and savage menace into the heart of Europe and the mayhem that ensues is curbed only by the *noblesse oblige* intervention of the detective," *Darkly Perfect World: Colonial Adventure, Postmodernism, and American Noir* (Columbus: Ohio State University Press, 2010), 6.

16   Stephen Knight, *Form and Ideology in Crime Fiction* (London: Macmillan, 1980), 46.

17   Thomas, *Detective Fiction*, 133.

18   Hoffman, *Poe Poe Poe*, 114.

19   Warren Kelly, "Detecting the Critic: The Presence of Poe's Critical Voice in His Stories of Dupin," *Edgar Allan Poe Review* 4, no. 2 (Fall 2003): 80; Robert Daniel, "Poe's Detective God," *Furioso* 6 (Summer 1951): 49, 54.

20   Meyers, *Edgar Allan Poe*, 124.

21   Pollin, "Poe's 'The Murders in the Rue Morgue,'" 239.

22   Raymond Chandler, "Letter to James Sandoe, May 20, 1949," in *Raymond Chandler Speaking*, ed. Dorothy Gardiner and Katherine Sorley Walker (Boston: Houghton, 1977), 57.

23   Thoms, "Poe's Dupin," 137.

24   This information comes from the first chapter of Robert K. Merton and Elinor Barber's fascinating book about serendipity, which was written in 1958 but published forty-six years later as *The Travels and Adventures of Serendipity: A Study in Sociological Semantics and the Sociology of Science* (Princeton: Princeton University Press, 2004).

25   In another famous instance, this one involving a missing person rather than an animal, Pierre-Augustin Caron de Beaumarchais, in a 1776 letter to the *Morning Chronicle*, minutely describes a woman he has never beheld who left behind a cloak at the Pantheon in London, "Cloak without Dagger," in *The Delights of Detection*, ed. Jacques Barzun (New York: Criterion, 1961), 345–48.

26   Daniel Stashower, *The Beautiful Cigar Girl: Mary Rogers, Edgar Allan Poe, and the Invention of Murder* (New York: Penguin, 2006), 7.

27   Ibid., 249.

28   Meyers, *Edgar Allan Poe*, 135.

29   Ibid.

30   For an important reading of Poe's story in connection with the Mary Rogers case, see John E. Walsh, *Poe the Detective: The Curious Circumstances behind "The Mystery of Marie Rogêt"* (New Brunswick: Rutgers University Press, 1968). For an eye-opening discussion of the tale in the light of nineteenth-century attitudes toward abortion, see Laura Saltz, "'(Horrible to Relate)': Recovering the Body of Marie Rogêt," in *The American Face of Edgar Allan Poe*, 237–67.

31   Patricia Merivale, "Gumshoe Gothics: Poe's 'The Man of the Crowd' and His Followers," in *The Metaphysical Detective Story from Poe to Postmodernism*, ed. Patricia Merivale and Susan Elizabeth Sweeney (Philadelphia: University of Pennsylvania Press, 1999), 101–16.

32   Terence Whalen, *Edgar Allan Poe and the Masses: The Political Economy of Antebellum America* (Princeton: Princeton University Press, 1999), 236.

33 Collins's comic tale pits two experienced police professionals against an arrogant and narrow-minded amateur, the last three letters of whose name, Sharpin, but not his sleuthing skills, recall Dupin's. An admirer of Poe's tales and poems from his youth who published a story in 1883 in which a ghost declares himself the "embodiment" of Poe, Doyle frequently acknowledged his profound debt to Dupin's creator, Michael Sims, *Arthur and Sherlock: Conan Doyle and the Creation of Holmes* (New York: Bloomsbury, 2017), 74–75. Notably, in staging the first meeting of John Watson and Sherlock Holmes in *A Study in Scarlet* (1887), Doyle evokes his American forerunner.

34 Hoffman, *Poe Poe Poe*, 116.

35 Peeples, *Edgar Allan Poe Revisited*, 126.

36 Knight, *Form and Ideology*, 58.

37 Hoffman, *Poe Poe Poe*, 118.

38 David Reynolds, *Beneath the American Renaissance: The Subversive Imagination in the Age of Emerson and Melville* (New York: Knopf, 1988), 247.

39 In *Edgar Allan Poe and the Dupin Mysteries* (New York: Palgrave, 2008), Richard Kopley compares the situation in which the Queen finds herself in "The Purloined Letter" to that of two other Queens "of problematic reputation" in famous literary texts that serve as important precursors to detective fiction—Jocasta in *Oedipus the King* and Gertrude in *Hamlet*, 87–88.

40 Thomas, *Detective Fiction*, 142.

41 For a reading that links Poe's detection to another myth related to yarn or thread, that of Theseus and the Minotaur, see John T. Irwin *A Mystery to a Solution: Poe, Borges, and the Analytic Detective Story* (Baltimore: Johns Hopkins University Press, 1996).

42 David Van Leer, "Detecting Truth: The World of the Dupin Tales," in *New Essays on Poe's Major Tales*, ed. Kenneth Silverman (New York: Cambridge University Press, 1993), 66.

43 Hervey Allen, *Israfel: The Life and Times of Edgar Allan Poe* (New York: Farrar & Rinehart, 1934), 408.

44 Thoms contends that Dupin's "concealment of a story of moral crime" in "Murders" serves "to shield his own behavior," for "to examine the legitimacy of the sailor's project and, more particularly, his cruel domination of the orangutan would be to raise uneasy questions about the detective's own employment of power" (138).

45 Saltz, "'Horrible to Relate,'" 237.

46 Van Leer, "Detecting Truth," 80, 88.

47 Thomas, *Detective Fiction*, 144.

48 Peter Thoms, *Detection and Its Designs* (Columbus: Ohio State University Press, 1998), 70.

49 Peeples, *Edgar Allan Poe Revisited*, 126.

50 Irwin, "A Clew," 152.

51 In "The Reader as Poe's Ultimate Dupe in 'The Purloined Letter,'" *Studies in Short Fiction* 26 (1989), Hal Blythe and Charles Sweet fault Armstrong for not going far enough in linking Dupin and D-----, asserting, "Simply put, in 'The Purloined Letter' there is in actuality no real Minister, and the reader who fails to perceive this point misses 'the very simplicity' of the story and is as guilty as the Prefect of overlooking the obvious" (312–13). Without enumerating the many questions raised by their largely unsubstantiated claim that Dupin has spent years creating his alter ego the Minister so that he can write the letter to the Queen, steal it from her disguised as D-----, hold on to it until the reward has been doubled, and then sell it to the Prefect, I would observe that this can hardly be described as a simple solution to the mystery. Similar to Ronald Thomas and others who focus on Dupin, conflating him with Poe, Blythe and Sweet, by reading D----- as an alter ego created by Dupin, fail to see the detective himself as one of the devices concocted by Poe to manipulate readers.

52 G. K. Chesterton, "The Blue Cross," in *The Innocence of Father Brown* (New York: John Lane, 1911), 9.

53 Valerie Wilson Wesley, [Interview], 2003; John Cullen Gruesser, *Race, Gender and Empire in American Detective Fiction* (Jefferson: McFarland, 2013), 166.

54 Raymond Chandler, "Casual Notes on the Mystery Novel," in *Raymond Chandler Speaking*, 69.

55 Chandler, "Letter to James Sandoe," 57.

56 Jon Thompson, *Fiction, Crime, and Empire: Clues to Modernity and Postmodernism* (Urbana: University of Illinois Press, 1993), 49.

57 Lee, "Edgar Allan Poe (1809–1849)," 370.

58 Chandler, "Casual Notes on the Mystery Novel," 70.

59 Although I have emphasized these three forms of competition in this chapter, I could have included a fourth—metacriticism in connection with Poe's detective fiction. In discussing Barbara Johnson's critique of Jacques Derrida's critique of Jacques Lacan's critique of Poe's "Purloined," Irwin observes in *A Mystery to a Solution*, "As with Derrida's reading of Lacan, the wit of Johnson's reading of Derrida lies in the way that she doubles Derrida's own insights back upon themselves to make them problematic. Thus, in dealing with Derrida's attempt to be one up on Lacan . . . , Johnson assimilates their opposed readings of the tale's numerical structure to the game of even and odd" (6). Irwin suggests that despite her efforts not to become embroiled in such competition, Johnson cannot completely avoid doing so because by reading Derrida the way she does she places him in the same position that he places Lacan. This intellectual game of one-upmanship, of course, also holds true for Irwin himself vis-à-vis Johnson and can be continued ad infinitum. On the competitive nature of critical readings of "The Purloined Letter," see also Peeples, *Edgar Allan Poe Revisited*, 130.

Chapter 5

1 "Why Do People Read Detective Stories" (October 14, 1944), "Who Cares Who Killed Roger Ackroyd" (January 20, 1945), and "'Mr. Holmes, They Were the Footprints of a Gigantic Hound'" (February 17, 1945); reprinted in *Edmund Wilson: Literary Essays and Reviews of the 1930s & 1940s*, ed. Lewis M. Dabney (New York: Library of America, 2007), 657–61, 677–83, and 684–90.

2 *Selected Letters of Nathaniel Hawthorne*, ed. Joel Myerson (Columbus: Ohio State University Press, 2002), 123.

3 Kopley, *Edgar Allan Poe*, 88; George Dekker, *The American Historical Romance* (New York: Cambridge University Press, 1987), 324.

4 Walt Whitman, "Life and Adventures of Jack Engle," *Walt Whitman Quarterly Review* 34, no. 3/4 (2017): 301, 314. (Subsequent citations will be listed in the text.)

5 Franklin R. Rogers, "Introduction," in *Simon Wheeler, Detective*, by Mark Twain (New York: New York Public Library, 1963), xii.

6 The fact that the audience knows that Oedipus himself is the pollution that plagues Thebes does not make him any less of a detective figure. Similarly, even though viewers learn the identity of the killer at the start of each episode of the old *Columbo* television series, this does not make the eponymous police investigator any less of a sleuth.

7 Nathaniel Hawthorne, *The Scarlet Letter and Other Writings*, 2nd ed., ed. Leland S. Person (New York: W. W. Norton, 2017): 51. (Subsequent citations will be listed in the text.)

8 Chillingworth's statement that he needs to look deeper into Dimmesdale's "rare case" to advance the cause of science, "Were it only for the art's sake, I must search this matter to the bottom" (86), recalls to some extent Dupin's remark that "an inquiry" into the Rue Morgue killings "will afford us amusement" (*CW*, II 546).

9 J. Gerald Kennedy, "The Limits of Reason: Poe's Deluded Detectives," *American Literature* 47, no. 2 (May 1975): 186.

10 Brook Thomas, "Citizen Hester: *The Scarlet Letter* as Civic Myth," *American Literary History* 13, no. 2 (2001): 443.

11 Hawthorne reiterates the point in Chapter XIV when the narrator declares, "In a word, Old Roger Chillingworth was a striking evidence of man's faculty of transforming himself into a devil, if he will only, for a reasonable space of time, undertake a devil's office" (104).

12 Zachary Turpin, "Introduction to Walt Whitman's 'Life and Adventures of Jack Engle,'" *Walt Whitman Quarterly Review* 34 (2017): 225–26, 240. (Subsequent citations will be listed in the text.) David S. Reynolds associates *Jack Engle* and yet another literary form, "the city mystery novel, a popular genre of the day that pitted

the 'upper 10 thousand'—what we would call the 1 percent—against the lower million," Jennifer Schuessler, "Path to 'Leaves' in Lost Novel by Whitman," *New York Times*, February 21, 2017, A1. Without denying this connection, I argue below that Whitman's short novel includes key elements of detection.

13 *Jack Engle* ran from March 14 to April 18, 1852, in *The New York Sunday Dispatch*.

14 In both *Jack Engle* and "Revenge and Requital," a story which Whitman published seven years earlier, a lawyer named Covert makes inappropriate advances toward his young female ward and tries to cheat her and a young man out of their rightful inheritance, "Revenge and Requital; A Tale of a Murderer Escaped," *The United States Magazine and Democratic Review* 17 (July and August 1845): 105–11.

15 Walt Whitman, "Life and Adventures of Jack Engle: An Autobiography," *Walt Whitman Quarterly Review* 34 (2017): 280, 318. (Subsequent citations will be listed in the text.) "Revenge and Requital" likewise characterizes a member of the bar named (Adam) Covert as "unprincipled," the adjective that Dupin uses to describe D----- in "The Purloined Letter."

16 Moreover, by referring to the necessity of digging deeper than an opponent in order to come out on top, the language here anticipates that used to describe the battle between Sherlock Holmes and Professor Moriarty in Arthur Conan Doyle's "The Final Problem" (1893).

17 That is, "watchmen," "officer," "police," "victim," "clue," "investigate," "mystery," "evidence," "murder," "prison," "jailor," "fraud," "swindling," and so forth.

18 Delbanco, *Melville*, 230.

19 For an article that provides fascinating historical background relating to Melville's novella, see Greg Grandin, "Who Ain't a Slave? Historical Fact and the Fiction of 'Benito Cereno,'" *The Chronicle of Higher Education*, December 16, 2013, http://www.chronicle.com/article/Slavery-in-FactFiction/143551. See also Grandin's *The Empire of Necessity: Slavery, Freedom, and Deception in the New World* (New York: Metropolitan, 2014).

20 Kevin J. Hayes, *The Cambridge Introduction to Herman Melville* (New York: Cambridge University Press, 2007), 80.

21 "Benito Cereno," in *The Piazza Tales and Other Prose Pieces, 1839–1860*, 114. (Subsequent citations will be listed in the text.)

22 Delbanco, *Melville*, 242.

23 Although Dekker stops short of calling Delano a detective, he does acknowledge the American captain's obtuseness in his comments on this episode (202–03).

24 Poe's ingenious straddling of two types of Gothic stories—ones in which supernatural events actually occur and ones in which there is a rational (if highly improbable) explanation for apparently occult phenomena—makes his best tales unforgettable and ripe for critical debate. At the start of "The Fall of the House of

Usher," as he approaches the edifice, the narrator raises the question of whether the mansion has its own atmosphere. Although he dismisses this "strange fancy" as "ridiculous" and later as "a dream" (*CW*, II 399), he nevertheless provides a possible explanation for the existence of a meteorological system peculiar to the House of Usher by referring to the gaseous haze that appears to envelop the mansion as "an atmosphere which had no affinity with the air of heaven, but which had reeked up from the decayed trees, and the gray wall, and the silent tarn—a pestilent and mystic vapor, dull, sluggish, faintly discernable, and leaden-hued" (*CW*, II 399–400). Later, Roderick asserts that the house not only has its own atmosphere but has exerted a "terrible influence" on his family, "mould[ing] the destinies" (*CW*, II 408) of his ancestors as well as himself and his sister. In response to this statement, the otherwise voluble narrator says only, "such opinions need no comment, and I will make none" (*CW*, II 408). Even though he has had a similar impression about the mansion, the narrator adopts the pose of the hyperrationalist here, suggesting that Usher's beliefs do not even merit consideration. His self-imposed silence, however, is telling. A clear-thinking rationalist would analyze Roderick's contentions, dismissing those rooted in fantasy rather than reality and recognize that there are two issues here. First, have the decaying trees, the vapors of the tarn, and the house's isolation and antiquity indeed somehow combined to create a distinct atmosphere around the house? If they have not, then Usher in this passage and the narrator at the start of the tale and elsewhere are deluded. However, if the mansion does, in fact, have its own meteorological system, then it is necessary to address the second part of Roderick's claim: Are the fates of the two Houses of Usher preternaturally linked? If they are, then the storm raging outside the mansion reflects the turmoil in the family caused by Roderick burying Madeline alive. However, to believe there is such a connection between the edifice and the Ushers requires the acceptance of the existence of supernatural phenomena, a position that a rationalist could never embrace. Whatever one's opinion on the presence of a separate atmosphere and the affinity between the house and the family may be, the narrator's hyperrationalist claim that Roderick's contentions deserve no comment must be seen as disingenuous and evasive. Moreover, despite Usher's weird habits and the very real possibility that he planned and carried out the premature burial of his sister, he distinguishes reality from illusion much more effectively than the narrator in the final pages of the tale. Whereas Roderick awaits the imminent arrival of his sister, the narrator tries to ignore the noises that he hears emanating from the subterranean crypt in which he and Roderick sealed Madeline and rejects Usher's seemingly implausible explanations for them. Clinging to the pose of the rationalist, the narrator attempts to find a more prosaic explanation for the gradual opening of the chamber door, attributing it to "the work of the rushing gust" (*CW*, II 416). He immediately corrects himself, however, reporting that

Madeline is indeed there and that she falls dead upon her fatally terrified brother. As bizarre as the events the narrator describes are, they may have rational (as opposed to supernatural) explanations, as unlikely as these may be. If Madeline is cataleptic and if Roderick suffers from pathological fear, then it is possible—at least within the realm of Poe's fiction—that (1) Madeline may not have been dead when she was put in the crypt and, after struggling to free herself from her coffin and tomb, may have sought out the brother who buried her alive and ignored her cries for help, *and* that (2) upon seeing and being seized by his emaciated, vengeful, and moribund sister, Roderick may have died of fright. Similarly, there may be a rational explanation for the collapse of the House of Usher. G. R. Thompson suggests a bolt of lightning touching off gunpowder in the mansion's underground vault, *Poe's Fiction: Romantic Irony in the Gothic Tales* (Madison: University of Wisconsin Press, 1973), 94, but it could simply be the whirlwind toppling the ancient and already fissured edifice. Perhaps the would-be rationalist narrator, if he were simply reading or hearing about the events *chez* Usher rather than experiencing them firsthand, could himself postulate natural explanations for these occurrences. In order to compensate for the unnerving effects that Roderick, Madeline, and their ancestral home have had upon him, however, the narrator adopts a hyperrationalist approach. Roderick is mad, not the narrator; therefore, the uncanny effects Roderick believes the house has upon him and his sister cannot have really taken place, and Usher must be wrong about the sounds coming from the vault and the imminent appearance of his sister. Yet madmen often speak the truth. As strange as Roderick may be, at the end of the story he has a firmer grasp on reality than the narrator, so much so that it is Usher who impugns the narrator's sanity, twice calling *him* the "Madman," and he is within his rights to do so because to ignore one's senses willfully, as the narrator has done, is a sign of delusion. Because, as he admits, the Usher family and the house itself profoundly influence the narrator throughout the story, it is not surprising that seeing the simultaneous deaths of the brother and sister—the most bizarre of all the strange happenings in the House of Usher—unhinges the narrator's already unsettled mental state. An unaffected person would not "fle[e] [the house] aghast" (*CW*, II 417) but rather summon the servants, alert the authorities, and make funeral arrangements. Unable to provide a rational explanation for the events that occur just before he departs the mansion, the now-delusional narrator embraces Roderick's occult belief about the link between the family and the house and convinces himself that he witnesses the house fall into the tarn in confirmation of Roderick's superstition. In a similar manner but for different reasons, Captain Amasa Delano of Massachusetts adopts the pose of the hyperrationalist in connection with the events on the *San Dominick*.

25 Grandin, "Who Ain't a Slave?"

26 Robertson-Lorant, *Melville*, 349.

27 For an excellent discussion of the connections between the masquerade in the short novel and minstrelsy, see Jason Richards, "Melville's (Inter)national Burlesque: Whiteface, Blackface, and 'Benito Cereno,'" *ATQ* 21, no. 2 (June 2007): 73–94. It is worth noting that even after the capture of Babo, the blacks continue to use white prejudice to their advantage, tying a hatchet to a white clerk's hand to make him look like a "renegade seaman" (116) as the crew of Delano's vessel, the *Bachelor's Delight*, prepares to board the slave ship so that the Americans continue to believe that Spaniards rather than Africans control the vessel.

28 Eric J. Sundquist, "'Benito Cereno' and New World Slavery," in *Herman Melville: A Collection of Critical Essays*, ed. Myra Jehlen (Englewood Cliffs: Prentice-Hall, 1994), 186.

29 Robert Blake, *101 Elephant Jokes* (New York: Scholastic, 1964), 8–9.

30 One critic, Richard L. Kellogg, disagrees, asserting that "The Stolen White Elephant" "is neither parody nor pastiche," even though he subsequently refers to it as "the case of the purloined elephant," "The Twain Detective Who Was Not Sharp," *Baker Street Journal* 49, no. 4 (1999): 50–51.

31 Mark Twain to William Dean Howells, *Mark Twain's Letters, Vol. 3: 1876–1885*, ed. Albert Bigelow Paine, January 21, 1879, https://www.gutenberg.org/files/3195/3195-h/3195-h.htm#link2H_4_0003.

32 *The Stolen White Elephant, Etc.* (London: Chatto & Windus, 1882), 1.

33 Thomas, *Detective Fiction*, 244.

34 Walter Mosley, "Introduction," in *The Stolen White Elephant and Other Detective Stories*, ed. Shelley Fisher Fishkin (New York: Oxford University Press, 1997), xxxvi.

35 Alan Gribben, "That Pair of Spiritual Derelicts: The Poe-Twain Relationship," *Poe Studies* 18, no. 2 (Dec. 1985): 19.

36 Ibid., 20.

37 Kellogg, "The Twain Detective," 50; W. Keith Kraus, "Mark Twain's 'Double-Barreled Detective Story': A Source for the Solitary Oesophagus," *Mark Twain Journal* 16, no. 2 (Summer 1972): 12; Jeanne Ritunnano, however, has defended the story, reading it as a parody of Conan Doyle's *A Study in Scarlet*, "Mark Twain vs. Arthur Conan Doyle on Detective Fiction," *Mark Twain Journal* 16, no. 1 (Winter 1971–72): 10–14; and Jeff R. Banks declares it "one of the most delightful spoofs in the history of that ancient art," "Mark Twain: Detective Story Writer: An Appreciation," *Armchair Detective* 7 (1974): 176.

38 Peter Messent, *Mark Twain* (New York: St. Martin's, 1997), 10.

39 Ibid., 6.

40 Mark Twain, "The Stolen White Elephant," in *The Stolen White Elephant and Other Detective Stories*, 30. (Subsequent citations will be listed in the text.)

41 Lillian S. Robinson, "Afterword," in *The Stolen White Elephant and Other Detective Stories*, 9.

42 Harold G. Baetzhold, "Of Detectives and Their Derring-Do: The Genesis of Mark Twain's 'The Stolen White Elephant,'" *Studies in American Humor* 2 (January 1976): 194–95.

43 Robinson, "Afterword," 2.

44 Mosley, "Introduction," xxxiii.

45 Twain likely knew that the first printing of Poe's "The Gold-Bug" in the *Dollar Newspaper* featured two illustrations by the famous F. O. C. Darley.

46 Messent, *Mark Twain*, 2.

47 In a chapter devoted to Twain in *Detective Fiction and the Rise of Forensic Science*, Ronald Thomas offers a strong, contextualized reading of *Pudd'nhead Wilson* as a novel that, by indicting law and science "for promising certainties they cannot deliver, exposing them as coercive (and sometimes contradictory) instruments of social control instead of agencies through which to discover truth or establish justice," epitomizes the skepticism of American detection, 242. Oddly, and unfortunately, he makes no mention of "The Stolen White Elephant," even though he quotes statements Twain made about the genre during the period in which he was writing the story. With its depiction of an English civil servant whom detectives from the United States rob of his life's saving, the story, as Thomas argues about *Pudd'nhead Wilson*, "clearly presents itself as a restaging in the detective mode of the fundamentally conflictual relationship between British and American culture" (245), that he perceives in much of Twain's fiction. Perhaps Thomas steers clear of "The Stolen White Elephant" because addressing it would force him to do something that both he and Messent are reluctant to do: take the parodic dimension of the tale, and of detection generally, seriously.

48 Quinn, *Edgar Allan Poe*, 639. Similar accounts can be found in other biographies (by James Harrison, James M. Hutchisson, J. Gerald Kennedy, and Philip Van Doren Stern). In *Midnight Dreary: The Mysterious Death of Edgar Allan Poe* (New York: Palgrave, 2000), John Evangelist Walsh convincingly casts doubt on the theory that Poe was a victim of cooping; however, his contention that the blame rests with the relatives of Poe's first love, the Richmond widow Sarah Elmira Royster Shelton, likewise strains credulity.

49 Quinn, *Edgar Allan Poe*, 629.

50 Gribben, "A Couple of Spiritual Derelicts," 6.

51 Twain's prefatory admonition to those seeking to find a "motive," "moral," or "plot" in *Adventures of Huckleberry Finn* may also be relevant here.

52 Ibid., 20; Rogers, "Introduction," xii.

53 J. R. Hammond, *An Edgar Allan Poe Companion* (Totowa: Barnes & Noble, 1981), 104, 194n.

54 Catherine Ross Nickerson, *The Web of Iniquity: Early Detective Fiction by American Women* (Raleigh: Duke University Press, 1998); Kathleen Gregory Klein, *The Woman Detective: Gender and Genre*, 2nd ed. (Urbana: University of Illinois Press, 1995); Stephen F. Soitos, *The Blues Detective: A Study of African American Detective Fiction* (Amherst: University of Massachusetts Press, 1994); and Frankie Y. Bailey, *African American Mystery Writers: A Thematic Study* (Jefferson: McFarland, 2008).

Chapter 6

1 See the *Edgar Allan Poe—"The Gold-Bug"* page of the website of the Baltimore E. A. Poe Society, https://www.eapoe.org/works/info/pt042.htm.

2 Burton R. Pollin, *Images of Poe's Work: A Comprehensive Descriptive Catalogue of Illustrations* (Westport: Greenwood Press, 1989). Beyond the tale's popularity, the reasons for this include its comparatively high word count, its appeal to juvenile as well as adult audiences, and its unique combination of elements, namely detection/cryptography, the adventure of the treasure hunt, the fantasy of the acquisition of fabulous wealth, pirate lore, and local color/racial humor.

3 "Art. XXII—Poe's Tales," *Aristidean*, October 1845, 317, E. A. Poe Society of Baltimore, https://www.eapoe.org/works/criticsm/ara45pe1.htm.

4 Liliane Weissberg, "Black, White, and Gold," in *Romancing the Shadow: Poe and Race*, ed. J. Gerald Kennedy and Liliane Weissberg (New York: Oxford University Press, 2001), 133.

5 Toni Morrison, *Playing in the Dark: Whiteness and the Literary Imagination* (New York: Vintage, 1993), 32.

6 See Terrence Whalen, "Average Racism: Poe, Slavery and the Wages of Literary Nationalism," in *Romancing the Shadow*, 17, 27.

7 Paul Christian Jones, "'Her Little Maid Mandy': The Abolitionist Slave Owner and the Rhetoric of Affection in the Life and Early Fiction of E. D. E. N. Southworth," *J19* 2, no. 1 (2014): 53–82. See also Robert Yusef Rabiee, "'The Little Mistress': Chivalry, Autonomy, and Domestic Relations in E. D. E. N. Southworth's *The Hidden Hand*," *J19* 6, no. 1 (2018): 147–65.

8 Whalen's "average" is not evaluative but rather descriptive, synonymous with "standard," "typical," and "pervasive"; moreover, "average racism" was certainly banal but by no means benign. Another of Whalen's terms, "neutral," used to describe Poe's position on slavery, does not refer to an actively pursued middle position between abolition and unchecked slavery but rather to silence about or evasion of the issue.

9   Jacobs completed a version of *Incidents in the Life of a Slave Girl* in 1858, before the initial serialization of *The Hidden Hand* in 1859; however, *Incidents* was not published until 1861.

10 Jean Fagan Yellin, *Harriet Jacobs: A Life* (New York: Civitas, 2005), 145.

11 John Cullen Gruesser, *The Empire Abroad and the Empire at Home: African American Literature and the Era of Overseas Expansion* (Athens: University of Georgia Press, 2012), 113–26.

12 Andrew R. Black, *John Pendleton Kennedy, Early American Novelist, Whig Statesman, and Ardent Nationalist* (Baton Rouge: Louisiana State University Press, 2016), 149–51.

13 Morrison, *Playing in the Dark*, 58.

14 Thomas Nelson Page, "Marse Chan: A Tale of Old Virginia," *Century Magazine*, April 1884, 938, 942.

15 Whalen, "Average Racism," 4.

16 Nina Baym, "Introduction," in *The Hidden Hand* (Oxford: Oxford University Press, 1997), xviii; Paul Christian Jones, "'This Dainty Woman's Hand . . . Red with Blood': E. D. E. N. Southworth's *The Hidden Hand* as Abolitionist Narrative," *ATQ* 15, no. 1 (2001): 63; Michelle Ann Abate, "Launching a Gender B(l)acklash: E. D. E. N. Southworth's *The Hidden Hand* and the Emergence of (Racialized) White Tomboyism," *Children's Literature Association Quarterly* 31, no. 1 (2006): 40, 45; and Christopher Looby, "Southworth and Seriality: *The Hidden Hand* in the *New York Ledger*," *Nineteenth-Century Literature* 59, no. 2 (September 2004): 179–211.

17 See Joanne Dobson, "Introduction," in *The Hidden Hand or, Capitola the Madcap* (New Brunswick: Rutgers University Press, 1988), xxiv; Baym, "Introduction," xviii; Patricia Okker and Jeffrey R. Williams, "'Reassuring Sounds': Minstrelsy and *The Hidden Hand*," *ATQ* 12, no. 2 (June 1998): 135; Abate, "Launching a Gender B(l) acklash," 46; and Looby, "Southworth and Seriality," 198.

18 Beth L. Lueck, "Maniac Brides: Southworth's Sensational and Gothic Transformations," in *E. D. E. N. Southworth: Recovering a Nineteenth-Century Popular Novelist*, ed. Melissa J. Homestead and Pamela T. Washington (Knoxville: University of Tennessee Press, 2012), 113. In her essay, Lueck draws on the work of Paul Christian Jones and Teresa Goddu. As Jones discusses in *Unwelcome Voices: Subversive Fiction in the Antebellum South* (Knoxville: University of Tennessee Press, 2005), critics have been reluctant to categorize Poe as a Southern writer because, although his texts are not antislavery as some of Southworth's are, they are, in the words of G. R. Thompson, "virtually devoid of all regionalist sentiment" 88.

19 Lueck, "Maniac Brides," 118.

20 Abate asserts, "while Southworth named her character Capitola Black, she may more accurately be called Capitola Black(face)" 57.

21 It should be noted, however, that, early in the novel, the white infant Capitola, the story's protagonist, and Nancy Grewel, a free mulatta who saves her, are sold into slavery, only to be liberated when they are rescued following a shipwreck.

22 See Jean Fagan Yellin, *Harriet Jacobs* and *The Harriet Jacobs Family Papers*, 2 vols, ed. Jean Fagan Yellin et al. (Chapel Hill: University of North Carolina Press, 2008).

23 Harriet A. Jacobs, *Incidents in the Life of a Slave Girl*, ed. and introduced by Jean Fagan Yellin, enlarged ed. (Cambridge: Harvard University Press, 2009), 110. (Subsequent citations to this edition will be listed in the text.)

24 Jean Fagan Yellin, "Introduction," in *Incidents in the Life of a Slave Girl*, xli; Henry Louis Gates, Jr., "Introduction," in *The Classic Slave Narratives* (New York: Signet, 2012), 12; and Valerie Smith, "Introduction," in *Incidents in the Life of a Slave Girl* (New York: Oxford University Press, 1990), xxxi–xxxiii.

25 Daneen Wardrop, who sees multiple links between "The Purloined Letter" and *Incidents*, contends that the "loophole in the garret owes its success, in remaining impossible to expose, precisely due to the fact that it is so obvious," "'I Stuck the Gimlet in and Waited for Evening': Writing and *Incidents in the Life of a Slave Girl*," *Texas Studies in Literature and Language* 49, no. 3 (Fall 2007): 226.

26 According to Jean Fagan Yellin's biography of Jacobs, Cowper's phrase was used in 1838 in a column called "The Curtain" published in *Freedom's Journal* (373).

27 Born a slave in Richmond, Virginia, in 1839, Bowser was freed in 1851 by Elizabeth Van Lew, a staunch abolitionist, who bought and liberated Bowser's enslaved family members and sent Bowser to a Quaker school in Philadelphia where she was studying when the Civil War began. Van Lew, who had a reputation for dressing and acting eccentrically, earning her the nickname "Crazy Bet," arranged in 1863 for Bowser to work in the home of Jefferson Davis, where she was regarded as an unlettered and dimwitted but diligent bondwoman. In reality, she was not only free and well educated but also had a photographic memory that she put to good use in examining the documents crossing the desk of the president of the Confederate States of America. To transmit the intelligence she gathered to Van Lew and Thomas McNiven, a Union spy who disguised himself as a baker, she availed herself of everyday materials within the household, hiding military plans in empty egg shells, conveying messages by means of a food tray with a false bottom, and even using the clothes she hung up to dry to send coded messages. Perhaps because her real identity was suspected, Bowser fled Richmond in January 1865, attempting, unsuccessfully, to burn down the Confederate White House as she left. It was long believed that Bowser vanished after leaving the South; however, Lois Luveen, who wrote a novel based on Bowser's life, discovered that she returned to Richmond shortly after the war. The information Bowser provided from the heart of enemy territory was of such value that General Grant called it the best

intelligence he received from Richmond during the Civil War. Bowser was inducted in 1995 into the United States Army Military Intelligence Hall of Fame, which noted in its citation that "Jefferson Davis never discovered the leak in his household staff . . . although he knew the Union somehow kept discovering Confederate plans." Exploiting white assumptions about her mental abilities and slave status to make invaluable contributions to her people's struggle for freedom, Mary Bowser, astoundingly, managed to convert the headquarters of the Confederate war effort into a loophole of retreat. See Jasmine K. Williams, "Mary Elizabeth Bowser—Tea and Secrets," *New York Post*, March 27, 2008, 34; Elizabeth R. Varon, *Southern Lady, Yankee Spy: The True Story of Elizabeth Van Lew, A Union Agent in the Heart of the Confederacy* (Oxford: Oxford University Press, 2003); Vertamae Grosvenor, "The Spy Who Served Me: A Tale of Espionage from the 'White House' of Jefferson Davis," npr.org., https://www.npr.org/templates/story/story.php?storyId=1141977; and Mary Elizabeth Bowser, "African American National Biography," https://sites. fas.harvard.edu/~aanb/SHTML/DOWNLOADS/Sample%20entries%20for%20 Web%20site.pdf.

28 Anne Bradford Warner, "Carnival Laughter: Resistance in *Incidents*," in Harriet Jacobs, *Incidents in the Life of a Slave Girl*, ed. Deborah M. Garfield and Rafia Zafar (New York: Cambridge University Press, 2000), 219; Michelle Burnham, "Loopholes of Resistance: Harriet Jacobs's Slave Narrative and the Critique of Agency in Foucault," in *Incidents in the Life of a Slave Girl*, by Harriet Jacobs, ed. Nellie Y. McKay and Frances Smith Foster (New York: Norton, 2001), 278.

29 Burnham, "Loopholes of Resistance," 281–85.

30 "Retreat," of course, likewise has a military and a nonmilitary connotation.

31 Confronted by the black-white and slave-free oppositions dominating antebellum America, Jacobs chose to emphasize gender in her narrative, asserting the common sisterhood of Northern white free women and Southern black slave women and exhorting the former to take a personal and political stand against the moral abomination of slavery.

32 Hazel V. Carby, "Introduction," in *The Magazine Novels of Pauline Hopkins* (New York: Oxford University Press, 1988), xxix–l. Kristina Brooks discusses the serial in connection with racial stereotypes in "Mammies, Bucks, and Wenches: Minstrelsy, Racial Pornography, and Racial Politics in Pauline Hopkins's *Hagar's Daughter*," in *The Unruly Voice: Rediscovering Pauline Elizabeth Hopkins*, ed. John Cullen Gruesser (Urbana: University of Illinois Press, 1996), 119–57. Stephen F. Soitos in *The Blues Detective* and Catherine Ross Nickerson in *The Web of Iniquity* address Hopkins's use of detection in the novel (as do I in *Race, Gender and Empire*). Janet Gabler-Hover in *Dreaming Black/Writing White: The Hagar Myth in American Cultural History* (Lexington: University Press of Kentucky, 1999) reads Hopkins's

narrative in connection with other American novels relating to the biblical figure of Hagar. Eugenia DeLamotte shows how Hopkins draws on and reworks the female Gothic tradition established by Ann Radcliffe in "'Collusions of Mystery': Ideology and the Gothic in *Hagar's Daughter*," *Gothic Studies* 6, no. 1 (2004): 69–79. In a chapter of *Pauline E. Hopkins: A Literary Biography* (Athens: University of Georgia Press, 2005), Hanna Wallinger focuses on the figure of the tragic mulatta. Meanwhile, in her own Hopkins biography, *Pauline Elizabeth Hopkins: Black Daughter of the Revolution* (Chapel Hill: University of North Carolina Press, 2008), Lois Brown argues that the serial pays homage to John Milton's epic poem *Paradise Lost* as well as to the first African American novel, William Wells Brown's *Clotel*. Alisha Knight claims that it critiques the American Gospel of success, *Pauline Hopkins and the American Dream: An African American Writer's (Re)Visionary Gospel of Success* (Knoxville: University of Tennessee Press, 2011), and Jill Bergman devotes a chapter of *The Motherless Child in the Novels of Pauline Hopkins* (Baton Rouge: Louisiana State University Press, 2012) to *Hagar's Daughter*. More recently, Lauren Dembowitz has charted Hopkins's extensive borrowings from 1880s and 1890s popular fiction in her first serial novel, most of it published in *Frank Leslie's Popular Monthly*, "Source Chart and Bibliography for *Hagar's Daughter: A Story of Southern Caste Prejudice*," in *"Inspired Borrowings": Pauline Hopkins's Literary Appropriations*, ed. JoAnn Pavletich, Pauline Elizabeth Hopkins Society website, http://www.paulinehopkinssociety.org/inspired-borrowings/. On the subject of what some call Hopkins's plagiarism and others her "inspired borrowings" in connection with her other serial novels, see JoAnn Pavletich's, "'We are going to take that right': Power and Plagiarism in Hopkins's *Winona*," *CLA Journal* 59, no. 2 (Dec. 2015): 115–30; and Gregory Sanborn's "The Wind of Words: Plagiarism and Intertextuality in *Of One Blood*," *J19: The Journal of Nineteenth-Century Americanists* 3, no. 1 (Spring 2015): 67–87.

33 Hopkins's novel signifies on *Jane Eyre*, thereby anticipating not only Zora Neale Hurston's *Their Eyes Were Watching God*, a female bildungsroman about a character named Janie (whose five marital statuses parallel the five locations that structure Jane Eyre's life), but also to some extent *Wide Sargasso Sea*, Jean Rhys's counter-discursive postcolonial rewriting of Brontë's canonical text, in which Antoinette Cosway, aka Bertha Mason, becomes the protagonist and predominant speaker.

34 Hagar's circumstances, appearance, and bold actions recall those of Bertha Mason in *Jane Eyre*. Although not necessarily of mixed-race ancestry, Bertha is portrayed as an exotic colonial woman whose family wealth derives from slave labor. As Sandra M. Gilbert and Susan Gubar argue in *The Madwoman in the Attic: The Woman Writer and the Nineteenth-Century Literary Imagination* (New Haven: Yale University Press, 1979), she functions as Jane's dark double, embodying and acting on the rage that engulfs the protagonist at key moments in the novel. At Thornfield

Hall, Jane frequently hears a strange laugh coming from the third floor, which Rochester and the housekeeper Mrs. Fairfax attribute to Grace Poole but actually comes from Bertha. Jane first hears it in Chapter XI when a tour of the mansion takes her to the third story: "While I paced softly on, the last sound I expected to hear in so still a region, a laugh, struck my ear. It was a curious laugh; distinct, formal, mirthless. I stopped: the sound ceased, only for an instant; it began again, louder: for at first, though distinct, it was very low. It passed off in a clamorous peal that seemed to wake an echo in every lonely chamber; though it originated but in one, and I could have pointed out the door whence the accents issued," Charlotte Brontë, *Jane Eyre* (New York: Penguin, 2006), 126.

35   Pauline E. Hopkins, "Hagar's Daughter: A Story of Southern Caste Prejudice," in *The Magazine Novels of Pauline Hopkins*, 57–58. (Subsequent citations will be listed in the text.) The way in which the laughter of the two women builds and the use of the word "peal" serves to connect the passages in Brontë and Hopkins.

36   Brontë, *Jane Eyre*, 326–27.

37   Qtd. in DeLamotte, "'Collusions of Mystery,'" 73.

Coda: "A Crime of Dark Dye": Misreading Poe's Criticism

1   Henry James, "The Art of Fiction," in Walter Besant, *The Art of Fiction: A Lecture* (Boston: Cupples, Upham & Co., 1885), 71.

2   Review of *Twice-Told Tales*, by Nathaniel Hawthorne, *Graham's Magazine*, May 1842, 299–300. (Subsequent citations will be listed in the text.)

3   Although "Tale Writing—Nathaniel Hawthorne" contains laudatory comments, some of them taken verbatim from the earlier assessments, Poe greatly expands on his prior reservations about Hawthorne and denies him the "originality" previously accorded to him. In many ways, this final review serves as an occasion for Poe to launch a general attack on members of the New England literary clique, with whom he often feuded (especially after his calamitous reading in Boston in October 1845), and to target the Transcendentalists in particular. Poe likely associated Hawthorne with the latter group because the Preface to *Mosses from the Old Manse* describes fishing trips he took with Ellery Channing and identifies the rented house where many of the stories were written as the one where Emerson wrote *Nature*. Poe makes his true targets clear in the rhetorical flourish that concludes the review, urging Hawthorne to "get a bottle of visible ink, come out from the Old Manse, cut Mr. Alcott, hang (if possible) the editor of 'The Dial,' and throw out of the window to the pigs all his odd numbers of 'The North American Review'" (256).

4   The tale first appeared in *The Token*, an annual Christmas gift book, for 1836, which means that it was published in 1835. A review of *The Token*, written by

Henry F. Chorley for the November 7, 1835, issue of the London *Athenaeum*, identified "The Minister's Black Veil" as one of "two stories of dark colour" with "singularity enough to recommend it to the reader." This positive notice caused Hawthorne, no doubt with typically self-deprecating irony, to refer to himself as "a very famous man" in a January 25, 1836, letter to his sister Elizabeth. A year and a half later, in early March 1837, the story was reprinted in *Twice-Told Tales*, Hawthorne's initial collection of fiction and the first time one of his publications appeared with his name attached to it, Lea Bertani Vozar Newman, "One Hundred and Fifty Years of Looking At, Into, Through, Behind, and Around 'The Minister's Black Veil,'" *Nathaniel Hawthorne Review* 13 (Spring 1987): 5, 8. A review of *Twice-Told Tales* in the *Boston Daily Advertiser* commended "The Minister's Black Veil," which it found to be of "more fearful interest" than many of the other selections in the book. By June 1837, despite the onset of a severe economic depression, well over half of the print run of one thousand copies of the book, which had been financed without Hawthorne's knowledge by his friend Horatio Bridge, had been sold, Brenda Wineapple, *Hawthorne: A Life* (New York: Random House, 2004), 93.

5 There have been, to my knowledge, just four exceptions to this oversight: that of D. A. Miller who is not sure which "young lady" Poe is talking about, "The Administrator's Black Veil: A Response to Hillis Miller," *ADE Bulletin* 88 (1987): 50; that of Peter K. Garrett who likewise finds Poe's reference to the "young lady" somewhat unclear, *Gothic Reflections: Narrative Force in Nineteenth-Century Fiction* (Ithaca: Cornell University Press, 2003), 39; that of Paul Emmett who acknowledges that the story also describes Elizabeth as a "young lady," "Narrative Suppression: Sin, Secrecy, and Subjectivity in 'The Minister's Black Veil,'" *Journal of Evolutionary Psychology* 25 (March 2004): 106; and that of Leland Person, who points out the ambiguity of Poe's comments in a footnote to the story in the new Norton Critical Edition of *The Scarlet Letter and Other Writings* (New York: W. W. Norton, 2017).

6 Gilbert Voigt, "The Minister's Black Veil," *College English* 13, no. 6 (1952): 338.

7 E. Earle Stibitz, "Ironic Unity in Hawthorne's 'The Minister's Black Veil,'" *American Literature* 34, no. 2 (1962): 183.

8 Leland Person, *The Cambridge Introduction to Nathaniel Hawthorne* (New York: Cambridge University Press, 2007), 48; Eamonn Dunne, *J. Hillis Miller and the Possibility of Reading: Literature after Deconstruction* (New York: Bloomsbury, 2010), 89. As several critics have discussed, Hawthorne's ambiguous description of the funeral raises the possibility that something of an occult nature takes place. As he leans directly over the dead woman, Hooper realizes that she could perceive his naked face were she alive and quickly presses the veil to his skin. In a passage often cited as evidence of Hooper's guilt in connection with the young woman's demise, we are told, "A person, who watched the interview between the dead and the living, scrupled not to affirm, that at the instant when the clergyman's features were

disclosed, the corpse had slightly shuddered." Yet Hawthorne's narrator appears to dismiss the whole thing immediately thereafter by identifying a "superstitious old woman" as "the only witness to this prodigy," Nathaniel Hawthorne, "The Minister's Black Veil," in *The Scarlet Letter and Other Writings*, 180.

9 Judy McCarthy, "'The Minister's Black Veil': Concealing Moses and the Holy of Holies," *Studies in Short Fiction* 24, no. 2 (1987): 135.

10 H. J. Lang, "How Ambiguous Is Hawthorne?" in *Hawthorne*, ed. A. N. Kaul (Englewood Cliffs: Prentice-Hall, 1966), 92.

11 Cynthia S. Jordan, "Poe's Re-Vision: The Recovery of the Second Story," *American Literature* 59 (March 1987): 1–19; David Leverenz, *Manhood and the American Renaissance* (Ithaca: Cornell University Press, 1989), 229.

12 Carl Ostrowski, "The Minister's Grievous Affliction: Diagnosing Hawthorne's Parson Hooper," *Literature and Medicine* 17, no. 2 (Fall 1998): 200, 204.

13 Lydia G. Fash, "The Chronicle and the Reckoning: A Temporal Paradox in Hawthorne's *Twice-Told Tales*," *Narrative* 21, no. 2 (2013): 240.

14 W. B. Carnochan, "'The Minister's Black Veil': Symbol, Meaning, and the Context of Hawthorne's Art," *Nineteenth-Century Fiction* 24, no. 2 (1969): 183, 186.

15 Miller, "The Administrator's Black Veil," 50.

16 George E. Haggerty, *Gothic Fiction/Gothic Form* (University Park: Pennsylvania State University Press, 1989), 111.

17 G. R. Thompson, "Literary Politics and the 'Legitimate Sphere': Poe, Hawthorne, and the 'Tale Proper,'" *Nineteenth-Century Literature* 49 (September 1994): 187.

18 Joel Porte, *In Respect to Egotism: Studies in American Romantic Writing* (New York: Cambridge University Press, 1991), 142.

19 These statements come from Richard Kopley's unpublished respondent comments to the January 2016 Modern Language Association Convention Poe Studies Association panel in which I first presented my reading of critical misreadings of Poe's reading of Hawthorne's story. I am grateful to Richard for sharing his comments with me.

20 "Moore's Alciphron," eapoe.org., https://www.eapoe.org/works/stedwood/sw0611.htm.

21 Carnochan, "'The Minister's Black Veil,'" 183.

Index